To. K

From. D——.
All the best for 1981.

THE PHILATELIST'S
COMPANION

THE PHILATELIST'S COMPANION

Bill Gunston

DAVID & CHARLES

NEWTON ABBOT LONDON VANCOUVER

0 7153 6384 0

Set in 12 on 13 Bembo and printed in Great Britain by Redwood
Burn Ltd Trowbridge & Esher for David & Charles (Holdings)
Limited South Devon House Newton Abbot Devon

Published in Canada by Douglas David & Charles Limited
3645 McKechnie Drive West Vancouver BC

Contents

Preface

A century ago the collection of postage stamps was something practised by a lot of children and a very small number of adults who were, in consequence, considered rather childish. Today the adult collectors probably outnumber the children, and even the hundreds of millions of people who have never deliberately 'kept' a single stamp are keenly aware that these trivial bits of paper can sometimes be extremely valuable. Almost everyone on Earth able to read has heard about stamps of priceless rarity, or common stamps which happened to be incorrectly printed and thus came to be worth thousands of times more than the ordinary specimens. Very gradually stamp-collecting has come to have strong overtones of money – indeed the theme of this book is the basic law that the amount of profit you can show from the collection of postage stamps is roughly proportional to your knowledge of the stamps you collect.

This may disappoint some who have visions of 'getting rich quick' and wondered whether this book might contain some magical hints on how to do it through stamp-collecting. Such a belief is a pipe-dream. But for the collector prepared to turn into a philatelist – a term which is indefinable but is generally taken to mean a stamp-collector who studies some particular class or group of stamps or postal material and so has a deep knowledge of it – the path to profit is as sure a highway as he could wish for, unless he is incredibly silly or unlucky.

I did not become interested in stamps until 1966. Just as the route to classical music usually lies by way of Johann Strauss and Tchaikovsky, so did my route to philately lie in bright stamps from faraway places. If my office had a letter from Venezuela or Thailand, I acquired the envelope. One day a philatelist said 'Instead of collecting bits of paper, why don't you pick a "good" country, concentrate on it and become an expert?' Since then I have spent far more on philately than on any stocks or shares, savings certificates or any other investment; and I can show results that I defy any traditional investment broker to match.

There is nothing different about stamps to separate them from any other business commodity (apart from the fact that they are exceptionally small and convenient). Certainly they obey the basic laws of supply and demand. It is important never to forget that there are two sides to this equation. Too much supply or too little demand means low prices, just as it tends to with any other commodity. It is a pretty universal rule that a stamp, or a cover, or any other philatelic item is worth exactly as much as someone is prepared to hand over in exchange for it. This sum of money may be less or more than a figure written in a printed catalogue. As explained in Chapter 7, 'catalogue values' are a useful guide, especially to the inexpert collector, but it must never be thought that they are in any sense rigid or even correct – apart from the fact that they are probably the prices at which the publisher of the catalogue is prepared to sell. The more you practise philately, the better you will be able to judge stamp values. And perhaps it is a good rule never to spend much money on stamps until you have gained this ability.

Some high-class stamp dealers might not thank me if I advise rich aunts and uncles not to spend large sums buying little Johnny material that neither he nor they can properly judge; they would do him a better service either to bank the money until he could spend it wisely for himself, or else ask an expert to do the buying. Moreover, many postal administrations would not thank me if I suggested that the belief that every newly issued stamp must appreciate in value is nonsense. All over the world people queue at post-office counters on the first day of a new issue in order to buy copies of the new stamp, and either stick it on a self-addressed 'first day cover' or else salt it away as an investment. However, those who purchase these stamps for fun, or to keep a collection complete and up to date, will have no reason to be disappointed. The rest will one day wish to sell, and the material they have to sell is likely to be exactly what a million other people have to offer. The chief beneficiaries of this kind of collecting are the people with heavy postage bills, because they can always go to an auction and buy sheet after sheet of recent commemorative stamps – all good for postal use – at significantly less than face value.

Millions of people have already discovered this fact the hard way. Their proud collection of swans suddenly turned out to be an almost unsaleable lot of ugly ducklings, and left them with a smouldering feeling that stamp-collecting is a giant confidence trick. In fact it is not. Every year skilled stamp-collecting becomes an increasingly better investment. I shall continue, hopefully for many years, to spend more on stamps than on anything else apart from the necessities of life. This book is intended to encourage others to do likewise, and to help them obtain the greatest possible benefit from whatever their resources may be.

Bill Gunston

I
Stamp-collecting

The notion of 'collecting' is lost in antiquity. Undoubtedly some prehistoric men collected stones, shells and other objects that they considered pretty. Modern collecting is practised for various reasons. Something may be pleasing to the eye, or in some other way aesthetically desirable. It may be thought worth preserving for posterity. Or it might be considered an object likely to become rarer and therefore more precious. Again, in the basest terms, it might be a good investment that could later be turned into cash. The last three reasons are not quite synonymous, but considerations of money are seldom far removed from most types of collecting. In any case, stamp-collecting is a most agreeable hobby – a fact advertised in current British and French stamp-cancellation slogans – in which almost everyone can participate. After all, used stamps are available to anyone who cares to search for them, and the tools of the trade can be quite minimal.

Most experienced philatelists are experts on a restricted range of the overall subject, having chosen to concentrate on a particular country, a particular time, or a particular group or class of items. I believe that all of these people have felt a great and enduring kinship and affinity with the place and time of their choice. This close psychological link is powerful and probably wholly good; and it can be brought to life by picking up a single stamp, which can transport one back, say, to a vividly pictured England of the 1840s, or wherever and whenever else the stamp was used. Stamps are also highly educational. A director of Stanley Gibbons, the famed stamp dealers and publishers, was asked at the age of about eight to list some countries of the British Empire. The rest of the class stopped at about five names; he made himself notorious by reciting about 150! And he knew where they were, and much of their history.

To the young collector a desirable stamp is bright, superficially interesting, and from an exciting-sounding far-away place. To the philatelist it is more likely to be an indecipherable dull-looking rectangle of aged paper. An album filled with hundreds of these dull-looking rectangles can send him into transports of delight and keep him deeply interested for hours. The appeal of stamp-collecting is enormously strong yet infinitely variable. The fact that it can be highly profitable is a rather large bonus.

Most readers of this book are probably not yet able to appreciate the intense beauty of a hundred dull rectangles that all look just alike (except to the expert). Very few casual collectors are likely to want to acquire this appreciation as a deliberate project, but would be happy if it gradually came of its own accord. In the meantime they are satisfied with less-specialised stamps whose appeal is more overt and immediate. Except for the really young collector, they are unlikely to be misled when the world's biggest publisher of stamp catalogues (the aforementioned Gibbons) increases the base-line price for the cheapest and most common stamps to 5p (equivalent to about 12c in the USA) to cover his overheads; but they are invariably depressed if they take their collection to a dealer to try and sell it. Although the collection may contain only perfect stamps, lovingly arranged and cared for over many years, the dealer is likely to break the news that this is exactly the material he has fifty times over, and it is what his customers have too. What his customers do not have is usually what he does not have either; not only truly valuable classic stamps, but the annoying elusive items

12

that hardly anyone thinks of collecting when they are on sale and which suddenly seem to vanish off the face of the earth. Curiously, some of these elusive items are catalogued with all the common junk at 5p, but this does not mean that many dealers and experienced collectors would not give much more for them. It is these elusive items that the IMP (investment-minded philatelist) ought to notice.

Most of this book is written mainly for the IMP, into which little Johnny with his 'thematic' collections of space flight and football stamps is likely to develop in the course of time. But how did philately start in the first place?

The vast subject of postal history is concerned with all forms of conveyed written communications. Such communications have a recorded history of at least 5,500 years, but, so far as anyone knows, it is only in the past 100 years or so that postal items have been collected for the sake of their postal markings. Postal history is rather outside the scope of this book (although see Chapter 2) because the worth of a letter or other item is strongly determined by the eminence of the writer or addressee, by the interest of its content, and by other factors that are only marginally philatelic. Although there are thousands of letters much more than 200 years old, I am going to concentrate on the philately of the adhesive postage stamp – again, as far as anyone knows, there were no such things before the year 1840. Then, as described in the next chapter, mass-produced labels were printed in Great Britain which could be stuck on letters as prepayment of postage. It is impossible to say today how many of the earliest stamps were deliberately 'collected', but we certainly have a number of covers dated on or before 6 May 1840 which was the first official date of use of the original 1d stamp, the 'penny black' – undoubtedly the most renowned of all classic stamps and, by any yardstick, an outstanding example of graphic design.

These superb stamps, officially issued as 'adhesive labels', emerged into a world in which collecting, as a pastime or for investment, was very well established. But the collectors were almost exclusively from the upper strata of society, and they were interested only in *objets d'art* considered to be of both beauty and value. That the utilitarian bits of paper used to confirm the prepayment of mail could be thought to possess either attribute, would have been considered debatable if not preposterous. Admittedly the British public had from the start evinced a passing interest in what these labels looked like, but the only citizens outside the post office and the company which manufactured the stamps to take a deep interest in them were the growing number who discovered that the black stamps could be cleaned and used again. As the threat of transportation and other harsh punishment did not deter this practice, the post office decided to change the colour of the 1d stamp to a dull red-brown, and obliterate (cancel) it with black. When this happened, very few people thought of keeping a sheet or two of the black stamps to see if they would ever be of more than face value.

It is doubtful that more than one person in every million of the population did this. In December 1840 trial printings of the 1d stamp were made in the red-brown ink and also in two of the blue inks used to print the accompanying 2d value. If such a thing had occurred today there would almost have been fighting in the streets to try to get hold of mint — or, perhaps better still, used — copies; as it was, hardly anyone knew about it at the time, and nobody took the slightest interest. But one or two oddballs must have been collecting used stamps even at this time, possibly as a deliberate eccentricity, because in 1842 *Punch* took the trouble to ridicule such a fatuous waste of time. Indeed *The Times* still has on file a copy from the previous year containing a small advertisement for 'used stamps' inserted by a Dr Gray of the British Museum, who declined to say what he intended to do with them. Another newspaper carried an advertisement from a lady collector, but it transpired she merely wanted to paper a room!

During the next ten years several other countries adopted the practice of issuing stamps for postage, but perhaps the most significant issue of all, in September 1847, came from the little British island of Mauritius in the Indian Ocean. The wife of the governor was anxious for the island to have its own postage stamps to put on

14

envelopes containing invitations to a fancy-dress ball, and the resulting stamps (an orange-red 1d and a rich blue 2d) created great interest from the start. They were probably the first stamps in the world to be associated with the idea of philatelic value, and they were probably also the first ever to be worth more than face. This was partly because to most people Mauritius was a distant and exotic place, and partly because the number printed was measured not in millions but in hundreds, and the locally engraved copper die resulted in stamps that looked slightly amateur and thus interesting. Probably this issue, more than any other, gave rise to the notion that collecting postage stamps could be something more than an eccentricity or a childish pastime. By this time there were dozens of stamp-issuing countries, and so in every country there were plenty of 'foreign stamps' to collect, to exchange, or sell. In 1852 a Belgian bookseller, Jean-Baptiste Moens, started to deal in stamps as a sideline. In 1856 young E. S. Gibbons did the same, in the back of his father's pharmacy in Plymouth, and in 1865 he published the catalogue of the world's stamps which did much to make the name of Stanley Gibbons famous. Today this catalogue has expanded into a shelf-full of volumes.

By about 1870, although the world's postal authorities were wholly disinterested in anything but their prime duty of organising the mail service, and like most adults still scorned stamp-collecting as trivial, the proportion of used stamps and covers that found their way into the hands of collectors was not very different from the proportion today, although, of course, the number of items in absolute terms was much smaller. The vast majority of people, even in the 'developed' countries, hardly ever sent or received mail, and many were illiterate. The volume of commercial correspondence was large because there was no other means of communication, but it was still tiny compared with that of today. To most people the receipt of a letter was a major event, and postage stamps of any kind were common in only a few in every million of the world's households. These favoured households were almost exclusively upper-class ones, and in the 1850s these were invariably imbued with a deep sense of duty and industry. Children were permitted only a limited range of hobbies, and any new pastime had to be demonstrably creative or useful. Collecting stamps was not.

So it is not to be wondered at that in 1864 a British magazine editor told his readers, 'I am sometimes asked whether used postage stamps can serve any useful purpose. Such stamps have no use whatever, and are certainly not to be collected as has lately been done by thoughtless children.' Five years later a sort of 'editorial auntie' was more helpful: 'If you have lots of old postage stamps do not be so foolish as merely to paste them into an album where you can do no more than look at them. The best thing to do with them is to make them into a stamp snake. This is done by threading the stamps on to a long piece of fine string or stout thread. Either thread the string on a needle or else make a good hole in the centre of each stamp so that you can push the string through. You will need at least 1,000 stamps of the ordinary size for the body of the snake and at least 100 of the biggest size for the head. If you are very clever you will be able to finish off by tapering the last few dozen stamps down, smaller and smaller, cutting them ever more closely to produce a fine, pointed nose!' This advice will give any modern philatelist apoplexy, especially if he recalls that in 1869 there were hardly any stamps of 'the biggest size', and those that did exist were bound to become valuable. But it does show that people were interested in used stamps and pasted them into albums. I sometimes come upon the paste; after more than 100 years it needs careful handling, as outlined in Chapter 8. I also often find old stamps with holes in the middle!

It was inevitable that collectors should conceive the 'stamp album'. Albums were in use long before stamps; The Shorter Oxford Dictionary gives the date as 1651 for the earliest use of the word in the context of 'a blank book' for autographs, pictures and other essentially two-dimensional items. The first stamp albums were blank books made for other purposes, but by 1870 several publishers were producing printed albums tailored to the collection of stamps. All the earliest ones appear to have been designed to contain stamps of all the stamp-issuing countries, and by 1875 it was common for albums to contain printed rectangles ready to receive one stamp of each basic type, with a printed list on the facing (left-hand) page.

This exerted a big influence on what was then a fast-growing hobby. It tended to discourage specialisation, and encourage the almost impossible objective of having 'one of everything'. It strongly retarded the growth of philately by making no provision for any study of the stamps of one issue; when you had one stamp of any particular type you threw all the rest away, or used them as 'swaps'. It established the principle that a collector always stuck his stamps on to an album page, and this practice soon spread to mint stamps. Indeed by 1890 there was a strong body of opinion that used stamps were defaced and imperfect, and that only mint specimens would suffice. Then these were solemnly licked and stuck into the album! Finally, the printed rectangles made no provision for wing margins (the extra area of unprinted paper often left at

a   b   c   d   e

Fig 1   Some early stamps were printed from plates which were divided into 'panes' by broader gaps between the stamps of adjacent panes. These early British 4d stamps were printed by a plate (plate 12) divided into left and right panes by a broad gap down the centre. Stamps from the vertical columns next to this gap therefore have 'wing margins'. These examples come from the F column (see letter in each lower right corner). The first example (a), used in Sevenoaks, has the margin cut down and damaged, and is worthless; (b) used at Mortlake, London, has the margin neatly trimmed by scissors; (c) used in Malta, has the margin cut off and cunningly reperforated; (d) used in Edinburgh, has it intact; (e) used in Alexandria, Egypt, is a fine copy worth a premium. Stamp (c) is the sort of minor fake that is easy to miss.

the side of many early stamps). The consequence was the growth of a vague belief that the part to be collected was the printed design. Wing margins were cut off with scissors, the priceless margins were cut off early imperforate stamps and in countless cases the perforations were snipped off perforated stamps. What was left was a nice, neat rectangle of printed paper. Occasionally one still comes across albums full of these pathetic sights. They are included in big 'junk lots' in auctions containing many thousands of stamps which may fetch £1, or $1, from someone prepared to plough through it in the hope of finding a single good stamp.

These early printed albums did, however, serve one useful purpose in imparting a sense of organisation to an otherwise hopeless and haphazard business. They showed a collector in broad outline what had been issued, and helped him identify his 'gaps'. Thus they made collectors search for elusive items of which they would otherwise have had no knowledge, so that many copies of rare stamps became rescued for posterity. I believe this is the main advantage of the printed album. Without it the casual collector can remain ignorant of a rarity, or simply disguise its absence. With the printed album, he has a gap staring at him like a sore thumb, and he may be able to fill it. Philatelists will be able to think of countless stamp issues where one particular value, colour, perforation or other characteristic stamp is worth far more than all the others in the set. The printed album does often encourage collectors to track these difficult items down, and if this is done while the rarity is still in current use a copy will be saved from oblivion.

Today the philatelist (as distinct from the mere collector) seldom uses a printed album. It is far too restrictive and superficial; he may fill several volumes with seemingly identical stamps, but he will have a roomful of catalogues. The earliest catalogues, such as the classic effort issued by young Gibbons in 1865, were merely lists arranged country by country, with issue dates and face values (the postal duty or rate usually printed on the stamp and almost always the price paid over the post-office counter). Nearly all catalogues are published by people who deal in stamps, and so they are also price lists. The prices are normally given for mint and used stamps, and may be qualified by a note on how the price might alter for stamps in varying condition. The concept of condition is something often ignored by the very young collector, but to the real philatelist it is of overwhelming importance. I cannot emphasise too strongly the importance of condition, and it is discussed in Chapters 7 and 8. Obviously, no publisher would bother to consider any common or modern stamp that was not wholly perfect, but in the case of valuable stamps he might add a premium for 'well centred, lightly cancelled copies'; or he might offer to supply 'second quality' or 'inferior' copies at a small fraction of the listed price. For example, several early stamps were imperforate and had a printed design that was round or octagonal; sometimes these were cut to shape, either before being stuck on the letter or by an industrious early collector, and a catalogue may comment that such copies can be supplied for a relatively small sum.

It is not too much to claim that the catalogue is the basis of all serious collecting. This does not mean that the casual collector cannot get fun out of just picking up whatever comes along, but

a   b   c

Fig 2 Many countries have used stamps which were not rectangular in shape, yet which were laid out on the printing plate in a regular (non-intermeshing) rectangular pattern. When the sheet was cut up, some stamps survived with their original rectangular shape preserved, but most were cut to shape, either before being used or else because an early collector thought this looked nicer. The first stamp (a) is a fine copy of the British 10d of 1847. It is worth about fifty times as much as copy (b), cut to shape but not cut into. In turn (b) is worth much more than poor (c), which is badly cut into.

this 'simple life' technique can never be more than fun. Any collection of value, and any link between philately and investment, demands catalogues, study, and experience. Today the enormous accumulated knowledge of generations of painstaking experts can be picked up for a small sum by buying catalogues of successively greater specialisation and depth. They tell in considerable detail exactly what stamps have been planned or designed, which have been printed, and which have been issued to the public. The development of the catalogue is very largely the story of the development of philately.

Most very young collectors are content to ignore all but the obvious differences between one stamp and another. In the same way, the original Gibbons catalogue of 1865 simply listed a pair of stamps issued in Great Britain in 1840: a 1d (penny) black and a 2d blue. They were obviously different, because even though the designs were identical, they were different colours and bore different postal duties, one having twice the face value of the other. In 1841 the 1d stamp changed in colour to red-brown, though it was at first printed from the same plates. The 2d stamp stayed its original colour but suddenly appeared with horizontal white lines at the top and bottom. These were obviously two more different stamps. During the rest of the nineteenth century, one or two keen-eyed collectors noticed characteristics peculiar to particular specimens of these four basic stamps, but such things were regarded as trivial. The same is true of other countries; there were plenty of collectors who amassed big collections of seemingly identical stamps, and could hardly fail to notice many peculiarities and unrecorded 'varieties' of particular specimens, but this was all of no more than passing interest – except on one or two occasions when even this superficial study unearthed what appeared to be obvious mistakes. But imperceptibly, as the present century dawned, the collection of stamps developed into philately, a subject of such vast breadth and depth that no one can know more than a small fraction of it.

The reasons for the increased interest in stamp-collecting were varied, one being that the whole subject had become a little less trivial and more respectable. In Britain the collection of stamps even acquired royal patronage; in 1893 young Prince George became an Honorary Vice-President of the Philatelic Society of London, establishing an enduring interest in philately which he continued as King George V and handed on to his granddaughter, the present sovereign. Several other notable heads of state thought it quite proper not merely to continue a childhood interest, but to let the fact be known, thus rather spiking the guns of the arrogant adults who still scorned the whole topic.

A further very important point is that by 1900 the early juvenile collectors had grown up. Many of them had an enquiring mind and high intelligence; indeed, many were scientists, doctors, and engineers whose training taught them to look into things, measure everything measurable and write it down, and then, if possible, draw valid conclusions or inferences. A further influence was the dawn of a belief that two apparently identical stamps might not have identical values. The wide publicity accorded the discovery of printing errors, odd 'varieties', forgeries, and other departures from routine, gradually gave rise to the understanding that, as people were prepared to go out of their way to buy such things, they could be equated with an enhanced value in terms of hard cash. So by the start of the twentieth century there had grown a network of philatelists in almost every civilised country.

These men and women had the enthusiasm, the insight, the mental faculties, the financial resources, and the spare time to conduct deep study into particular issues of stamps. They organised themselves into groups, either corresponding with each other by private letter or by forming philatelic societies and study groups. By choosing particular types of stamp and studying them by the hundred or by the thousand, they were gradually able to work out the entire history of how that stamp was made. In the early days of stamp printing, flat plates carrying a number of impressions of the stamp were forced down on to a sheet of paper slightly larger than the plate. The process involved a lot of hand work, and as even skilled operatives can seldom repeat their actions precisely, it so happened that many of the stamps bore evidence of slight mistakes, corrected mistakes, and other distinguishing characteristics. Stamps are printed by 'security printers' who seldom record details of their manufacturing processes and certainly do not make them available to the public. So the early philatelists were discovering things that would otherwise have been lost, because with the passage of time it has become increasingly difficult to amass the great numbers of quite rare stamps needed for proper study.

The early philatelists sought to create order out of chaos, and this is one of the hallmarks of what philately is all about. The first groups of stamps ever subjected to such study were the original British stamps of 1840, the 'penny black' and 'twopenny blue'. Late in the nineteenth century there were at least a million of these in collectors' hands, but virtually nothing was known of their manufacture because it had not occurred to anyone to find out. Brief handwritten records had been left by the printers, Messrs Perkins Bacon & Co, and other records existed at the General Post Office, but none of these had been made public. So, solely on the basis of the characteristics of the issued stamps, the pioneer philatelists sought to 'plate' every stamp: to work out from which plate it had been printed, and the position of the stamp within the rectilinear pattern on the plate. Before long it was discovered that corrections or repairs to the plates caused visible changes in the stamps printed from them, and values began to be assigned to particular stamps showing prominent characteristics, and even to stamps printed from particular plates. Obviously this research was of profound interest to the philatelic industry which was then fast growing up in many countries. Each successive edition of the established catalogues contained fresh and more detailed information, and specialised catalogues emerged dealing only with stamps from one country, or even stamps of a particular issue.

Since the beginning of this century there have been two classes of stamp-collector. One class is interested in any stamp that comes along. In his right hand he used to hold a pot of horrible flour-paste, but today he holds a packet of adhesive hinges. The other class is the philatelist. In his right hand he holds a powerful magnifying glass, or a perforation gauge, perhaps even a micrometer or an optical instrument not normally found outside a laboratory. Show him a stamp from his own group, and he will immediately treat it as he would a lifelong friend, identifying it in complete detail and at once spotting anything that might be unusual about its printing or the way it was used. Show him any other stamp, even a valuable classical stamp, and he will say 'I don't really know much about those.' In buying and selling he is the master in his own field, but he would never dream of straying outside it.

The picture I have painted borders on that of the absent-minded professor, whom the rest of the world regards as a cranky eccentric. Nothing could be further from the truth. Almost all philatelists are very busy people and use philately as their relaxation. They are far from being 'cranky' but merely appreciate that, if you are going to be an expert, you have to narrow your field. Nobody today can be an expert in the world's stamps – although most stamp dealers have to try – and nobody can seriously try to collect the world's stamps, except for fun. But anyone with reasonable resources in terms of money and leisure can become quite expert in the stamps of one particular country, or the stamps printed within a particular period by a single printer, or any other obviously related group in terms of paper, printing, or use. Other types of grouping, such as the 'thematic' collection based on the subject portrayed on the stamp, such as flowers, spacemen, or wild animals, is obviously sheer 'fun collecting' and impossible to use as the basis for philatelic study, because there is no connection between any one stamp and any other apart from its theme. Such a collection might, however, be of interest to the artist and graphic designer from a purely pictorial viewpoint.

Today, stamps are printed in vast quantities by economic, fast presses. The translation of the stamp designer's finished design into the printed stamp is still a long process calling for plenty of manual skill by craftsmen, but on the whole it is an automated operation in which the possibility of error or deviation from a standard is kept very small indeed. Out of every million stamps printed, only a very few show any significant departures from the norm, and hardly any of these escape detection at the printer's factory. Very,

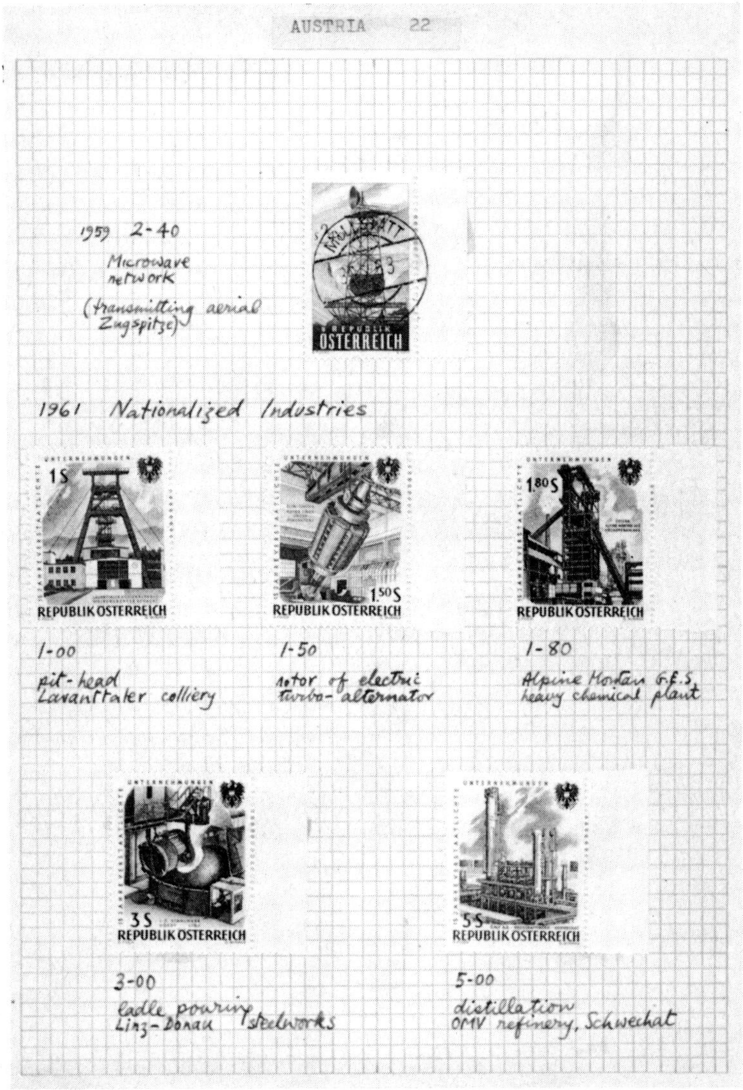

1959 2·40
Microwave
network
(transmitting aerial
Zugspitze)

1961 Nationalized Industries

1·00
pit-head
Lavanttaler colliery

1·50
rotor of electric
turbo-alternator

1·80
Alpine Montan G.E.S.
heavy chemical plant

3·00
ladle pouring
Linz-Donau steelworks

5·00
distillation
OMV refinery, Schwechat

Fig 3   A typical page from the album of an ordinary stamp-collector. Such a
collector might have stamps from over 100 countries, laid out in neat 'sets' as
these are. Incidentally these stamps are all examples of modern line-engraving or
recess printing, described later.

24

POLAND
M.N. Kilinski

SINGAPORE
Timber tong-kong

E. AFRICA
M.V. Umoja

THE LEBANON
felucca

HONG KONG
poled native craft

GIBRALTAR
S. S. Canberra

GUERNSEY
S.S. Dasher

FRANCE
round-the-world
vessel of
Alain Gerbault

YUGOSLAVIA

INDIA
M.V. Jalausha

AUSTRALIA
Abel Tasman's ship

UK
S.S. Great Britain

Fig 4   A page from the album of a thematic collector. This album is devoted to ships on stamps. It might start off with separate sections devoted to merchant ships, warships, native craft, and so on, but may eventually degenerate (as here) into a hotch potch, with stamps stuck in as they come along. Thematic collecting can be instructive about the chosen subject, and possibly of interest to a graphic designer, but it is poles apart from philately.

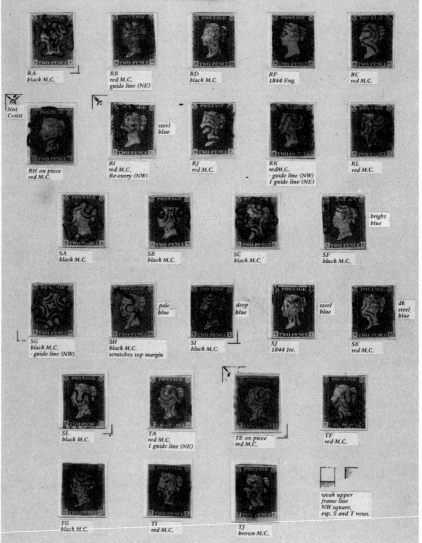

RA
black M.C.

RB
red M.C.
guide line (NE)

RD
black M.C.

RF
1844 Eng.

RC
red M.C.

Not
Const

RH on piece
red M.C.

steel
blue

RI
red M.C.
Re-entry (NW)

RJ
red M.C.

RK
redM.C.
- guide line (NW)
1 guide line (NE)

RL
red M.C.

SA
black M.C.

SB
black M.C.

SC
black M.C.

bright
blue

SF
black M.C.

pale
blue

deep
blue

steel
blue

dk
steel
blue

SG
black M.C.
- guide line (NW)

SH
black M.C.
scratches top margin

SI
black M.C.

SJ
1844 Ire.

SK
red M.C.

SL
black M.C.

TA
red M.C.
1 guide line (NE)

TE on piece
red M.C.

TF
red M.C.

TG
black M.C.

TI
red M.C.

TJ
brown M.C.

weak upper
frame line
NW square,
esp. S and T rows.

very few indeed slip through to reach the public, and these are at once equatable with a sum of money many times their face value. It follows that today's philatelist either deals in classic stamps or he follows slightly different procedures. I have no doubt there are philatelists whose speciality is the USA definitive 20c or 21c air mail stamp, or the French 0,05 definitive, or the Indian 15p 'plucking tea', or the current Great Britain definitives. I very probably have a thousand of each of these, because I could not stop them flooding in. The idea of anyone making a study of such a stamp seems at first to be an unrewarding task. There is no possibility whatever of 'plating' them. They are printed on rotary presses and the output is such that scores of printing cylinders are used in the course of the stamp's life, and each cylinder differs from the previous one only in microscopic ways. I suppose one could look at, say, ten thousand used 3p stamps a day for a month and be no nearer classifying or grouping them, or discovering much about their printing. I say a little more about this at the start of Chapter 5.

The basic point to be made is that old-style philately is largely inappropriate to modern stamps; but one has to try very hard to take a long-term view. Almost always the stamp of value is the one that was ignored in its own time because it was not worthy of study. Philatelic study of even the most common mass-produced stamps might just unearth varieties very richly deserving catalogue status. A change of frame size, of colour, of paper, of perforation, of 'phosphor' bands or coatings, could all be quietly introduced or used for a particular reason for a short period, and thus create a sub-group of considerable value years later when the situation had been fully identified. Sometimes changes are announced – then the philatelic trade may well suggest that either the old stamp or

Fig 5   A page from the album of a philatelist. To the ordinary 'stamp-collector' such a page might be supremely boring, especially when the other pages in the album all look the same! But to the philatelist who knows the country concerned, such a page is a happy meeting with old friends. Like people, the stamps are generally similar, yet in detail no two are alike.

the new one will be of great value, and that a sheet or two would be a good investment. This is seldom the case; history shows that on such occasions the good investment had already jumped to a price which it is unlikely to exceed for many years, largely because thousands of 'investors' bought a sheet or two.

The best changes come quietly. During and after World War I the ordinary British definitive stamps were printed in inks of a marvellous range of hues. I do not know any comparable diversity of colours in any other set of stamps. The $\frac{1}{2}$d was green, the 1d red, the $1\frac{1}{2}$d brown, the 2d orange and the $2\frac{1}{2}$d blue, but these mere words give no hint of the fabulous richness of shades that can be found in mint specimens. When they bought them over the counter, people sometimes noticed that the stamps were unusual shades of colour, but not many thought them worth collecting. So today the more extreme shades are worth at least a thousand times face value; indeed some, with a certificate that they are genuine, can change hands at over £100 or $250. And these are stamps which, at the time, were considered so common as to be quite beneath the notice of a true philatelist.

It is therefore short-sighted to dismiss common modern stamps as being of no philatelic interest; the answer is 'wait and see'. I know a number of collectors who have formed, for very little cost, impressive collections of common modern stamps that are liberally sprinkled with printing flaws, ink shades, paper changes and other variations, some of them admittedly fairly trivial. Have we not all gone through albums belonging to hopeful collectors who have written in comments on 'varieties' that can barely be seen with the naked eye? I doubt that such collections will fetch any more than the stamps would as ordinary copies, devoid of such scrutiny and painstaking 'writing up' (see Chapter 5). Yet the world population of real philatelists, interested in the innermost details of the stamps they collect, has never been so high, and it appears still to be growing fast. A fair guide is the sales curve plotted opposite. This is enormously encouraging, yet the great boom in stamp-collecting, which is a global phenomenon of massive proportions, would have happened without there being any experts at all.

One of the influences behind this boom is a more liberal and philatelically orientated post office administration in almost every land. Led by Great Britain, many administrations once haughtily looked down on the suggestion that they should issue frequent pictorial or 'commemorative' stamps, claiming that this would in some way be debasing. For example, in 1936 the then postmaster general claimed that 'This present policy [of not issuing any but definitive stamps, with very rare exceptions] carries with it a definite international prestige value.' But by 1960 it was clear that deliberate encouragement of philately can bring returns in terms of hard cash that may be more valuable than a vague 'international prestige'. From then onwards the UK has poured out as many special issues as most other countries, and more than two-thirds of all British stamp designs date from 1960 or later. No one could fail to notice such a profusion of stamp issues, and a decade ago *Punch* printed a cartoon of a lady who was doubtless a mother asking at

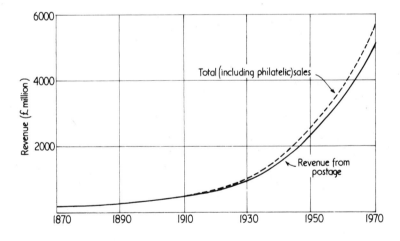

Fig 6   To show that stamps are not on the way out, this is a very approximate plot of the total world annual sale of adhesive postage stamps. Despite much greater use of telecommunications, and mail franking machines, growth in stamp sales has never been so rapid as today.

the post office for 'a twopence-halfpenny stamp commemorating absolutely nothing'. Even in the USA, Canada, Australia and many European countries, all of them with a long history of special issues, there was a definite trend in the 1960s towards an increase in the frequency of such issues, and especially in the total face value of new stamps issued each year.

This policy has netted substantial sums in extra revenue (see Chapter 9), although a country that pursues it to excess defeats its own objective in deterring the collector and depressing the value of its stamps. A secondary result of the more frequent issue of commemorative stamps has been to sustain the interest of the casual or young collector. There are two sides to this particular coin. The fact that about once a month millions of young people all over the world hand over their scarce pennies and cents in exchange for newly issued stamps is good for the post office, and good for the philatelic trade that supplies albums and accessories. But most of this mountain of stamps is almost immediately stuck clumsily into albums, creased, dampened, dirtied, and in countless other ways taken along an irreversible route of degradation that makes it virtually unsaleable (for the material is common). This means that the scarce pennies and cents have been wasted, if one regards the operation in business terms. On the other hand, the best way to learn philately is by collecting stamps, and a high proportion of these collectors gradually learn to make the transition from grubby degradation, which shows a financial loss, to diligent study and care, which can show a financial gain.

Precise statistics do not exist on the growth of philately, and the numbers obviously depend on what is meant by a philatelist, but I think it probable that the world total of 'serious collectors', who take the trouble to study what they collect, has doubled every twenty years from 1850. The total today is certainly not less than 15 million, and the total number of casual collectors is many times as great. All sorts of people collect stamps, from those ardent philatelists living in windy, leaky shacks on the Rand or the outskirts of Rio or Hong Kong, to those who are wealthy and eminent – indeed the most important public figures cannot escape acquiring

a multitude of philatelic items. Particular professions are also favoured, and in many countries doctors and sometimes dentists receive a flood of 'first day covers' containing mailing shots and
samples from the pharmaceutical industry and other medical suppliers. Doctors have all the necessities of the serious philatelist apart
from adequate spare time.

What are these necessities? The first is undoubtedly enthusiasm,
and this is something that cannot be injected from outside. Anyone
can stick stamps in a book, but for real philately one must either
wait for a particular bug to bite, or else take the advice of an undoubted connoisseur and make a firm decision to pick a particular
country or group of stamps and try to become an expert. Nobody
can become an expert without spending years literally surrounded
by the actual stamps in question, and it cannot be done only by
reading books or magazine articles. There is absolutely no substitute for the 'hardware' itself, in the biggest possible quantities. For
example, whenever you can spare the time, go to a stamp auction,
or 'view' the lots to be sold in that auction which are of interest to
you. Even if you can seldom afford to buy, this will help you to
gain the essential familiarity with the stamps in question. If you
read up all about them you will soon know what to look for, so
that every minute spent inspecting an auction lot, or stamps in a
dealer's shop, or a friend's collection, will be put to good use.

A second necessity is adequate money and time. Like learning a
foreign language, you cannot be an expert philatelist by devoting a
furiously intensive evening to the subject and then dropping it for
a month. A few minutes every day is a better idea, even if you
merely read a page from a specialised catalogue. Probably this
question of time will cease to be as important as it was in the past
because the 90-hour working week is now consigned to history.
According to most international statistics we shall all enjoy a
superabundance of leisure in future, and philately seems to be a
much better way of occupying one's time than watching a television screen. The money factor obviously reflects the field of interest. It is possible to run a good and profitable philatelic
operation with very little capital, especially if you can get the

pickings of the envelopes of a large office, and best of all if the office receives mail bearing high-value stamps, but such matters are obvious. The important point is that you do not have to be a Rothschild.

A third necessity is good eyesight, and an ability to distinguish between shades of colours, and to identify a shade correctly even when seen against an unhelpful background. This is discussed in Chapter 5. In many classes of philately, shades play little or no part, but good eyes and an alert mind are always vital. A schoolboy with a few coins in his pocket can walk into a large stamp retailer's shop and take them for a substantial sum – quite fairly and quite legally – merely by having sharper eyes or better knowledge than the professional behind the counter. He can walk into an auction room and outbid a hundred experts who just failed to notice something that he spotted in one of the lots for sale. He can sort through piles of waste paper and extract not the brightest or prettiest stamps, but the ones that he knows are going to be saleable years hence. Over the long term he will make philately pay handsomely. In doing so, he is bound to accumulate piles of stamps and other material outside his own field, and in disposing of it he may well help someone else. The philatelist must resign himself to giving away, or selling for a purely nominal sum, stuff he does not understand. If he acquires a lot of Nicaragua, he can give it to an expert on Nicaragua. Do not try to become an instant expert on any country, unless you really do mean to take that country seriously. In my experience, accumulations obtained as office waste, or as unwanted bits of big auction 'junk lots', are likely to be made up of at least 99 per cent common and almost unsaleable stamps. It really is not worth your time spending many hours going through it with an unfamiliar catalogue, hoping to find a rarity.

What does one actually do as a philatelist? Obviously one can join clubs and study groups, engage in correspondence and chat with friends, but the essence of it is acquiring stamps (and, if you wish, also disposing of others) and building up order out of chaos. One can acquire stamps in many ways, as outlined in Chapter 10.

Merely buying stamps from the post office and salting them away for the future is not in any sense philately, though it may, with care, be a good investment. Going to an auction, inspecting a single good stamp and buying it as an investment is philately, since it requires knowledge and judgement. The best philately of all is lifting material from the mire and putting it in a worthy setting. I derive immense pleasure in buying old album pages for next to nothing, that a dealer or friend cannot be bothered to go through in detail, and carefully attending to what is on them. An evening's relaxation can convert filthy, creased pages covered with tatty-looking stamps into a pile of perfect copies waiting to find their proper places in a valuable collection filling dozens of volumes. The techniques of the conversion process are discussed in Chapter 8. In general, the process is intended to restore each stamp as closely as possible to a perfect state, whilst both bringing to light any hidden damage and avoiding causing any damage where none exists.

The process has much in common with the buying of derelict old habitations, 'doing them up', and selling them at an enormous profit (with the important exception that one cannot add to or improve a stamp). In many countries, properties ripe for improvement are hard to find, and the process is less attractive when everything has already been done. Will the efforts of the great world population of philatelists ensure that, one day, every interesting stamp will be in place, fully identified, in a high-quality collection? One thinks wistfully of the early philatelists, who rummaged through material that had never before been seen by expert eyes. One of them found strips and blocks of the Austrian stamps of 1850 with crosses attached. Another found an envelope bearing a copy of the British 1869 sixpenny from the rare plate 10. It is fair to assume that such items will never pass out of the world of top-flight philately. They will never be absent-mindedly given to little Johnny, whose collection will later appear on a street-trader's barrow. But a rung or two down the ladder there is a reverse process in operation. Every day some philatelic material of very substantial value gets lost, overlooked, sold by someone who doesn't

understand it, given to little Johnny, or left in the effects of a philatelist who failed also to leave clear details of what it was and how
it should be disposed of. It is this global reverse process which
enables philatelists, even in the 1970s, to keep on finding unex-
pected good material. Unfortunately, the reverse process also results in a little good material being lost or destroyed. If this can be
held below about 5 per cent, the main result will just be sharper appreciation of the rest. But for a true philatelist to cause damage or
destruction, which can happen through forgetfulness, tiredness or
rank carelessness, is tragic.

The basic objective of most philatelists is, first, to add to the
storehouse of knowledge on his own speciality, and, second, to
build up a collection to bring pleasure and profit. This involves
arranging all the material in albums in such a way that no other
expert can be left unaware of the value. Rarities are pointed out
and described, and the condition and cancellation and other variables are commented upon. If, for any good reason, a stamp is included that has any kind of damage (a very rare thing indeed) this
fact is pointed out. Some collectors may be tempted to hide
damage and other imperfections. What they do to maximise their
own satisfaction is their own affair, but if they have a collection of
some value and wish to sell it, they are strongly advised to remove
every damaged or imperfect item, or else make sure it is clearly
indicated. Only in this way will a dealer or auctioneer take pains
to see that the collection realises its proper price.

There are many guides on how to arrange and write up a collection. In my own case, I have gone broader and deeper and simply
used common sense. It helps enormously if one has some artistic
accomplishment, a sense of good layout, and the ability to write
uniformly and legibly. An intelligent adult collector can decide
for himself how to arrange things. For example, as a general rule a
single album page does not contain both mint and used stamps,
but this rule can be waived to show mint and used examples of a
particular variety, a stamp with a particular marginal marking
(such as a 'control'), or a rare shade of colour. In my own case, I
mount the mint stamps first, on one or more pages, and the used

34

FOURPENCE   PLATE 3

With the ninepenny, this was the first surface-printed
       stamp to have corner letters

Dates: 4 February 1860   decision to insert corner letters
               to   4d, 6d, 1s when plates had to be renewed.
         No warrant issued for 4d value until after proofs.
         29 June 1861   die proof, no inscription or corner letters
         28 November 1861   Treasury Warrant issued
         29 November 1861   Registration
         30 November 1861   Put to press.
         Date of issue: believed to be 15 January 1862
               (earliest postmark 16 January)

Paper: large garter, hand-made, white

Plate: as Pls. 1 and 2 (see diagram)

Issued colour: described as scarlet; actually shades of
       deep to pale vermillion and bright to dull red

EK unused
horizontal crease

B1
possibly regummed

In the design of this fourpenny stamp the Board, on the
instructions of the GPO, incorporated features showing the plate number
(the line engraved stamps then being prepared all did this).
The number was shown by insertion of a single vertical white line,
said to represent a Roman I, in the lower border just inboard of
the lower corner squares.

The new electro-plating of silver was used, after experiments by
Warren De la Rue, to protect the copper plates from attacking
the vermillion which had to be used, instead of true scarlet,
to make the ink fugitive.

Fig 7   A page from the author's volume of British stamps of 1862–4. This page
introduces plate 3 of the 4d issue of January 1862. Two unused copies are contained in protective (Hawid) mounts, while the background facts and dates are
set forth in handwriting.

SG. 79 bright red

CK
In perfect original state;
later the K in SE square
became a white blob
(see SG. 80 for example)
London

KJ
466 Liverpool

AD (short stamp, A row)
Ireland 215 ?
　　Ennistimon

DI
London

GB
Ireland
309 Longford ?

copies on the pages immediately following. True mint stamps, with gum undisturbed, are always mounted in a transparent folder (many types are available) even if they are of supposedly common modern types; who can say what difference undisturbed gum will make a century hence? But I have no fetish about 'unhinged mint'. A dealer once told me how angry he became at the stupid way a customer spent several minutes studying the back of a fine old stamp with a magnifying glass to see if it had ever been hinged. Eventually he took the stamp from the customer, stuck a hinge on and said 'Well, it's hinged now!' About one-quarter of my unused stamps, a century and more old, appear to be truly unhinged, and these are in transparent mounts. The rest are on light hinges, which cannot affect the value of the stamp. Indeed some gum on old stamps may have to be removed entirely (see Chapter 8).

A philatelist with some artistic ability can lift his collection out of the common rut by adding drawings, diagrams and other illustrations showing the layout of the original sheets of stamps, the marginal markings, the printing of the colours or phosphor bands, and many similar topics which interest the philatelist but not the casual collector. Indeed, I know one or two collections which are full of pictures of rarities even though these are beyond the owner's reach! Why not? It adds vastly to the interest of an otherwise ordinary collection, and may even add to its value. But there remains the basic problem of the investment-minded philatelist of very limited means. He cannot really get very far with pictures of classic rarities. Probably the only contribution to philately he can make is to build up a comprehensive collection of a common modern stamp, or set of stamps, embracing every possible vari-

Fig 8   The next page following that shown in Fig 7 is the first of many such pages each containing five stamps in the bright-red shade; then follows a group of pages displaying used copies in less-bright shades. Each copy is identified by its corner letters and place of use, together with comments on the stamp or its usage. The arrangement is completely flexible and the collection can grow as the philatelist wishes.

ation in printing and usage (including, of course, unusual uses, cancellations, franking slogans and anything else the collector can think of).

This can be quite a satisfying thing, and done for next to nothing; but what will it be worth a few decades hence? I sometimes see vast accumulations of common old stamps, and in general they are boring. There are some exceptions. Again choosing an example from Great Britain, the 1864 'penny plate numbers' can be made to fill volumes; but, although they all look alike, each bears the number of the plate from which it was printed, and this at once divides the collection up into at least 151 parts. Common modern stamps bear no such distinguishing features, and sorting a giant collection could well be a waste of time – even though it could make a genuine contribution to philately. Predicting the future is often uncertain, and the philatelist with very scant resources must always ask himself 'What is this likely to fetch, if I should want to sell?' and try to decide how many other people are likely to be making similar collections. He should also try to judge what his time is worth, and whether he is really making the best use of it.

But at least a person who asks such questions will never buy up modern stamps in the firm belief that they will appreciate in value. The mere process of buying and storing a commodity does not automatically yield a profit, and the more widely it is done the less profitable it is. Yet millions of people do not understand this, and continue to buy newly issued stamps, each printed in astronomic quantities, and to store them in a way that frequently causes positive degradation in value. These people would probably not think it reasonable that they should run a business with no skill, no knowledge and no input of work, and yet show a profit; and there is no law which says that a common object, stored all over the world in vast quantities, is bound to appreciate in value.

In the final chapter of this book I offer further advice on how to collect at a profit. I will conclude this opening chapter with some universal golden rules which are common sense but often hard to follow.

1 Stick to your last; never become involved with stamps you

know little about, even if something appears to be a marvellous bargain.

2 Always be vitally concerned with condition; when encountering a rare or valuable stamp for the first time, try to examine it in good lighting in a disbelieving frame of mind which expects to find imperfections, faking, touching-up, regumming and all sorts of other dodges.

3 Try to acquire a keen eye and alert mind so that you never fail to notice anything worth noticing.

4 Before buying anything, always be in a position to know pretty accurately the answer to the question 'What can I sell this for?'

5 Consider what you intend to do with your collection in order to maximise your enjoyment, as well as your ultimate profit, and then do it in a deliberate and planned way (so that, for example, you never find yourself committed to an album arrangement which proves too narrow and restrictive and has to be done all over again).

6 Never buy even one expensive stamp until you have acquired much knowledge and familiarity with the stamp trade, retailers, auctions and clubs, and are fully able to judge what you are doing.

7 When you wish to sell, be sure you know exactly what you are selling and what it ought to fetch; if you do not, but are sure it has some value, put it into an auction.

2
Postal History

Postal history is an enormous subject, far greater than the study of mere adhesive stamps. But nine collectors out of ten are interested almost solely in stamps, and so this chapter is very brief, giving a broad outline of how today's posts developed.

Many of the early civilisations appear to have had splendid systems for written communication, at first using clay tablets and then early forms of parchment or even paper. The Persian emperor, Cyrus, laid the foundations for one of the first empire-wide postal systems, the later Egyptian Pharaohs undoubtedly had excellent systems of which many records or allusions remain, and probably the finest of all the early postal organisations was that of the Romans. Then, like so many other advances, everything fell apart for centuries. I do not know of any medieval country in which there was any postal system at all, apart from an *ad hoc* conveyance by horsemen of the king's messages. It was not until 1482 that the British king thought it worth while setting up a semi-permanent organisation to carry his despatches. In that year Edward IV decreed that a rider should be waiting every twenty miles; but this was still only along a particular road of interest to the king. The sole people who had any sort of postal system, and probably the only ones who realised the need for such a system, were the merchant guilds and the universities, which set up their own post-riders to carry their messages throughout much of Europe.

Henry VIII created the office of 'Master of the Postes' soon after his coronation in 1509, but an early holder found he could not rival the fine national systems growing up on the continent because of the parsimony of the Treasury. The post-boys or constables who carried the mails had no horses, but had to borrow them from carters and ploughmen! In 1591 Elizabeth proclaimed her right to a national post system for all international correspondence, which was aimed at stopping the university and merchant traffic and increasing the volume and revenue of the national post. Very gradually post offices were established, the original ones in London and Calais being supplemented by such obvious ones as Bristol, Holyhead (for Ireland), Berwick and (appropriately in 1620, the year of the Pilgrim Fathers) Plymouth. James I in 1603 improved the 'packet post' for official mail but forced private communications to go by the 'thorough post' [sic] at the rate of 2½d *per mile*. There follow two centuries of argument, improvement, abuse, graft, folly, and various attempts by individual entrepreneurs to organise commercial post systems. On a national basis Britain, and the other European countries or principalities that had post systems, provided for letters to be sent only between a small number of 'post towns' along particular roads. Mail was left at the post town nearest to the addressee, who was expected to ride in from time to time, see if there was any mail for him, and often to pay for the postage before he could collect it.

In 1784 the first mail coach ran from Bath (some records say Bristol) to London, thus doubling the speed of the through journey and greatly increasing the possible payload. The rates charged varied over the years, but, to the surprise of many, the big coaches were soon costing less to run than the old teams of post-boys. Any modern transport expert will know that speed, big traffic flow, and low unit costs go together, but in 1800 this was not understood. It was not the supposedly expensive coaches but the

41

Napoleonic war that made the postal rates climb to 4d for 15 miles rising to 17d (almost an average week's wage) for 700 miles. By 1815 the General Post Office was earning £1.5 million a year, costing £0.5 million, and supplying the balance to help fight the French. The government continued to milk the service for another twenty-five years, until a great reformer, Rowland Hill, managed through pamphleteering and public discontent to get a uniform rate. On 5 December 1839 this was fixed at 4d, throughout the United Kingdom, and on 10 January 1840 this was changed to Hill's target: 1d. At last economic sense prevailed, and the massive increase in mail volume eventually more than made up for the sharply decreased revenue on each item.

When, in 1839, Hill's reform had been accepted in principle, the Treasury organised a national competition to see who could devise the best method of ensuring that everyone who sent a letter paid his penny, or whatever higher charge might be levied for a letter contained in a separate envelope (then counted as two items), a very large letter, or a postal packet. Many extremely ingenious answers were forthcoming, most of them based on the concept of a pre-gummed printed label, bearing an image defying easy forgery, which could swiftly be affixed to the postal item. Several entrants suggested labels with designs either embossed or else printed with intricate patterns originally engraved by special machinery to give a result at once distinctive and difficult to copy. One man who was ahead of his time designed a coil-dispensing machine for issuing embossed 1d stamps from a £1 roll of 240 stamps, each stamp

Fig 9   In 1839 the British Treasury held a competition for the design of a postage stamp that could be manufactured in advance and stuck on a postal item to show postage had been paid. This was a novel idea, and over 2,600 entries were received. One entrant, Charles Whiting, submitted many marvellously complex 'stamps' (a) to deter forgers. James Chalmers hit on the idea of 'cancelling' the stamp with the place and date (b). Nobody suggested a delicate representation of the queen's head, which was the design finally adopted.

a

b

emerging when a 1d coin was inserted. He was awarded one of the four £100 prizes, but none of the submissions was considered wholly acceptable. Eventually Hill himself, guided by an 1819 report on preventing forgery of banknotes, which suggested that the design should be immediately identifiable by 'the common observer' who should be able to detect any manipulation or forgery decided that the central feature of the design of the proposed label should be a likeness of the queen. Further notes on the design of this stamp appear in Chapter 3.

In those days most people were even more suspicious of new ideas than they are now, and many refused to trust the stuck-on labels and continued to hand their money to the postmaster who wrote '1d' or 'paid' on the item. But in the long term this revolutionary development was a great success. The concept of universally prepaid mail, carried at a known cheap rate, was a massive spur that combined with increasing literacy to foster the growth of commerce and written communication. In 1839 the number of letters carried in Britain was some 80 million. In 1840 it was about 170 million. By 1870 it reached 800 million, by 1928 it passed 3,000 million and today it is about 12,000 million. And, of course, today the Post Office handles telecommunications, savings banks, money orders and many other services, just as it does in other countries.

This brief outline of the British postal service has close parallels with the stories of the posts in most other long-developed countries, especially in Northern and Western Europe. In the USA the embryonic postal service established in Massachusetts in 1639 was growing fast when there came the traumatic break with Britain in 1775–6 and it was reorganised under Congress. In 1791, when there were some eighty post offices, the service became a subsidiary of the US Treasury, but in 1823 it was made a separate department which gradually grew to cover the country as it was opened up westwards, with railroads supplementing and then replacing the horse. By the late 1920s, when the number of US post offices topped 50,000, there were twenty air mail routes operated by commercial firms (embryonic predecessors of the giant passenger airlines) under fixed-rate contracts. Experimental air mails had

been operated for short periods at Allahabad, India, in February
1911, and between Hendon and Windsor, England, in September
of that year; and the Zeppelin airship airline sustained a regular
passenger and mail service in Central Europe in 1911. After World
War I the RAF flew a scheduled mail service to Cologne and then
to other continental destinations, while in 1919 the first sustained
air services by aeroplanes (except for a flying-boat route in Florida
in 1914) began to link all European capitals.

From about 1850 mail carried by train had borne special postal
markings in many countries. Some of the mail was sorted en route,
and TPO (travelling post office), 'sorting tender', and special sta-
tion postmarks are today eagerly sought by postal historians. Ship
mail has a much longer history, and again there is a wealth of
special postal markings often worth considerable sums. For a century, mail has been actually posted aboard passenger vessels, and
this generally bears the international cancellation 'PAQUEBOT'
which, though a French term originally meaning a packet – a frequent and fast mail-boat – has long been used on all sorts of mail-
carrying ships and is something quite distinct from the 'packet
letter' dating from the first steam packets of about 1835. One can

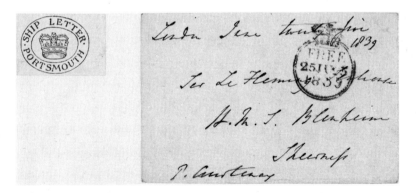

Fig 10   Postal historians are interested in postal items of all kinds, starting with
clay tablets! These two items, a hand-struck 'ship letter' stamp and a hand-
struck 'FREE' stamp, both date from the days when there were no adhesive
'postage stamps' as we know them today.

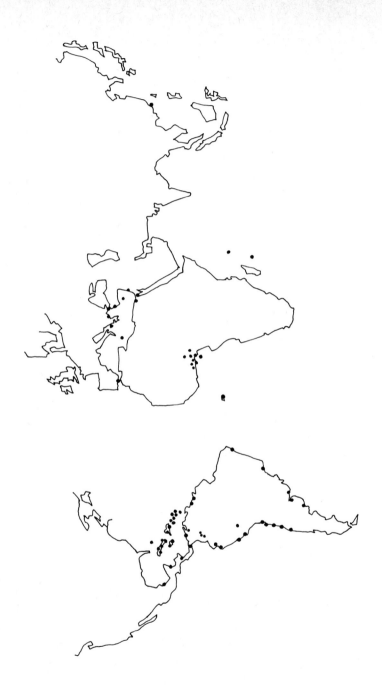

find many letters bearing the paquebot cancellation and the date-stamp of a distant foreign port, yet with postage stamps appropriate to the nationality of the vessel.

In the same way, many postal administrations organised offices and mail services outside their own territory, in the absence of any other postal service, leading to the important subject of postage stamps 'used abroad'. The British had by far the biggest overseas postal service, extending throughout the Mediterranean, Middle East, West Indies, and Central and South America. Many other countries provide examples of stamps used in unusual territories, and in every case the special cancellation enhances or even multiplies the value of the stamp. Sometimes a stamp – or, better still, a complete cover – becomes enormously valuable because of its place of use. British stamps were used in India, although this is not often shown in catalogues, and there are many islands and outlandish or temporary offices whose mail invariably commands high prices.

Thus the postal historian keeps his eyes peeled for special cancels out of the common rut, such as those of exploratory missions, military campaigns, foreign offices used only for a short period, and particularly prized cachets such as 'PAR BALLON MONTÉ' used on letters carried by balloon out of besieged Paris in the Franco-Prussian War of 1870 – surely the first of all air mails. There are special postmarks for early experimental rocket mails, special cancellations for mails posted in advance for delivery on Christmas Day, rare obliterations by early experimental machines (in the days when it was all done by hand), and countless distinc-

Fig 11 Setting up a world-wide postal system took a long time. In the nineteenth century the posts in many countries were run by the British Post Office, and British stamps (often accompanied by local national stamps) were stuck on the mails. The black dots show the British post offices where British stamps were used in the last thirty years of Queen Victoria's reign. Today all these places have their own postal service.

a

b

COMMEMORATING THE   BICENTENARY OF THE
FIRST VOYAGE OF   CAPTAIN COOK TO
NEW ZEALAND   1769–1969

c

A SOUVENIR FROM NEW ZEALAND
NATIONAL STAMP EXHIBITION, NEW PLYMOUTH
6TH–11TH OCTOBER, 1969

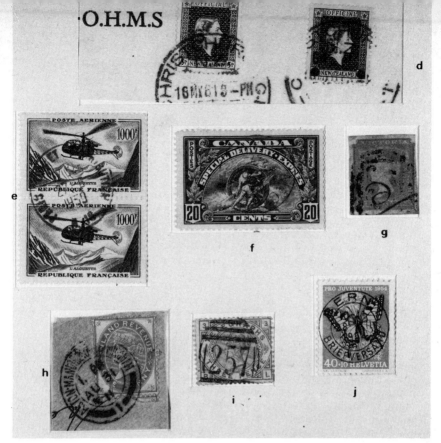

Fig 12 Some examples of different types of stamps: (a) a letter card, an example of printed postal stationery, with a 'stamp' printed in upper right corner (this one has been sent overseas, and so extra adhesive stamps had to be added); (b) a bisect, used when an office runs out of stock of the necessary value (in this case, a 2d bisected and used as a 1d); (c) a miniature sheet, a purely philatelic item (in this case containing four different stamps, each of which could also be bought as a complete regular sheet in the normal way); (d) two 'official' stamps, for postal use only by government departments (one of them is an example of a value overprint); (e) high-face air mail stamps; (f) an express or special-delivery stamp (not used for normal postage but paying a surcharge for specially quick delivery); (g) a registration stamp (not used for normal postage but to pay a surcharge for registration of a valuable postal item); (h) a revenue stamp that has been (quite legally) used for postal duty; (i) a telegraph stamp that has been (again legally, but most unusually) used for postal duty; (j) a charity stamp, in which the original purchaser has to pay a surcharge which (often after various deductions for overheads) is given by the post office to a named charity (in this case the postal duty is 40 centimes and an extra 10 centimes is charged on behalf of the Swiss Children's Fund).

tive cancellations for exhibitions, sporting events and all sorts of commemorative occasions.

Postcards were introduced in Austria in 1869, and spread like wildfire. Soon the picture postcard was flowing from holiday-makers in cities and resorts, forming a collectable item in its own right. Books and newspapers have in many countries been sent at reduced rates, often with special postmarks or cancellations, and there are instances of reduced postal rates for commercial samples. Parcels have heavy and usually unsightly obliterations, and in many countries registered mail, carried for an additional fee, has borne distinctive stamps or cancels and is often sent in special printed envelopes. In Britain and many other countries these envelopes bear embossed stamps covering the registration and sometimes also the postage. This puts them in the big class of printed or embossed stationery, which has a history just as old as adhesive stamps and is avidly collected by specialists. Many postcards also come into this category, it being especially convenient to buy a postcard, or a pack containing several, already bearing the postal duty in the form of a 'stamp' printed on it. In the early days of adhesives some authorities issued special 'Too Late' stamps bearing extra duty to speed up their transmission, and in many countries this has continued to the present day with the issue of 'express' or 'special delivery' adhesives of a distinctive design different from the regular definitive stamps. Of course, many countries also issue definitive 'Air Mail' stamps, usually portraying aeronautical motifs, and there is a big range of special air mail stationery ranging from lightweight envelopes (generally with a border frame coloured to match the national flag) to 'aerogrammes' which often have a 'stamp' printed on them.

From the earliest days of adhesives it has generally been possible to equate a postally valid stamp directly with money to the value of the postal duty, so that one can hand the stamp back to the post office in exchange for cash. This fact was not lost on the employees of firms and government departments dealing in large numbers of stamps, and the employers equally swiftly sought ways of protecting themselves against theft or improper use of their stamps. Some printed their names on them, but in Britain this was forbidden by the Post Office which, instead, allowed them to have their names printed on the back, in the same ink as used for the face, so that it was visible under the gum. (The Oxford Union Society defied this rule and continued to print its initials on the face for many years.) An even more potent deterrent was the perforation of the firm's initials right through the stamp, a procedure agreed by the British Post Office in 1868. Ever since, thousands of companies, local authorities, and other organisations have used only 'perfin' stamps. Some people have made great collections of them, while others hold that a 'perfin' is relatively valueless.

For a while in Britain official departments used stamps over-printed with their name or initials, and although this was discontinued in 1904 it persisted in many other countries, often just with the single word 'OFFICIAL', or its equivalent in the language concerned. Today it is more common for official mail to be sent in a printed envelope requiring no adhesive to be affixed at all. If anyone else sends mail without prepayment of the correct rate, the deficiency (or sometimes a multiple of it) is usually indicated by the postal authority affixing Postage Due stamps and cancelling them on the item. Oddly, although they have only a negative 'face value', dues are now keenly collected as mint stamps, as well as in used form, and are bought at face value from certain post offices.

Inland mail in any country is carried throughout by the one postal organisation, but international mail obviously has to be carried by two or more services. To organise international mail traffic, ensure its reliable and speedy transit, and lay down rules regarding such basic questions as the postal rates and the definitions of different classes of mail, some international agreement was inevitable, and after long discussions in Paris in 1863 and Berne (Switzerland) in 1874 the International (now Universal) Postal Union came into being. To a philatelist its more obvious results have been a vague international agreement on the colour of some definitive stamps used for specific rates, and a rash of special Postal Union commemorative issues by member states. Today

51

almost all the world's countries belong to the union, and their joint agreement is essential on all fundamental matters.

Such agreement is particularly important in view of the increasing need to replace expensive manpower by machine-power, in such routine operations as gathering outward letters into a neat pile, arranging every letter so that the address is uppermost, with the stamp(s) at the upper right-hand corner, and then cancelling the stamps. To any automation expert it was obvious the job could best be done by making the envelope or the stamp(s) respond to an electrical or optical stimulus in a way that could be detected by the machine through which the letter was passing. The first British experiment on a large scale was the issue in November 1957 of stamps having narrow black lines printed on the back, under the gum. Each line was in effect an electrical conductor of graphite, so that as the stamp passed close to a coil of wire through which a current was flowing, the resulting field caused a reaction in the graphite. It would have been possible to print the graphite as a closed loop on each stamp and then energise the stamp so that a current would flow, but the open-ended graphite lines could not carry current; instead they caused a local distortion in the magnetic field of the machine. The machine was designed to locate where on the letter this distortion took place; it was then easy to make the machine turn the envelope the right way for the stamp(s) to be cancelled automatically. The machine was called 'ALF', for automatic letter facing.

Later it was found that better and more economic results could be had by printing 'phosphor' bands on the face of the stamp. A phosphor is a substance which either glows by itself in the dark or else emits visible radiation (light) when some other electromagnetic radiation (such as ultra-violet) falls upon it. It was no easy matter to choose the best phosphor material and make it up into a precisely repeatable form that could be economically and quickly printed on the stamp, which would not spoil the look of the stamp, which would not wash off in the rain, and which would stay active for years. British phosphor stamps came on sale in November 1959 (they happened previously to have been printed with graphite lines on the back) in conjunction with a revised letter-facing machine which scanned the mail not electrically but with ultra-violet 'light'. The radiation was invisible, having wavelengths appreciably shorter than the violet end of the visible spectrum, but it made the phosphor bands on the stamps glow — green on the first issue, blue on the next and violet on all subsequent ones. There were two bands on most stamps, but only one on the stamp bearing the duty for second-class mail, and three or even four bands on wide commemorative stamps.

Other countries had conducted their own experiments, and had often decided to print the phosphor over the whole stamp or even

Fig 13 Modern stamps in the busiest postal administrations are 'tagged' or printed with ink containing a phosphor, or else contain a phosphor in the paper. When illuminated with ultra-violet 'light' the phosphor glows, usually with a visible colour, to trigger a machine that places the postal item in the correct way for the stamps to be cancelled. These stamps bear single (left and centre) or double bands of phosphor printed on the face.

to incorporate it into the smooth surface coating of the paper (see Chapter 4). By 1965 there were thus millions of stamps with phosphor surface coatings, either under or over the ink of the visible design, which could not be seen unless illuminated with ultraviolet radiation. In contrast, the British banded stamps could easily be detected by looking at the stamp almost edge-on, when the band(s) showed up clearly. This move into modern technology, though taken for economic reasons in the same way that computers can replace armies of clerks writing with pens in great ledgers, at once exerted a large influence on philately.

A second, and much more difficult, objective is to devise a machine which can reliably read the address on a letter. Sorting the mail has always been one of the biggest tasks in handling written communications, and in many modern postal services it costs more than the straightforward task of moving the mail from A to B. For many years electronic or electro-optical machines have been able to read specially prepared writing, such as the magnetic-ink characters printed on modern cheques, and more recently machines have been developed which can unfailingly read the results of bad typing or printed handwriting. What is far more difficult is deciphering the ghastly scrawl that many people call handwriting. In years to come there are bound to be big developments here. Today the best that can be done is to devise a national 'post code' or 'Zip code' system to supplement the old-fashioned 'address' and to use special typewriters on which a post employee can encode the address on the envelope in magnetic or phosphor ink – but he has to read it first!

When the whole process of arranging, franking, sorting and checking the mails has been automated, there will be a fresh supply of rare and valuable postal items – the first day of automatic address scanning, for example. Such items will be pure postal history, and the covers may not bear stamps at all because in business correspondence there is an increasing tendency to replace adhesive stamps by automatic high-speed franking machines called, ambiguously, postal meters. Some of these print a 'stamp', a 'town /date-stamp' and a slogan direct on the postal item, while others merely print on a gummed strip which is then torn off and affixed by hand. To most stamp-collectors, metered mail is a disappointment, especially when it comes from a distant country and carries a high rate of postage. Yet there are plenty of people who collect nothing else, just as there are people who collect slogan postmarks and almost fail to notice the stamp that these postmarks are cancelling. Above all, there are the real postal historians who study the mails of particular places and times as keenly as any philatelist ever studied an adhesive stamp. They go to big auctions and bid vast sums for priceless old covers. To an ordinary 'stamp-collector' it seems odd to watch this, because you may see hundreds of such covers and never find one with a stamp on it.

3

Designing Stamps

All over the world modern stamps are usually designed with at least one eye, if not both, on the philatelic market. The fact that the purpose of the little adhesive label is to confirm the prepayment of postage has become secondary, and in many lands the enduring objective of having every stamp instantly identifiable because of strong and sustained national characteristics has been forgotten. Britain, which used to lead the world in this lofty ideal, now issues millions of stamps which, were it not for a small and discreet sovereign's head tucked away in a corner, could be a trading stamp, a charity stamp, or any other small printed label. In such an environment the original prime requirements of the postage stamp have been blurred if not lost, and it may be worth repeating what these are.

The design should be instantly recognised, and distinct from all other labels. It should have the postal duty clearly marked on it, preferably in figures rather than words. It should be easy and cheap to manufacture in very large quantities. It should be difficult to forge. It should be grossly and indelibly changed in appearance by being postally cancelled. And it should withstand all the conditions of use that might reasonably be expected (for example, it should resist repeated folding without bad cracking of the design, and should be strong both dry and wet). In the modern world the stamp must also trigger a letter-facing machine.

Some of these factors affect the design in an engineering sense, but in this chapter I am concerned with design only in a graphical context. In the early days of stamps, postal administrations were overwhelmingly concerned to prevent forgery. The background to the original British stamps was an engine-turned pattern that virtually defied duplication (though one needed a magnifying lens to see it clearly). The central head of the young queen was a masterpiece, not only of fine engraving but as a subject that, while familiar, could not be reproduced in any easy way (as the government proved to its own satisfaction when it arranged for the 1d stamp to be 'officially forged'). But, as already noted, the black stamp could be cleaned and reused, and its colour had to be changed, while the accompanying 2d blue was reissued with 'fugitive' ink which it was thought would inevitably be defaced by any attempt to remove an obliteration. In Spain the design of the stamps was completely changed every year from the first issue in 1850 until 1855, but a design that did remain unchanged was forged so often that it was changed in 1860 and again every year or two for more than twenty years.

Today, considerations of forgery and fraudulent reuse are much less important. When Britain introduced completely new definitive stamps in 1967, the most common values, the 4d and 5d, were so dark as to be almost 'penny blacks' all over again, while the highest face value of all, the £1, was printed in true black and is often hardly changed at all in appearance by a light cancellation. Today, people usually have more and more money, and more calls upon their spare time, and in general the forger of current postage stamps, or the fraudulent reuser of them, must be something of an eccentric. This has had a marked effect on the design.

For the first hundred years of adhesive postage stamps, the central feature of the design was very often a human head which is a peculiarly evocative shape and one which the human eye appreciates very quickly in great sensitivity of detail. Usually the head

57

was that of the monarch, president or other national ruler, but some countries, such as France and Greece, preferred characters from their mythology, or allegorical subjects suggestive of national pride and industry. The quality of the head, always in those days produced by direct hand engraving on a metal die, varied very considerably. In Britain it never wavered from a consistently superb standard. In the USA the standard was not quite so high, but it was consistent and characteristic – and the same style was seen throughout all the Americas, because most early stamps from the Canadian Arctic to the tip of Argentina were produced in the USA. Most British colonies used stamps printed by the established British printers, but some did their own, with varying results. Those of Mauritius, already mentioned, and the early stamps of New South Wales, Victoria, Van Diemen's Land (Tasmania) and India were local productions and looked crude; the Indian stamps had a design resembling a poor copy of the British engraved stamps, with an unrecognisable Victoria in the centre. New Zealand, after a few months using printing plates made in England, carried on alone and maintained a fine standard.

Of course there is no special advantage in high-quality printing,

Fig 14   Many of the earliest adhesive stamps were printed from plates made by rather unskilled engravers, and frequently the stamp impressions on the plate, or between one plate and the next, were visibly different. These New South Wales stamps are supposed to be identical, but close inspection shows that no two parts are quite the same. A philatelist would bring out his magnifying glass, but one difference that especially stands out is the size of the letters in SOUTH at the top.

and these crude early stamps are without exception of great philatelic value today. Experts identify them by their errors, their individual peculiarities and the characteristics of primitive handprinting where hardly any two stamps emerge quite alike. Perhaps recognising the difficulty of printing in high volume and at low cost while still yielding a good result, many countries settled for less-demanding stamp designs. Some, such as Egypt and Japan, contrived to find fairly complicated designs that would not easily be forged, yet which did not look crude even when executed by engravers of modest skill. The Portuguese included a head, but for many years left it a plain white outline without attempting to fill it in. So, for that matter, did Gambia, a British colony, which for the first thirty years had plain white (but embossed) Victorian heads produced by the most experienced stamp printer in the world, De La Rue & Co.

A stamp dominated and almost filled by a central head does not leave very much freedom to the graphic designer, although the company just mentioned, De la Rue, brought a revolution in stamp appearance in 1855 as the result of a new method of printing (as described in Chapter 4). But even small differences can be of interest to a public which has grown familiar with an unchanged design over many years. Sometimes a small change actually makes a big difference to the public. For example in the winter of 1897–8, the Canadian post office issued a fine new definitive set of stamps which was one of the few ever to bear a good likeness of Queen Victoria after sixty years on the throne (in most other parts of the commonwealth, including Britain, she was still portrayed as an unchanged young girl). At once the French-Canadians protested that there were no figures on the new stamps, and that they had no intention of trying to read the English inscriptions of face value. So by the summer of 1898 the issued stamps were hurriedly being replaced by a completely re-engraved set in which the duty was clearly shown in figures as well as words.

Today it is rare for any stamp to be issued without the duty being shown in numerals, although this was the case with British definitives of George VI from 7d to 1s, of 1952–67 from 5d to 7d, and a few commemoratives. What exactly is the apparently clear distinction between 'definitives' and 'commemoratives'? In fact there is no clear division at all. The definitive, often called in North America a 'regular issue', is basically a standard series of stamps, usually of fairly small size, printed in vast numbers over a period of years. Often a set of values are printed to identical or obviously related designs, and some administrations would claim that such stamps were not designed primarily to attract the casual collector. The commemorative is basically a stamp, or a set of stamps, whose design features some past event, an organisation, a place, natural flora or fauna, or some other special subject. The definitive may well also have a theme (in some countries it always does), but the essence of the commemorative is that it is on sale for a relatively short time. Some commemoratives do indeed commemorate either an occasion at the time of issue, such as a state wedding or the opening of a large construction project, or the anniversary of one in the past. In the case of an anniversary it is reasonable to expect that it will be something like a tenth anniversary, or a twenty-fifth, or a hundredth or some other round figure, but there is no law about this; in January 1964 India issued two stamps commemorating the '67th birth anniversary' of one national figure, and followed the next month with the eighty-fifth birth anniversary of another. A very great many so-called commemoratives are not linked with any particular date or event at all. It has become traditional for the USA and Canada to issue one or more 'commemorative' stamps every few weeks which simply recall, honour or portray something that the post office has decided is desirable. Many 'commemoratives' would be better called 'feature stamps' because what they do is not commemorate but feature a particular topic. In many countries this is sometimes done as a public service; for example the topic may be road safety, wildlife conservation or preventing litter.

It is often argued that the first 'commemorative' was a little red stamp issued by Peru in 1871 when that country opened its first major rail route. It showed the simplest design approach: the border contained the postal duty and the names of the three cities linked by the new railway, while in the centre were the national arms surmounted by an outline of the locomotive and tender. Sometimes one sees modern stamps where it looks as if the artist has merely put in the essential ingredients and not worried too much about the design, but most modern commemoratives are the result of a long period of hard thinking, trial and error, and a gradual approach to what often seems an elusive goal. This is true even when the bulk of the design is already fixed, as in the case of a stamp featuring a famous painting or a coat of arms. The road to the stamp on sale in the post office is always long and usually rather difficult.

Before I briefly outline a typical design process, I must mention policy, because this determines what the designer is asked to do. Undoubtedly the most significant single event in the history of stamp design was the British Treasury competition of 1839, because not only did this explore practically the whole realm of what was attainable with contemporary printing technology, but also the design finally chosen exerted an enormous influence over the stamps of many nations for many years. A close second in importance was the wish of the US Post Office to do something rather special in stamps inscribed '1492–1892' for the 400th anniversary of Columbus's discovery of 'America'. Just how far it was 'America' and what part Columbus played in discovering it is immaterial. There is no doubt that the resulting set of sixteen stamps was a landmark in graphic design, fine printing, and establishing the concept of the big, pictorial stamp to commemorate great events. The USA followed up with a second very fine set of stamps in 1898 featuring the push of the frontier westwards and linked with the Trans-Mississippi Exposition in Omaha. Several other countries took up the idea. New Zealand produced the 'commemorative series of 1906', Canada issued a Quebec Tercentenary set dated 1608–1908, Portugal commemorated Vasco da Gama's voyage to India with a set dated 1498–1898, and even tsarist Russia issued a pictorial set in 1905 with a surcharge to help Russo-Japanese War charities. Almost every country has issued pictorial or feature stamps, and many of the younger nations appear to issue hardly anything else.

61

There are several ways in which pictorial or feature stamps can be issued. Some administrations, such as the USA and France, frequently issue a new design of stamp of a denomination (face value) appropriate to inland letter post. This is done for general interest and to serve such subsidiary purposes as honouring worthy causes, getting across messages or codes of behaviour, and keeping stamp-collectors from drifting away. In such countries the revenue derived from philatelic sales is usually less than 1 per cent of the total revenue of the mail service. The special stamps almost always supplement long-enduring regular stamps of the same value. Undoubtedly the outstanding exponent of this system is the USSR, whose issues of special low-value (letter-post) stamps practically defeat my attempts to count them.

A second system is to decide to have, say, six new issues in a year. One or two of the issues will be obvious (for example, Christmas); the rest will be chosen from a very long list of possible items, some of which may be true commemoratives and some of which may be purely pictorial. This is the technique followed in Great Britain. A flood of British stamps has appeared in which the design is merely evocative of a subject, such as 'British discovery and invention', or just a picture of some countryside or some wild flowers. The next issue may be a set of three or four stamps commemorating totally unrelated events or organisations. The postal duty may be appropriate to letter post but also frequently takes in much higher values to increase the philatelic revenue extracted from collectors who are reluctant to leave anything out (and, say the Post Office, so that the special stamps shall be seen by the recipients of parcels or overseas air mails).

If this is done to excess it defeats its own objective. Britain has just managed to tread a tightrope between her former role as a splendid philatelic country (see Chapter 9) because she had practically no special stamps, and the disastrous abyss of being a philatelic outcast because she tries to milk collectors for all they are worth. Everyone can think of countries – usually small ones – which have dived headfirst into this abyss. They regard postage stamps primarily as a useful source of extra revenue, almost in the category of something for nothing. One is reminded of the persistence and enthusiasm of the early collectors over 100 years ago. In the face of derision, they laid the groundwork for a vast industry which has had the effect of assigning quite high monetary values to tiny bits of printed paper for reasons unconnected with postage. These values are many times what the bits of paper cost to print, so some states have considered it a good idea to bring out new issues of stamps as rapidly as possible, regarding them as saleable philatelic items rather than as labels confirming the prepayment of postage. High-value (high face) stamps abound; several small states have issued new designs of stamps to a face value exceeding £10 ($25) a year after they took over control of their own post offices. They have sought to minimise their outgoings by issuing a big set of stamps, then reissuing it with an overprint, and then issuing the overprinted stamps with yet a further overprint! Such practices do at least offer an opportunity for superb artwork, because the whole purpose of the stamps is not postage but pictorial appeal. Unfortunately almost all the opportunities have been wasted, and many designs have been disasters. For example, some of these philatelically orientated sets have dealt with space flight. Many nations have space programmes and could have provided good references for illustrations, yet time after time these worthless stamps appear portraying fictitious rocket vehicles utterly unlike anything ever flown.

This travesty of the postage stamp art brings its own downfall, because only the very young collector at present would be interested in countries issuing such stamps. It could be that the wheel will turn full circle, and in fifty years these bits of paper may become valuable for the very reason that they are at present widely despised, but it is my personal view that every postal administration ought to agree with the following beliefs: (*a*) every postage stamp is a label intended primarily for postal use; (*b*) every postage stamp inevitably acts as a widely distributed poster advertising the originator's choice of design and quality of execution; (*c*) reconciling the presumed objectives of suitability for postal use, aesthetic appeal and minimal production cost is a considerable challenge yet also a very great opportunity.

In fact the actual cost of designing and manufacturing postage stamps is very seldom more than about 0.1–0.125p (USA $\frac{1}{7}$c) per stamp, although this can rise sharply if an administration is determined to depart from conventional methods of manufacture. With modern multi-cylinder presses it costs very little to add additional colours, so the design can be printed in up to eight or even nine colours with no trouble. This opens up new possibilities. Most colour printing in periodicals and books is done with only four inks, typically magenta (purplish red), yellow, cyan (bright blue) and black, and from overprinting these it is possible to synthesise all other hues. Modern stamp printing can use up to nine inks to obtain a greater range of tonal values and clearer or brighter

Fig 15   Some contrasts in modern stamp design. The 1.00 (franc) is one of the fine French 'art' series. All the designer had to do was copy the chosen painting and add the necessary inscription, value, and artist's name in the most discreet way possible. The 2.00 is a regular air mail, an ordinary picture of an executive jet. The 0.90 is anything but 'regular' – a special commemorative, it taxed the designer in getting in all he wished to depict: mountain scenery, skiing, a Japanese train, and two Olympic symbols. The 0.50 is a regular definitive with an interesting design tailored to production at the rate of millions a day.

colours, and can use silver or gold in a way quite beyond the capacity of the traditional four-colour press. In fact the stamp designer has a wealth of possibilities open to him (or her), and although their designs often seem deliberately contrived to challenge the stamp printer, it is now extremely rare for real trouble to be experienced in stamp manufacture.

There are occasions when a stamp design is based on a drawing by a child, a classic painting or a photograph, and in these cases the stamp designer may have quite a difficult task in fitting in something that was originally created with no thought of stamp printing. But most stamps are designed by an experienced professional who starts off with the knowledge that he is going to design a stamp that it is to be a definitive or a pictorial stamp on a particular topic, and that it will be printed by a particular process. In some countries the designer is appointed to the job, or he may even have a permanent employment as the national stamp designer. In most countries he competes with others, and he may be self-employed, a member of a large graphic studio, or even an employee of a stamp printer. Again, he may know which printer will receive the contract to print the resulting stamps, or he may only know that the printer will be chosen from a select group. Until recently one company printed all British stamps, apart from high-value definitives, but today several rivals are competing with this famous firm (Harrison's) to try to win particular contracts. Obviously, it helps if the would-be designer can talk over the proposed issue not only with the customer post office but also with the printer. Certainly the designer and printer have to work together in the final stages before manufacture starts.

In the next chapter it is emphasised how totally different are the ways in which stamps are printed. Almost all stamps are printed in very large quantities, and, although individual stamps are very small, the numbers needed are so great that it is usually a big, high-volume printing job. It is very much a task for the specialist supplier, and these suppliers tend to be equipped for one printing method. It follows that many nations have strong characteristics in their stamps resulting from a particular choice of printing method and a corresponding type of stamp design. Look at a modern British stamp (not a high-value one); then look at a stamp from France. The contrast in printing is obvious, and it strongly influences the whole approach of the designer, who from the start works towards a mental picture based upon the printing method used.

A graphic designer must be an individual artist, and it is impossible to lay down any precise technique or process common to all. But most stamp designers, after spending a lot of time thinking and vaguely 'doodling', get down to their drawing-board with some rough sketches. Sometimes they are very well informed on the subject matter (of course, in the case of a definitive, this may hardly arise), but often they need to spend a long period trying to become an expert. A stamp may feature a historic battle, a national costume, a famous writer, or a philanthropic organisation. In each case the designer reads every book he can on the topic, and in particular seeks every possible picture. Before long he has dozens of

Fig 16 Contrasts in stamp printing: although they form a single set, these four stamps are printed by totally different methods. The 4d and 7½d were printed in Australia by the recess (line-engraving) process; the 1s was printed in Britain by offset litho, and the same method was used to print the 2s in Switzerland.

possible ideas. Some may be pedestrian, some dramatic, some technically difficult; and always in the back of his mind he may have to remember that he is designing a stamp. This does not only mean his design will end up very small; it also means it must suit a customer, whose customers in turn are the public (and, indeed, stamp collectors all over the world). Many brilliant and dramatic designs have been rejected because they were 'too clever'; many postal administrations have accepted only stamp designs where the message was virtually spelt out in capital letters, so that not even the dimmest person could fail to understand it.

In British stamps, the designer has the great advantage of not having to include the name of the country; it was not considered necessary in the original stamp design of 1839–40, and the tradition has been jealously guarded ever since. For almost a century the British stamp tended to be a rather busy design (with the notable exception of the austere 'lilac or green' issue of 1883–4), but the new art of the 1930s suddenly broke through with the dramatic new stamps designed for the reign of Edward VIII. As it is also traditional to include the head of the sovereign, these stamps were about as simple as a stamp could be. In general this is a good thing; especially in a small definitive stamp there is everything to be said for a simple uncluttered design. This is doubly so with photogravure printing, introduced in Britain shortly before the Edward VIII stamps were designed, which allows for tonal values to change gradually.

The first British gravure stamps were the George V issue of 1934, and in these the existing designs were changed as little as possible. The original 'Georgian' stamps of 1911 were designed around a photographic portrait of the new monarch, and this proved too much for the designer to cope with because, when it was translated into a typographic (letterpress) printing plate, the head printed dark and blotchy. The head was then completely re-engraved, yielding in 1912 a better-looking stamp of identical design. In the same year the designer started again with a fresh head which was based not on a photograph but on the same designer's profile for a medal. This was much more successful, the head being in sharp side profile. A second designer used the same head in the higher values of the same series. It was these stamps that, in 1934, began to be re-issued in photogravure. They looked different, and no member of the public failed to comment on the hitherto impossibly subtle grading of the tones, but it was not until the Edward VIII stamp of 1936 that the possibilities became obvious.

In one stroke this short-lived issue transformed British stamps from cluttered designs intended for typography to clean 'tonal' design intended for gravure printing. There was, of course, a storm of criticism because many people cannot accept change of any kind, though *The Times* in a perhaps remarkable leading article welcomed the new stamps and their absence of 'petty detail'. It is rare for a designer to be able to produce such a stamp. Usually he is instructed to include at least one, and possibly two, pictorial scenes, as well as at least one ruler's head, probably two sets of inscriptions, and the postal duty. In the case of stamps of the British Commonwealth, the ruler's head was formerly either the central feature or, with notable exceptions, at least the dominant one. Among the exceptions are the original stamps of New South Wales, which showed the seal of the city of Sydney with a delight-

a   b   c   d

Fig 17   Development of the same design: (a) the original British ½d of George V, designed in 1911 with the head copied from a photograph; (b) as issued on 1 January 1912 with the whole design re-engraved; (c) as issued in January 1913 with the head sideways, copied from a medal; (d) as issued in November 1934, with the method of printing changed from letterpress typography to rotary photogravure.

ful 'view' of the town itself; all nineteenth-century stamps of Western Australia, which showed the famed (or fabled?) black swan; the earliest issues of New Brunswick and Newfoundland; and the outstanding pictorial set of New Zealand of 1898. In all these the designer was relatively unfettered, but in British stamps the sovereign's head had to be bold and prominent, and this often interfered with the design or upset its balance. But in 1966 the queen's head appeared as a plain white outline and it has now shrunk to a small but characteristic shape with which many designers have contrived to come to terms (though the Duke of Edinburgh made a comment about head-shrinking!).

It is my view that the happiest stamp designs do not contain a mandatory head divorced from the main design. In the case of 'GB' stamps the royal head is undoubtedly essential, for it is the only thing that distinguishes some recent 'commemoratives' from mere printed labels. Some designers tried to do without this vital head – indeed the 1965 'Battle of Britain' se-tenant (see glossary) block of six different stamps was originally proposed with the queen's head on only the upper right stamp in each block, so that the other five would have been plain labels bearing striking air-

Fig 18   As the British leave the name of the country off their stamps, they have been able to produce some classically simple stamp designs. The original stamp of 1840 contained only three words; the short-lived Edward VIII stamps contained only one word; British definitives contained no word at all. Most graphic artists would probably agree that simple designs are better than cluttered ones.

battle silhouettes. They would have been possibly improved as labels, but I believe the Post Office was right to suggest that a stamp that does not bear the name of the country ought at least to show the head of its ruler. This being so, I think by far the best British stamps have always been the definitive issues, both low and high values, and especially those currently in use.

As the issuers of more different stamp designs than any other country, the USSR has kept its designers extremely busy. Usually they have had to pack rather a lot in, so that the result is often cluttered. Without doubt the most effective Soviet stamps are those featuring a single, close-up portrait. A particular feature of the multitude of Soviet issues is their great variety of sizes and shapes. Usually a nation's stamp-manufacturer cannot cope with more than two or three variations, and many countries manage with one. On the other hand it is doubtful that varying the size or shape is of very much help to the designer except in the special cases of a gross increase in size or a gross increase in one linear dimension, both of which open up new possibilities.

Most graphic designers are well schooled in typography and lettering, and this is nowhere more important than in a stamp. All the earliest British stamps had letters in their corners which identified the stamp as coming from a particular place in the sheet. The usual arrangement was twenty rows of twelve stamps, the top row being lettered AA to AL, the second row being BA to BL and so on down to the final row lettered TA to TL. Philatelists began to study these letters around the year 1900, and by 1910 they had sorted out most of the stamps into individual plates, largely because of the different characteristics of the letters. In 1870 there appeared a halfpenny stamp that, after nineteen different 'essays' by the printer, was finally squeezed into half the usual size. There was

Fig 19   How do you design a figure 1 for maximum clarity? These examples show some of the answers found by stamp designers. The latest of all, on the new British £1 definitive, is no longer a 1 at all but a capital I.

no room for any writing other than '½d' and the corner letters. Today it is common for British stamps to have no inscription at all other than the postal duty, this having also been a feature of the 1948 Silver Wedding and Channel Islands/Great Britain 'seaweed' issues. This makes the numbers used for the postal duty doubly important, and it is worth commenting that in the British decimal issues the figure 1 is always replaced by a Roman I; indeed in 1972 a redrawn £1 stamp was specially issued in order to make this change, which can only be regarded as highly undesirable.

Students of numerals will find that throughout the Americas the earliest stamps were characterised by extremely bold, condensed and highly characteristic numbers which persisted until about 1933 (when, via a pair of stamps using Roman numerals, a change was made to ordinary and more legible forms). Until recently it was also thought essential to use capital letters exclusively – a practice also found in advertisement hoardings, name boards, public-transport destination boards and all manner of other notices – but gradually, with Britain very much in the lead, it is being appreciated that the more legible 'caps and lower case' (small letters) are especially desirable on stamps.

It has often happened that a designer has had more trouble with numbers, letters, or inscriptions than anything else. Some designers

Fig 20　These sketches illustrate how a great stamp design was created. The artist, William A. Smith, wanted to design a 'blockbuster' (a block of stamps forming a single picture) to commemorate the Boston Tea Party of 16 December 1773, when angry Americans threw cargoes of tea (on which the British made them pay tax) into the harbour. This touched off the American Revolution. At first Smith sketched a block of four stamps (a). Then he sketched a wider scene that would split into five vertical stamps (b). He did not like the strip of five, and at (c) returned to the block of four. The breakthrough came at (d) when a better picture was made to fit the same shape. At (e) is the 'rough' of the final design, and at (f) are the stamps as issued by the US Post Office on 4 July 1973.

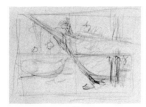

a

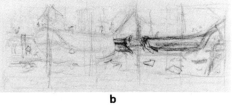

b

c

d

e

f

have left behind sketches and 'roughs' suggesting that they had to change their entire approach after spending a great deal of time refining a design while ignoring the inscriptions. But eventually they arrive at a design they consider wholly suitable and submit the most perfect piece of artwork they can prepare, together with instructions on their objectives, the inking or any other factors they feel need explanation. The most common size for a final proof is four times the size of the stamp, this being at once the smallest possible size for perfect hand artwork and the largest size capable of giving a clear impression of what the stamp will look like. It is at this point that the winning design begins the long and highly skilled process that translates it into usable stamps.

4
Making Stamps

At first sight it might be thought that, while a philatelist may have great interest in stamp design, he need know nothing about stamp manufacture. However, in my opinion the processes of manufacture are the basis of the whole of philately. It is the making of the stamp that actually creates the thing the stamp-collector studies, and the more experienced he is as a philatelist, the more he has to know about the 'hardware' of paper, ink, gum, and perforations, and such possible extras as overprints, phosphor materials, embossing and even such gimmicks as metal-foil printing and self-adhesives peeled off a backing sheet. Without a good knowledge of stamp manufacture he will neither understand half the terms of philately nor know how to care for his stamps.

Today stamps, printed in nine colours, can roar off the giant presses, if necessary with different parts printed by quite different printing processes, at such a rate that a five-hour shift yields a stack of five million finished stamps. Yet in 1840 everything was done by hand. Even the paper was made by hand, and paper must be the subject of the first part of this chapter.

Paper has always been basically a two-dimensional mat of cellulose fibres. Early hand-made paper began with piles of old clothes and rags, which were converted into a pulp by shredding and lengthy soaking in vats of water, sometimes with acid or alkali additives. In those days all woven fabrics were made of natural materials, such as cotton or linen. The result of the shredding and soaking was a vat full of loose vegetable fibres suspended in water.

The skilled papermaker would dip in a scoop like a large rectangular baking tin, but having a wire-mesh bottom. He would deftly fish out a trayful of fibres and shake these so that, as the water ran out through the mesh, the fibres would arrange themselves into a uniform layer over the base. When most of the water had gone, he would tip this on to a sheet of thick felt. Further trays might be dumped beside the first load to make a 'mill sheet' of paper. The adjoining edges would be worked together to form the layer into a single pulpy mass, much thicker than cardboard, and this would be worked over by hand to fill any shallow parts and trim the edges. It would then be squeezed between two layers of felt to drive off more water, and finally put into a strong screw-press, at first with the felts and finally without. This process would convert the wet mass of pulp into dry paper, the sheet finally being hung in a loft so that the last molecules of water could evaporate.

This mill sheet would have a rather sharp, irregular edge. Some of the early 1839 proposals for stamps suggested that paper should be made in the form of a very long narrow strip, on which could be printed a single row of stamps sold as a coil. The edges of the hand-made paper, having this sharp but uneven form, would serve as a further deterrent to forgery, because to forge a single stamp would mean trying to reproduce this distinctive edge on each side. Such edges are still seen today on expensive hand-made paper for some Christmas cards or special book bindings. It can be seen on the margin of most stamp sheets up to 1870. As the light wooden border used in the final mould of the sheet was called a deckle, the edge is called deckled, or a deckle edge. Another important characteristic of all hand-made paper is that no two pieces are quite the same. Some are thick, some are thin, and any large piece varies slightly in thickness (though this would seldom be obvious on a single stamp). Often the skill of the papermaker

76

reduced this variation, and many countries printed their stamps with excellent uniformity, but an expert can invariably tell hand-made paper even by looking at a small piece such as a stamp. Of course we all know that even some modern paper occasionally has blotches, thin spots, thicker lumps, and pieces of foreign matter in it. This was much more common with hand-made paper, and a high proportion of early stamps show unwanted irregularities in the paper.

Around 1850 there came a great change in the composition of paper. The demand for paper was soaring, and outstripped the supplies of old rags. Inventors gradually perfected ways of pulping wood and other plant material. This was not a new idea, because papyrus had been made chiefly from long grasses, but the use of timber from trees opened up a huge new source of supply. Soft-

Fig 21 Early stamps were printed on hand-made paper which always had a 'deckle edge' – a thin (almost sharp) irregular edge which is everywhere unique and thus difficult to forge. As shown here, the edge was invariably off the printed part of the sheet, and so the deckle edge was not actually any help against forgery.

woods, such as fir and spruce, can be mechanically broken down either by cutting into chips or by grinding into a fibrous mass under sprays of water. The finely divided wood is then 'digested' in huge vats by any of several chemical processes – sulphite, sulphate or soda, for example – to yield wood pulp, a white, soft mass of fibres suspended in water. Depending on the process used, the pulp is left slightly acidic or alkaline. Experience showed that the pulp should be whitened by bleaching, and that a blue dye should be added to neutralise the natural yellowish tint, and improved by 'fillers' such as kaolin, 'hardeners', and other additives. In any case, paper has seldom been made entirely from wood pulp, but usually contains some rags, 'broke' (waste material from papermaking), and grasses. Almost all modern paper is made by machine.

Machine-made paper was introduced generally to stamp printing in the early 1860s (in Britain in 1867, though special machine-made paper incorporating silk threads was used twenty years earlier). Compared with hand-made paper it is more uniform, for a machine can better maintain a standard thickness and weight. The first surface-printed stamps (a term described presently), of 1855, were printed on fairly thick hand-made paper which was supposed to be deeply blued by adding potassium prussiate to the pulp (in the erroneous belief that this would prevent any attempt to erase a cancellation and use the stamp again). This paper was plate-glazed, meaning that in its manufacture it was given an increasingly good shine and smooth surface by repeatedly passing it between polished steel rollers under very high pressure. Only by this means could a good result be obtained with surface printing on hand-made paper. It was not until much later that stamp paper gradually developed into its modern forms.

Today a great variety of paper is available, each exactly tailored to its duty. For stamp printing the paper is nearly always made from pulp formed from wood, esparto grass and rags. Modern rags are much more expensive than formerly, because old clothing and other fabrics have to be carefully sorted to remove the major part of the mass in which some or all of the fibres are synthetic (eg nylon or Terylene) to leave just the vegetable fibres suitable for making pulp. Rag is used in an appreciable quantity only for very strong and expensive papers, and is generally confined to high-value stamps where the quantities are small and the 'shelf life' (storage time before use) is often long. The modern papermaker turns out a precision product, meeting a tightly controlled specification. Stamp paper then goes to a 'paper converter' for various surface treatments, such as the addition of phosphors or adhesives, before it is finally sent to the stamp printer.

Modern paper is made on a non-stop flowline basis. Wood chips or ground fibres, esparto grass, carefully sorted rags, possibly some broke, and a number of chemical additives are continuously poured in a measured flow into one end of a very large water-tank. All the solids are thoroughly beaten to a fine pulp to yield a thick white carpet gently flowing across the liquid surface. This is picked up by an endless belt of fine-mesh copper wire, or some other finely perforated screen. The water drains through as the pulp carpet leaves the tank, helped by suction from below. As the porous belt lifts the pulp from the vat, it vibrates to shake the fibres into the desired uniform interlocking mat. When the mat has passed through the first drying stage, on the perforated belt, it moves on to a thick felt belt of soft wool. A second felt comes down from above to make a sandwich which passes between a series of heavy rollers. The result is crude paper, strong enough to carry on through further heated steel rollers without support between them. These hot cylinders evaporate the rest of the water, giving a 'web' (endless strip) looking like white blotting paper. Further rolling between steel cylinders gives paper with a 'machine finish'. As the original pulp contained gums, alums, binders and fillers, this paper is strong and uniform – but it is probably not good enough for stamp printing.

In the early days the raw paper was coated with size, gums, starches or resinous coatings, some of which were positively harmful. The purpose of these was to give a flat, impervious surface so that ink would not run into fine dendritic (tree-like) patterns in the way ordinary writing ink runs on unsized paper. Today the finishing of the surface is all-important. First, the paper is calendered by

79

passing the web through a maze of twenty or thirty rollers, some of polished steel, some of vulcanised rubber, and some with soft cotton coverings. For an even better finish the paper is super-calendered by feeding it through a further set of rollers, under even greater pressure. These roll out the hills and valleys in the surface, giving a finish good enough for two-colour gravure printing. But most stamp paper is then coated, and this is done by the converter.

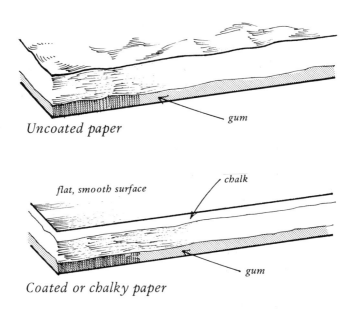

Uncoated paper

gum

flat, smooth surface

chalk

gum

Coated or chalky paper

Fig 22 Most paper has a more or less rough, irregular surface which on a microscopic scale is rather like a hilly landscape. The cross-section of uncoated paper shows how the gum smooths out the back, but the upper surface is still ir-regular and difficult to print on in sharp, fine detail. In contrast, coated paper (often called 'chalky' paper) has an almost perfect surface of chalky or china-clay material which is applied in an operation rather like plastering a rough wall. This coating gives a superb surface on which to print.

Early coated papers were used for British stamps in 1905. These are generally called 'chalky' or 'chalk-surfaced', although it is a mistake to think the coating is always literally crushed chalk (limestone). In 1905 the coating was introduced to give a dead flat, smooth surface, capable of accepting the printed image perfectly, and, especially, of giving a stamp image that would be immediately defaced by any attempt to wash off or erase a cancellation. Modern coated papers are made simply to suit the surface to the printing method. In general, recess-printed stamps, such as most of those of France, the USA, Canada, Sweden and most German, Austrian or Swiss definitive issues, need no surface coating at all. Gravure printing is often done on uncoated paper, but for the sparkling, bright effect of most modern stamps a coating is essential. The paper converter passes the web through a machine which spreads over the surface a thin, uniform film from a milky suspension of white chalky powder, and this is then rolled on to give a firmly binding and absolutely level and smooth finish. For web-offset litho printing the coating is of china clay, and thicker. Thus the coating gives a cushioning effect and provides a depth of surface into which the inking roller can press the ink.

Most modern stamps have no watermark, but these markings are of enormous importance in the philately of classic stamps. Watermarks were first used in Italian paper of about the year 1460. In hand-made paper the watermark was impressed by a raised die, usually made of heavy brass wire, soldered or wrapped into the bottom of the scoop mould. As the mat of fibres settled on to the porous mould base, the watermark die (called a 'bit') impressed itself to make an outline in the underside (later this becomes the upper surface) of the paper. Subsequently this part of the paper would be permanently thinner, and would actually contain a slightly reduced quantity of fibres. In other words, the paper is not just packed more tightly, because where there is a watermark there is less paper. The mark can never be erased or tampered with, and its main purpose has always been security, to prevent forgery.

In the planning of the original British stamps of May 1840 someone, doubtless Rowland Hill, hit on a brainwave: why not have a separate watermark on each stamp? Small crown shapes were made from wire and fixed in position in a regular pattern of twenty rows of twelve in the pulp mould so that when the complete sheet was finished there were 240 small crowns each positioned approximately in the centre of each stamp. Since then countless billions of stamps have been produced either with one watermark on each stamp or else on paper having an overall pattern of small watermarks. Often these watermarks have been made by bits punched from brass, and in modern papers the bits are often moulded in plastics. In modern papermaking the felted mass of fibres is passed over a 'dandy roll' on which the watermark bits are fastened to the surface of a mesh drum. Although it is still difficult to get delivery of a dandy roll inside two months, they are today mostly used in security papers other than stamps. In stamp printing the chief objection to the watermark is not so much the extra cost as the fact that the uneven paper surface tends to harm the print quality, and philatelically conscious postal authorities would

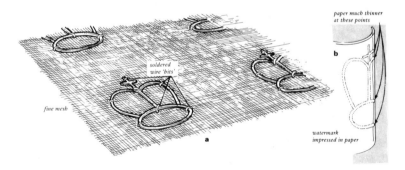

Fig 23   Many early stamps were printed on paper which was watermarked as an extra protection against forgery. When the paper was being made, the mat of pulp was deposited on a gauze mesh to which had been fixed 'bits' made of wire (later from metal sheet or plastics). Early British stamps had a separate bit in the centre of each stamp (a), shaped like a simple crown. This impressed itself into the paper (b) in a way that could not be rubbed out or forged (unless the forger made his own paper).

rather have a uniformly perfect stamp than one much more difficult to print at home! Anyone with access to British Edward VII
mint stamps printed on uncoated paper will soon find copies where
the Imperial Crown watermark can be seen as an outline of imperfect printing on the face of the stamp. The chalky coating filled in
the watermark cavity and gave a better result.

Several of the most important countries have hardly ever
bothered about watermarked paper, but some of them have experimented with other forms of security. One is to make the paper
from pulp containing fine chips cut from coloured artificial silk
fibres. Such paper, often called 'granite' because of the scattered
profusion of small coloured lines in it, is practically impossible to
duplicate accurately without a supply of the original silk fibres in
the correct colours. Such paper can be seen in many recent issues of
Switzerland. Another method, used in some very early stamps,
particularly in Britain, is to roll out the pulp around stretched silk
threads, so that the threads run through the interior of the finished
paper. This method worked well in early high-value imperforate
stamps, but could not be continued once stamp sheets began to be
perforated because, although the user could tear the perforations,
he could seldom break the threads. Yet another security trick is to
use coloured paper. In many nineteenth-century stamps the paper
was tinted by a dye added to the original pulp, while in some early
twentieth-century stamps the paper was one colour and the
'chalky' coating was another!

All modern stamps are printed on paper already coated by the
paper converter with adhesive. The earliest stamps in Britain were
coated with old-fashioned 'horse's hoof' glue, actually made from
vegetable starches, usually brushed on from a steaming gluepot by
hand after the printed sheet was dry. Later complaints of imperfect
adhesion caused the sheets to be given two coats – and filthy muck
it is when you get it in large quantities! For the embossed high-
value stamps of 1847 this thick glue was replaced by clear gum
arabic, applied before the embossed printing. Gum arabic, the
most important adhesive in the history of stamps, was in those days
a very pale yellow that happened to match the paper. In 1854 there

were complaints of embossed stamps that would not stick, and it was found that they had been printed on the gummed side. Just before these stamps were discontinued they went into production with gum tinted green, so that the printer could not go wrong again. But 'printed on the gummed side' has ever since remained a recurring item in philatelic catalogues, in all sorts of issues right up to the present time. They are valuable, and if they get wet they can be hopelessly damaged.

Gum arabic is prepared from the sap of acacia trees grown chiefly in the Sudan and Nigeria. The pieces of amber-coloured sap become mixed with pieces of tree bark, and are carried in sacks where they acquire a hairy growth of hemp, so one of the main costs in manufacture is filtering out the foreign matter. The purified gum is colourless, and the paper-converter rolls it on to the back of the paper to leave a bright, shiny coating which is often characterised by streaks or parallel lines. There have been instances of specially flavoured gums, but these are far more common in envelopes and postal stationery. People do not all like the same taste, and it adds greatly to the cost to prepare one copper boiling vat full of flavoured gum and then scrub it out before going back to the normal kind.

Early gum arabic stamps suffered in the course of time from the thick coating, usually brushed on hot, which eventually tends to craze and can even deform and crack the paper (see Chapter 8). By 1880 the best stamps used machine-made paper with machine-applied gum, a few stamps still used hand-made paper with animal or vegetable glues, many countries preferred the newer dextrins made from refined starch (such as corn starch or potato starch), while a great many countries sold their stamps ungummed. Habits die hard, and for a century afterwards stamps from these latter countries are still often found with the gum intact and the stamp stuck down by a great lump of home-made paste! You often find this with South America (especially Brazil).

In recent years newer and better adhesives have rapidly come to the fore. Yields from the traditional thorny acacia shrubs have to be sent round the Cape of Good Hope, adding to the cost, and an attempt to corner the market and force up the price merely had the result of hastening the switch to alternatives. By far the most important of these alternatives is polyvinyl alcohol. This is often loosely abbreviated to PVA, although the strict philatelist should prefer PVAl or PVOH (alcohols always having a molecule ending in OH) to prevent confusion with another adhesive, polyvinyl acetate (which is used, for example, on aerogramme forms). PVAl can readily be made in enormous quantities from standard chemical and plastics industry feedstocks. It usually costs a little more, even today, than gum arabic, but it can be spread in a thinner coat so that the cost per stamp is closely comparable. The thinner coat lies flat, does not curl the stamp sheet, has a matt appearance (so that people have complained of stamps lacking gum), can be put on the paper at a higher speed than gum arabic, and can more readily be given an anti-fungicide or anti-bacterial additive. PVAl is also better able to adhere when wet; thus, although the stamps do not wash off in the rain, the collector has difficulty in obtaining fine used blocks without the stamps separating along the perforations!

The gum is coated by machine on the reverse side of the paper; the stamp is printed on the face, which is the side where the watermark is usually impressed when the paper was made (and, of course, the side having any coating). Some modern papers have gone into production where both sides are identical. These are made 'vertically' on a new type of double-sided papermaking machine, but I do not believe any has yet been used for stamps.

Stamps are printed by special inks. Most are typical of those used for high-speed long-run printing, and these are quite unlike the bottled ink used in the home. The earliest inks, some 5,000 years ago, were prepared from ground-up carbon particles suspended in water. The ink used to print the penny black was not very different, though its finely divided carbon (lamp-black) was suspended in linseed oil with an additive of zinc white to give it greater body. The continually differing ratio of black to white resulted in the odd concept of different shades of black, ranging from 'intense black' to distinctive shades of deep grey. For other colours there were problems. The vast modern technology of dyes and colours had barely begun, and commercial dyes were based on organic materials from the madder plant, from cuttlefish and other unlikely sources, and the results were often far from stable. Moreover, many early coloured inks contained suspended particles which acted as an efficient abrasive and rapidly wore away the printing plate (or, in the case of individually embossed stamps, the die).

Early inks also often contained chemicals which reacted with the metal of the printing plate. In trials for a bright scarlet 4d stamp in Britain in 1861, it was found that the vermilion pigment in the ink contained mercuric sulphide which attacked the copper of the plate, delaying things until De La Rue coated the copper with electrolytically deposited silver. Later in the printing of the same stamp it was discovered that the silver could be eroded right through, or cracked or pierced, and so a way had to be found to make the plate with such a thick electroformed layer of silver that it needed no copper under it. Other early inks were deliberately given a small content of potassium prussiate, sometimes added to the paper at the pulp stage. This additive was intended to make the ink more fugitive, so that any attempt to clean off a postal cancellation would dissolve out the ink yet leave the cancellation. The original British 1840 blue 2d stamp, for example, was printed in a permanent ink. The 1841 stamp was printed in a supposedly fugitive ink, and white lines were added to the stamp design to make it immediately identifiable. The chemical additive caused potassium salts to precipitate out permanent prussian blue dye into the paper, often clearly visible on the back of the stamp and sometimes revealing the printed design on the back in quite sharp outline. This was a feature of many stamps produced by line engraving; later surface-printed stamps were sometimes printed on deliberately blued paper.

By the mid-1850s the discovery of aniline and coal-tar dyes had opened up a huge new colour industry based mainly on long hydrocarbon molecules. This made possible new colours and a highly fugitive series of inks which were very widely used in

Britain and some other countries between 1870 and about 1910 (a few such inks are found to the present day). The so-called 'doubly fugitive' ink is rapidly dissolved out of the pores of the paper by water, even after a century.

Today the specifications for stamp inks are the exact opposite. They are more like paint than the traditional watery bottled ink, and have much in common with some of the semi-solid inks used in ballpoint pens. Stamp inks are increasingly becoming very complex products, tailored to the correct chemical and physical properties so that they can be spread by the printing process in a very thin and uniform film. This film must have perfect 'covering power' with no thin or dry spots, it must go on in a very small fraction of a second, it must not 'run' in any manner visible to the eye and it must dry very swiftly. And, of course, the exact shade of each ink must be closely controlled. Some stamp inks will still fade or change colour if the stamp is soaked, or left in strong sunlight or ultra-violet light, but the objective today is long-term stability.

All the earliest stamps were printed by line engraving, which in 1840 was the universal way of reproducing illustrations for printing. Basically it was printing from a metal plate which originally had a smooth, dead-flat surface but which had the design to be printed cut or impressed in it so that the recesses could hold ink. In the case of the original 1840 stamps the makers, Messrs Perkins, Bacon & Petch, first took a block of soft steel about two inches square, gave it a surface like a mirror and then engraved on it a complicated pattern using a 'Rose engine', a machine invented early in the nineteenth century for making fine 'engine turned' repetitive patterns such as were soon introduced to bank-notes and silverware. The middle of the pattern was left blank in the form of an outline of the queen's head, and in this space a highly skilled engraver cut fine lines by hand, using engraving tools resembling miniature chisels, working from water-colour drawings to give the light and shade contrasts, and helped by a detailed sketch showing the crown. The design was completed by hand-engraving top and bottom borders containing the word 'POSTAGE', the postal duty, two corner 'stars' and two blank lower corners. This then

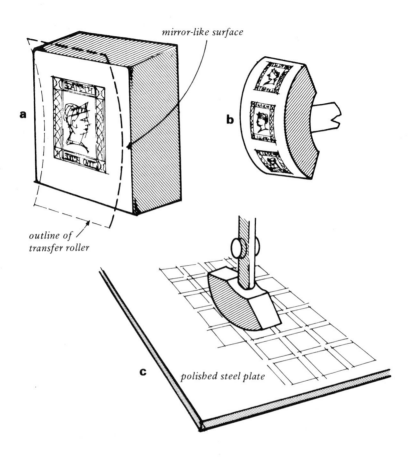

Fig 24 Early line-engraved (recess-printed) stamp designs were first engraved in perfect detail on a polished metal block (a). This was hardened and an impression (reversed left to right, ie the right way round) taken on a transfer roller (b). This was in turn made very hard, and then pressed with great force while rocked like a blotter to leave rows of impressions (again reversed) on the printing plate (c). Finally, the completed plate was itself hardened and then used to print sheets of stamps. The original die and transfer roller might be used again, though in their hardened state it would be difficult to repair damage or improve the clarity of the design.

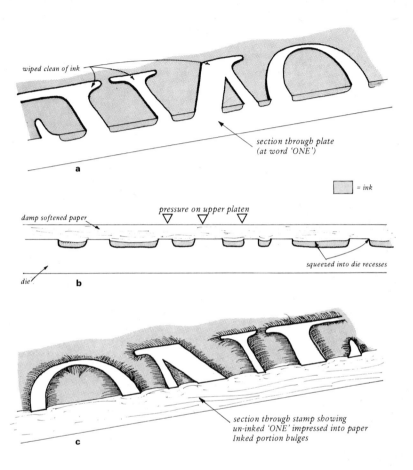

wiped clean of ink

section through plate
(at word 'ONE')

a

= ink

damp softened paper

pressure on upper platen

squeezed into die recesses

die

b

section through stamp showing
un-inked 'ONE' impressed into paper
Inked portion bulges

c

Fig 25 The line-engraved printing plate (Fig 24) had its design pressed into it
in sharp relief. When the plate was inked, the ink was worked right down into
all the fine furrows and crevices of the design (a). Then the plate was wiped
clean and burnished with the flat of the hand to leave the top surface free from
all ink. When the thick soggy paper was tightly squeezed in the press, it was
forced into all the ink-filled recesses of the impressions of the plate (b). As a result the uninked parts of each stamp were pressed into the paper while the inked
parts bulged slightly upwards (c).

89

served as a master die, and it was heat-treated to make it very hard.

A soft steel roller or shape like a small rocking blotter was then pressed down on top of the die and rocked to and fro under great pressure until it had taken up the impression in reverse. This 'transfer roller' was then in turn hardened, so that it could be used to transfer the pattern to the printing plate. Obviously the plate had to be designed to print as many stamps as possible simultaneously. For the original British stamps, the choice was a plate having a close chequerboard pattern of 240 impressions, in twenty rows of twelve. This was a good choice and was used in Britain until decimalisation when the definitive low values were changed to sheets of 200. To help the platemaker get his 240 impressions in the right places on the big, blank steel plate, fine lines were engraved to show the positions of one edge of each row and column. These guidelines were later erased as far as possible, but they sometimes fell just within the impression of a stamp, where they could not be completely removed and so showed on each stamp printed from that impression. The platemaker made the 240 impressions by rolling the transfer roller under great pressure in each of the 240

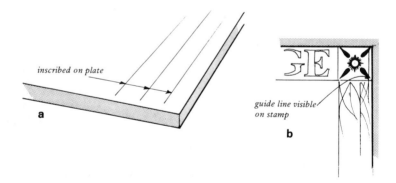

Fig 26 Fine lines were often scribed on the polished surface of the printing plate to help the platemaker 'enter' the impressions in good alignment (a). If the stamp impression overlapped the guideline, the latter was difficult to erase and so could leave a line on each stamp printed by that impression (b).

places. This was called 'entering'.

It sometimes happened that one impression, or even a whole row or column, might be in the wrong place or in some other way unsuitable. Each offending impression then had to be removed, and this was usually done by burnishing that part of the plate flat again (see Chapter 5). Then the design was impressed again, correctly. This was called a 'fresh entry'. It was frequently impossible to remove all traces of the original entry, and in any case the gradual 'cold working' of the metal surface of the plate while printing thousands of sheets of stamps very often caused the original entry to become increasingly visible. This resulted in a doubling of parts of the design. The same thing often resulted from repairs to the plate after it had been in use. Here a 're-entry' might be called for, either to correct damage or because the impression had worn too shallow to hold sufficient ink. With luck the plate-maker would re-enter the impression exactly over the old one. Such a 'coincident re-entry' could be philatelically recognised only by the later stamps from that impression suddenly becoming clearer and deeper-coloured. But the re-entry would often be non-coincident, so that the design would be partly doubled, just as in the case of a fresh entry done before the plate had been used.

Loosely, philatelists call all such doubled portions of the design 're-entries'. They are immensely important in all early stamps from all over the world, and are also important in some quite modern engraved issues. This is, of course, totally different from a stamp 'doubly printed'. The latter is very rare indeed, and generally affects the whole of a sheet or a major part of it equally, whereas all other sheets may be perfect. In contrast, a re-entry affects only one impression, but is seen in every stamp printed from that position in the plate. The subject is further discussed in the next chapter.

To finish the plate, measuring about 20in from top to bottom and 10in wide, required many – usually hundreds – of hours of handwork. In the case of a plate for British stamps, every impression had to be identified by the two check-letters. These were normally inserted by hand punch in the two vacant lower corners.

early print
weak, blurred

later print
strong, clear

Fig 27 A weakly entered impression (or one entered on a slight slant and thus weak on one side) could be re-entered by forcing the transfer roller on to the plate a second time. If the roller was re-entered in exactly the right place the result was a coincident re-entry (or 'fresh entry'), which would look clearer than the original one.

non-coincident
re-entry

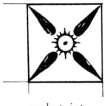 

early print

later print

Fig 28 If for any reason the second entry was not coincident with the first, and the first had not been erased, the result would be a non-coincident re-entry. Sometimes the fresh entry was deliberately made in a different place (for example to align the rows of stamps on the plate more accurately), and an example with a bigger shift than that shown here will be found in Fig 37 (p. 118).

There are several instances of stamps where it can be seen that the craftsman punched the wrong letter and then corrected it, and there is a classic case where one letter was completely left out and the plate was used for some time before the omission was noticed. Later, two cases occurred (one of them in surface-printed stamps) where stamps were printed with the wrong letters. Philatelists also discovered that, while different styles of hand punch were used for nearly all the early British stamps, a few had the letters engraved by hand. As well as adding these letters, which was a procedure not thought necessary by other postal administrations, the 'gutters' or white lines between the columns or rows of stamps had to be completely cleared, hundreds of flaws and burr marks had to be cleaned up, and in most printing plates (except for a very few countries) inscriptions had to be added in one or more margins. British stamps had instructions around the four margins of the printed sheet: 'PRICE 1d. Per Label. 1/- Per Row of 12. £1//-//- Per Sheet. Place the Labels ABOVE the Address and towards the RIGHT HAND SIDE of the Letter. In Wetting the Back be careful not to remove the Cement.' This was impressed into the plate by a die or transfer roller which seems to have had blank spaces for the values, which were engraved by hand (at the rate of 1d per stamp in the example given). Later, plate numbers and other markings were added.

The plate was then carefully inspected, mounted in a hand printing press and kept hot by a gas flame. Sheets of paper, sized to match the press, were dampened to make them soft, and kept handy in a stack. The pressman would ink the plate with a 'dabber', working the ink into each impression in turn. Then he would wipe off the bulk of the surplus with a metal ruler, carefully clean the entire plate with a rag so that the ink was removed from the whole surface except for the recesses and grooves intended to print, and would finally give the dry surface a polish with his hand. The paper was then positioned, and the impression made under high pressure. The ink would print the designs and the soft damp paper would be squeezed slightly into the recesses in the plate, giving a distinct slight embossing of the design which would have shown clearly even without ink. The paper shrank when drying, and this was allowed for in planning the size of the printing plate. When the ink was dry the sheet was gummed by hand as described later, then left to dry again and finally sent to the customer for issue to the public.

The only important change in this historic process was one made necessary by the large number of sheets of stamps needed. Most engraved plates, for books or for framed pictures, did not have to print quantities exceeding 1,000, but stamps were wanted in millions. It was soon found the plates were wearing, and early stamps often show obvious signs of plate wear in having thinned or almost colourless parts of the design where the recesses were too shallow to hold enough ink. It was therefore decided to heat-treat each plate to harden it. Different countries adopted different practices, but a common process was carburising, in which the finished plate is cooked at a suitable temperature (close to red heat) for a long period while surrounded by carbonaceous material, such as various forms of charcoal. This made the outer surface extremely hard, able to resist wear even after being used to print a million sheets. It also made the metal extremely brittle, so that sometimes the surface developed cracks, and narrow ridges broke off giving rise, for example, to what is called the 'O flaw' on many of the later British penny-black stamps, as described in the next chapter. It also meant that the hardened plate could not easily be subjected to further corrections or repairs. A hardened plate was unsuitable for attempting to re-enter an impression, and for hand engraving. For this reason, printers and platemakers continued to experiment with 'soft' plates, but these always wore very rapidly.

Today this classic method of printing pictures or designs is still of very great importance in making stamps. In the early stamps the method is called line engraving, or just engraving; today its modern counterparts, which differ in the details of making the plate and in the inks used, are more commonly called 'recess' or 'intaglio' printing. Since 1913 this method has been used for every British stamp of face value above 10p, except for one stamp in 1948 and another in 1965. It is used for the vast majority of Canadian stamps up to 1964, and for most issued since, for the bulk of recent definitive stamps printed in Australia, for most New Zealand stamps up to 1959, for many stamps of the USA, and for nearly all stamps of France, Sweden, Poland, Czechoslovakia and many other European countries.

Yet it was France which first had 'surface-printed' stamps. Since the days of Gutenberg and Caxton, most printing had been by the 'typography' or 'letterpress' method in which the pattern to be printed forms the raised printing surface, while the parts left blank on the paper are the intermediate spaces. The printing surface is inked quite lightly by a roller so that no ink gets into the cavities. The impression is then transferred by the inked upstanding surfaces, so that the method is the opposite of engraved or recess printing. Surface-printed or typographed stamps are in general flat both in fact and in appearance. If there is any surface relief at all it will be a slight indentation of the printed design. The printed image is often dull, but it can be brilliant with high-quality coated paper (look at British 'chalky' stamps of 1905–10).

It was in 1855 that the British decided to dispense with their cumbersome method of individually colour-embossing their high-value stamps (all over the value of 2d) and adopted the surface-printing method already used for some fiscal draft and receipt stamps. The firm chosen was Thomas De La Rue, the only British firm with the experience needed to create a surface-printing plate containing a large number of similar impressions. Like the engraved stamps, the process began with the hand engraving of a die, cut in soft steel forming a life-size mirror image of the printed stamp. When considered perfect, it was hardened and kept as a master. From it were then struck 'punches' in soft steel (each with the design in positive) which, after hardening, were then used to punch a set of secondary dies that were either duplicates of the first or else differed in the postal duty or in small details such as the plate number. To make a plate, the hardened secondary die was used to impress the image on to the same number of lead blocks as there were to be stamps in the sheet. Sometimes the lead was cast from the molten state against the die, as in modern type casting, but in

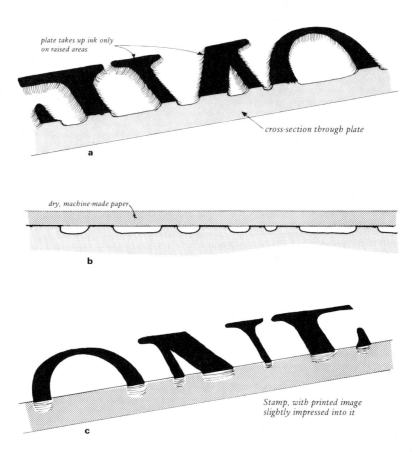

plate takes up ink only on raised areas

cross-section through plate

a

dry, machine-made paper

b

Stamp, with printed image slightly impressed into it

c

Fig 29 Most books, and very many stamps, are still printed by the method variously called surface-printing, letterpress or typography. In this case the ink is not allowed to permeate into the hollows but lies only on the upper surface (a). The paper is not damp and soggy but dry, and the raised parts of the design are the only areas of the plate that touch the paper (b). The result is a stamp in which the inked areas are very slightly impressed into the paper (c). With paper that has not been coated or heavily calendered, this slight indentation is needed to secure a good impression over the whole design.

96

the early British stamps the die was forced into the flat lead surface cold. The lead blocks, 240 of them in the original sheets, were then carefully mounted absolutely flat and in perfect alignment, in a chase (a tightly locked frame).

This was bodily dipped in a vat of dilute sulphuric acid close to a sheet of copper placed just in front of it, and parallel with the faces of the 240 blocks. The chase and the copper sheet were connected to the appropriate terminals of an electric cell so that the face of the lead blocks became coated with electrolytically deposited copper. The first atoms of copper lined the indented or recessed parts of the lead, forming a faithful reproduction of the stamp images. After an hour or so the copper would have built up a flat sheet, and after several hours the copper would be thick enough to be safely handled. The current would be switched off, the chase taken out and dried, and the thin copper sheet carefully detached. The rear surface of the sheet was then filled in with copper or type-metal to make it stronger. The backed sheet was then trimmed, carefully levelled and finally cleaned and inspected. Its 240 stamp images, formed in contact with the lead, were all flat and aligned with a single plane surface, though with the individual parts of each image either raised (to bear ink) or depressed.

To print the sheet of stamps, the copper plate was mounted on a heavy cast-iron slab and the surface level exactly adjusted by adding pieces of thin paper behind the copper printing plate wherever its level was too low. Different printers adopted their own techniques, but all the early surface-printed stamps were printed on hand presses, using a coloured ink applied over the plate by a roller. The first British issue was a 4d stamp printed in deep carmine (red) on highly calendered (plate-glazed) paper, which happened to be chemically tinted a deep blue. This impression was clear, but many of the early surface-printed issues contained very fine design and lettering and were printed on rather ordinary and deeply watermarked paper, creating a very difficult challenge to the printer; indeed the remarkable thing about these stamps is that they were as good as they were. The process was quite economical, and opened up possibilities that were impossible with engraving, but the soft copper plate wore rapidly and the process could not be used for the low-denomination stamps printed in huge numbers. The chemical attack by a vermilion ink on the copper of the plate caused a panic which was solved by inventing a way of using the electrolytic bath a second time to coat the copper printing surface with a very thin layer of silver, as noted earlier, which also made the plate last longer.

With modifications the same method is still used today for stamps described in catalogues as 'typographed'. The printing plate is now invariably made by one of the modern methods for making 'line blocks' and it is generally not copper but zinc or aluminium, and the surface is usually not silver but nickel or chromium. Modern printing plates can almost be guaranteed to last 300,000 sheets, even in the more severe printing conditions of high-speed presses. As described later, almost all stamps are now printed on rotary presses, but the traditional 'flat-bed' method is still often used for typographed or recess-printed stamps. Today the stamp printer has a wealth of options open to him, and typography is used for stamps printed in quantities below about 100 million where the printer happens to have all the equipment available and the design of the stamp is suitable. Generally, the printer uses paper already gummed, and, of course, does not damp the paper during the printing process; the ink is never water-based and has no effect upon the gum.

Newspapers are invariably printed by letterpress, and in them photographic illustrations are reproduced by the half-tone process. The same could be done with stamps, and as stamps are always printed on much better paper, the half-tone screen could be much finer, giving a better picture. But half-tone has very rarely been used in typographed stamps. Instead the photogravure method is employed, and today this is probably the most important method of stamp printing in the world. It was first used for a fine set of stamps of Bavaria (Bayern) of 1914, bearing a portrait of the kingdom's new monarch, Ludwig III, which was probably the first photographic, lifelike picture to appear on any stamp. It so happened that the British MI 7 counter-espionage organisation wanted to forge these stamps in 1917, and it is believed that the Waterlow company did the job.

Gravure has the ability, shared with another method – offset litho (pronounced lie-tho) – of achieving subtle and gentle tonal gradation to give a photographic type of result, in contrast to the two methods described earlier in which each bit of the stamp is either printed with the ink or left blank. Of course, when seen under a microscope the same holds true for all print processes; to obtain gentle shading it is necessary to use a fine half-tone screen. And it is hardly surprising that the gravure picture looks rather like a photograph, because in many respects the process is photographic. Practically all modern gravure stamp printing is on a rotary press, with a separate inking cylinder for each colour. Unlike ordinary four-colour printing using standard inks, most stamps are printed using 'facsimile inks' having hues specially chosen to match a particular colour. You can often see the colours from marginal check-dots or other markings in each ink.

Before starting the manufacturing process, the stamp designer and printer, and probably the customer, spend days or weeks discussing the desired result, studying enlarged reproductions in black and white called 'bromides' to refine the balance of the design and in particular the light and shade, and choosing the exact inks for each part of the design (assuming it is multicoloured). The next stage is an enlarged reproduction of the stamp in full colour, and this is then photographed through filters or 'scanned' electronically to separate it into one negative for each of the chosen printing colours. These are usually twice the final size, to allow for final hand retouching or improving the colour balance. When these master negatives are judged to be perfect, they are printed to yield stamp-size positives which can again be studied for colour balance. If the result is satisfactory, the stamp-size image is printed through a step-and-repeat camera, a device which can be programmed to print a photograph not once but many times in a row or in a rectilinear grid. The task with many definitive stamps is to print the image in, say, twenty rows of ten on a sensitised glass screen, each image being positioned within ± 0.0005 inch. The step-and-repeat camera is controlled by a punched paper tape which, as it is the same for each printing colour, should ensure perfect register of every colour plate.

The result is a stack of large glass plates called 'multipositives' each of which bears 200 – or even 960 – impressions of the printing to be done by one of the colours. (For a one-colour stamp, only one multipositive is needed.) The plates should register exactly. The multipositives are finished by hand by adding marginal markings, such as cylinder numbers, check dots, registration lines and any other details. Each multipositive is then used to print on to a 'carbon tissue', a delicate sheet of paper coated with a layer of orange-tinted gelatine which is sensitive to light. First, the carbon tissue, the same size as the multipositive and thus the same size as the stamp sheet, is exposed to light through a fine glass screen of black squares (or, looked at another way, of transparent lines crossing at right angles). This hardens the gelatine that happens to lie under the transparent lines, but not the parts under the opaque squares. The screen is very fine, each line of black squares having about 250 per inch, so the number of dots on a typical stamp is about half a million. Next, the carbon tissue is placed against the multipositive. This, like the crossing network of lines, is held closely against the carbon tissue by sucking the air out between them, and the exposure is made by a powerful 'point-source' light, so the exposures are made under identical conditions. The multipositive cannot affect the criss-cross of fine lines already hardened in the gelatine, but it can act on the tiny squares between them. The gelatine here is affected in direct ratio to the tonal variation on the multipositive. Where the latter is black, the light cannot penetrate to the gelatine, but everywhere else a smaller or greater amount gets through to reproduce the light and shade tones.

The result is a flimsy tissue, highly sensitive to light and to moisture, yet very much a precision product. The tissue is kept at constant humidity and near constant temperature, and with great care and in dull-red 'darkroom' lighting it is wrapped round the printing cylinder. This is a drum of steel or other rigid material surfaced with copper with a finish like a mirror. The cylinder is often sized to print two stamp sheets at once, so that each carbon tissue may go only halfway round its circumference. The cylinder is then immersed in hot water, at a precise temperature, and for an exact number of minutes. The carbon tissue backing paper comes away and the water dissolves out the softer gelatine, leaving the light-hardened parts in varying thicknesses proportional to the tones on the multipositive. Next the cylinder is etched in a bath of acid, with the time, temperature, and acid strength exactly controlled. This task, which is often done to a preset programme, etches microscopic square cells in the copper surface corresponding in size and depth to the depth of gelatine and thus to the tone of that part of the stamp design in that colour. The cell sizes, and thus the depths, are measured by a travelling microscope or other method capable of reading to within one or two microns (thousandths of a millimetre), and the final etching is often done with acid of different strengths poured on from jugs by hand. Skilled eyes judge the etch visually. When it looks right, a trial print is made and inspected, and any last-minute retouching is done. Then the finished cylinder is surfaced with very hard chromium, deposited electrolytically, and it can then be used to print millions of stamps.

In use the cells in the cylinder behave like the recesses in the old line-engraved method. The great rotary press runs at high speed, fed with a web (continuous length) of coated and gummed paper from a reel. The web is threaded through the machine past cylinders which each print in one colour. Each plate cylinder spins with its lower part immersed in a bath of the chosen ink. Although it is only in the ink for a fraction of a second on each rotation of the cylinder, the impression of each stamp picks up a coating of the ink and fills all its half-million or so square cells. A moment later the spinning cylinder carries the impression out of the ink, and it is at once scraped gently by a 'doctor blade', a perfectly straight knife-edge which removes all ink from the surface of the cylinder, leaving only the ink in the cells. The cylinder then brings the stamp impression into contact with the web of paper, moving past at exactly the same speed, which is pressed firmly against it by the 'impression cylinder' on the other side of the web. The plate cylinder transfers to the paper the ink from each microscopic cell. As the bigger cells are also deeper, they transfer more ink and make a richer colour than the smaller, shallower cells. A fraction of a

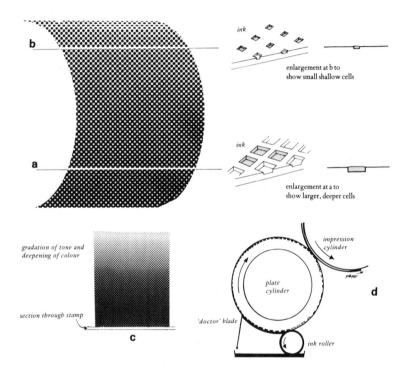

Fig 30   In rotary photogravure printing the image is etched into the surface of a polished metal cylinder in the form of a great number of microscopic square depressions. In some places the cells are large and deep (a), giving a deep shade of colour; in others the cells are small and shallow (b), and so hold less ink and give a pale shade. As the cells can be of any intermediate size, it is possible to have continuous gentle gradation in tone (c). The surface of the stamp is flat because the paper is printed between two flat rollers (d) and is not noticeably squeezed into the tiny ink cells. Gravure stamps have a characteristic appearance under a microscope.

second later the ink must be practically dry, because then the web passes between the plate and impression cylinders of the next colour, and so on until the complete range of colours has been printed. Some gravure machines are sheet-fed, in place of a rolled

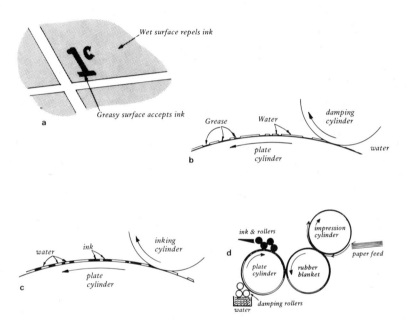

Fig 31 Offset lithography (litho) is based on the fact that grease repels water but will accept printer's ink (a). The design to be printed is deposited as a thin film of grease on the smooth surface of the metal 'plate cylinder'. This cylinder spins against a damping cylinder (b). Water from the damping cylinder wets the plate cylinder only where there is no grease. The plate cylinder, with its surface covered with a fine pattern of either grease or water, then runs against an inking roller (c). This immediately inks the greasy areas but the ink is repelled from the wet parts of the design. The result is a perfect inked impression. This is then 'offset' on to a rubber blanket cylinder (d) and it is this that actually prints the paper 'web' (continuous wide strip), which is then cut into sheets of stamps.

web. After the whole issue has been printed, the heavy plate cylinder is turned on a lathe until it is once more a smooth cylinder of copper, ready for its next job.

There is one other very important stamp-printing method: offset litho. It is based on the fact that oil and water do not mix. The old name 'lithography' means printing from a stone, but in the modern process the plate cylinder is covered with a curved sheet of aluminium, or aluminium–zinc alloy. The image is deposited on this metal surface in the form of an extremely fine greasy pattern, the molecules of grease being retained by the microscopic irregularities in the finely grained metal surface. The plate is then dipped in water, leaving a very thin film of water over all parts of the plate where there is no grease. This separates the metal surface into greasy areas which immediately retain ink and wet areas which repel ink, and the remarkable fact is that this can be done in the finest detail of an intricate design. To print the web, the plate cylinder is continuously rotated against damping rollers and inking rollers, keeping it replenished with the vital immiscible liquids. It also presses against a rubber-covered 'blanket cylinder', and it is this that prints the web of paper. Offset is a term meaning the transfer of a freshly printed pattern on to something else before it can dry. This transfer from the plate cylinder to the blanket cylinder, and thence to the continuous web, results in the method being called 'web offset', though the usual catalogue entry is just 'litho'. Wet stamps that press against the backs of others can leave a clear offset of their design in reverse; and an offset left on part of a printing press can sometimes leave the face of a stamp doubly printed. Such offsets can, of course, occur with any kind of printing.

There is no slick answer to the question of what is the best way to print stamps. Letterpress (typography) is certainly not the cheapest method for orders for thousands of millions of identical stamps. Probably the biggest stamp-printing machines in the world are used by the US Bureau of Engraving and Printing, and these print part of the design by direct intaglio (recess) and the rest by web offset. The only printing method designed specifically for stamps is De La Rue's 'Delacryl' process. This uses specially tailored papers and inks and seeks to combine the fine line quality of intaglio, the multicolour facility of gravure, and the economy and soft tones of web-offset litho printing. It must not be forgotten that whatever process is adopted, it must also be capable of printing any phosphor material unless this is incorporated in the paper. Early British phosphor inks were typographed, meaning that the printed web had to be run through a special letterpress machine just to print the bands. Today these important stripes or layers are printed

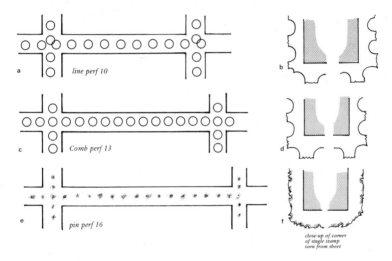

Fig 32   In line perforating (a) the sheet is first perforated by a succession of vertical or horizontal lines of holes and then by a second series of lines crossing the first at right angles. As there is no connection between the two sets of lines, they cross each other in unpredictable ways, so that the corners of a 'line-perf' stamp all look irregular and different from each other (b). Gauge 10 means there are ten spaces between hole centres in a distance of 20mm (0.79in). Comb perforating (c) finishes three adjacent sides of a stamp at one stroke, so that the vertical and horizontal rows all appear to cross perfectly (with one hole exactly in line with both rows); the stamp corners all look alike and regular (d). Pin perforating, sometimes called pin rouletting, does not punch out a set of paper discs but just makes small rough holes (e). The edges of a pin-perf stamp often tear badly (f).

by photogravure at the same time as the visible inks of the design.

The only significant thing left to do is the perforating. All the earliest stamps were issued as plain sheets, which were cut up by scissors or sharp knives (or sometimes by just tearing!) The most common method was for the post office counter clerk to cut each sheet first into horizontal strips. Then he could easily cut off however many each customer wanted. That is why vertical pairs and blocks are scarce. Late in the 1840s, Henry Archer invented a machine for perforating each sheet with rows of holes so that the stamps could be torn apart easily and accurately, and he not only patented the idea but persuaded the postmaster-general and Board of Inland Revenue to adopt it. At first he tried 'rouletting': the sheet of stamps was passed through a machine equipped with thirteen sharp-toothed wheels, looking like flat gearwheels, arranged on a single shaft with space for one stamp between each wheel. The rotating teeth made small slits down the vertical gutters. The sheet was then slotted along twenty-one rows from left to right in a second machine. The method was not very successful, and Archer then tried punching holes. In this case, the machine used a row of vertical prong teeth made of short lengths of rigid steel wire. The teeth descended through the sheet in the gutters between the stamps, the blunt end of each pin punching out a small disc of paper. At first there was great trouble with broken pins and other faults, and the sheets were often perforated in the wrong places (largely because of the great shrinkage of the wet paper after printing). For many years a lot of people continued to cut up sheets

Fig 33   The original British stamps were 20mm (0.79in) wide, allowing for half the inter-stamp gutter on each side (a) and when perforation was introduced the gauge was reckoned as the number of inter-hole spaces in a 20mm distance. Thus a stamp perforated 13 × 8 would have 13 'teeth' along its 20mm top edge and 8 teeth in a 20mm distance measured down either side. Even today many stamps are still just 20mm wide, and 24mm from top to bottom. Some are issued in 'end-to-end' coils, and they might be perf 9½ × imperf (b). Others, issued in 'sideways' coils, might be imperf × perf 9½ (c).

20mm

20mm

a

comb perf 13 x 8

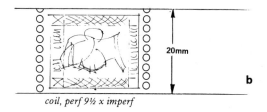

20mm

b

coil, perf 9½ x imperf

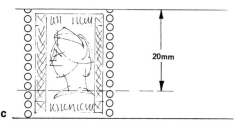

20mm

c

coil, imperf x perf 9½

with scissors even when they were perforated, but tearing through the holes gradually became universal.

There are many forms of perforation. The most common is comb perforating. The holes are punched, usually through a thick pile of stamp sheets cut from the freshly printed web and accurately stacked, by a 'comb head' which beats up and down from one edge of the sheet to the other, perforating one or more rows at a time. Each beat perforates both sides of every stamp in the row, and either the top or the bottom. Often the comb head has one pin working in a side margin, or it may perforate right through one margin, or the top or bottom. The finished sheet has a perfect grid of perforations, with vertical and horizontal rows exactly aligned and crossing through single holes at the corners of any four stamps. The alternative, invariably seen on stamps of the USA and Canada, is line perforating. Here each beat of the machine perforates one or more lines at a time; then the sheet has to be perforated along the lines crossing at right angles. There is no direct connection between the vertical and horizontal perforating, and where these lines of holes cross is a distinctive clue. Only by chance is there a single neat hole; usually the lines cross at a pair of overlapping holes, or one line may just miss the other.

Yet another early form was pin-rouletting. In this case the pins were not flat-ended but pointed. They did not punch out a disc of paper but just deformed it around the hole. There are even 'serrated perfs', 'zigzag perfs' and other unusual methods including early imperforate stamps that were separated by running a wavy-edged cutter (like a pastry cutter) between them. Philatelists are often interested in the diameter of the pins that punched the holes, and intensely interested in the 'perforation gauge'. This is the number of holes in a distance of 20mm (0.7874in). It so happens that most small definitives are about 20mm wide, including the unprinted margin. Thus a 20mm-wide stamp perforated to gauge 14 will have 14 projecting 'teeth' along its top edge, and the same gauge will give 17 teeth down each side. Sometimes stamps are issued in the form of coils, sold either from machines or over the counter. There is no reason to perforate the sides of such a coil, so

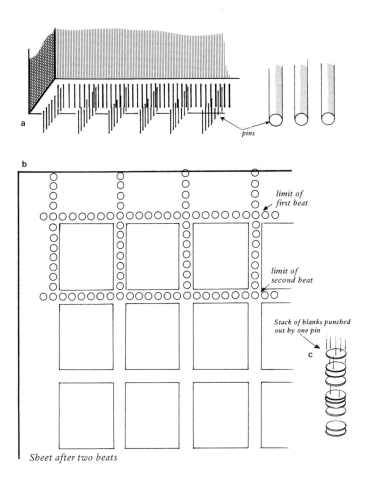

a

pins

b

limit of first beat

limit of second beat

Stack of blanks punched out by one pin

c

Sheet after two beats

Fig 34   A perforating comb has a long row of pins to strike through right across the sheet, plus short rows of pins at right angles to perforate the two adjacent sides of one row of stamps (a). Each stroke thus perforates the top (or bottom) and two sides of one row; or, if working from side to side across the sheet, it perforates top and bottom and one side. After two blows, a top-(or bottom-) fed machine will have done one margin and one complete row of stamps (b). The next stroke will finish the next row. Each hole goes through a stack of sheets, punching out a shower of tiny discs (c).

109

stamps from it might be 'perf 12 × imperf'. Or, in the case of a coil with the stamps printed sideways, the catalogue might list them as 'imperf × perf $9\frac{1}{2}$'.

To the casual observer, stamps issued in sheets, coils and booklets may all look identical, but in fact there are often important philatelic differences. Sometimes the coil or booklet stamps are deliberately printed with very slightly different designs. Coils are often made up of stamps of different denominations 'se-tenant' (many philatelic terms are French; this one means 'holding each other', in other words, joined together). For example a British coil of 1969 contained four different denominations: inserting a one shilling coin into the machine resulted in the ejection of five stamps, two at 2d, and one each of 3d, 1d and 4d! These stamps also differed from most sheet counterparts in each having a single phosphor band down the centre. In booklets it is common practice to design a special printing plate with half the stamps upside-down. The two halves are guillotined apart and made up into booklet panes

Fig 35 Se-tenant stamps are stamps of different denominations printed on the same piece of paper and issued joined together. These booklet panes contain stamps se-tenant horizontally (1d + 3d) and vertically ($\frac{1}{2}$d + $2\frac{1}{2}$d).

(pages), and if the paper is watermarked then half the panes have the watermark inverted. Sometimes ordinary sheets are printed with the watermark inverted, either by design or by accident. What is much rarer is for se-tenant stamps to be printed tête-bêche (another French term meaning that an adjoining pair of stamps are 'head to feet' or mutually inverted). This sometimes occurs with sheets printed for booklets being wrongly cut up, but in many stamp issues it was deliberate and is of no great value. There are countless variations resulting from the use of watermarked paper, some quite valuable stamps being distinguished by having the watermark sideways. This is commonly the case with coils prepared for side-delivery machines, but there are much rarer examples of sheets and booklet panes with the watermark sideways. Invariably the reason can be traced to the way the stamps were made, but such things are seldom explained in the catalogues.

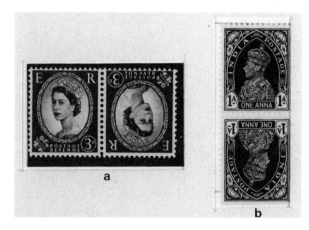

Fig 36   Tête-bêche stamps are 'head to tail', or mutually inverted. The British stamps are a sideways tête-bêche pair, and are the result of an error. The Indian stamps are a vertical pair, and were issued in this form.

5

Varieties

In general terms a 'variety' is a stamp which, in the course of its manufacture, was made to differ from most of its fellows. Sometimes the cause may be deliberate; for example, one of the finest varieties in the world is the British penny black deliberately printed in blue ink as a colour trial. Much more often the cause is accidental. It embraces incorrect colours, missing colours, printing flaws, mistakes in the design, paper, watermark, and countless other items. In most forms of collecting the connoisseur would instantly reject an item containing a flaw or error, or drastically downgrade it in price; in philately a mistake can multiply the value of a stamp a millionfold.

I must emphasise here that the value or significance of a variety is entirely one of degree, and of the extent to which it is obvious. So far, man has printed about 3,000,000,000,000 stamps, and if you inspect them carefully enough you will find that no two are alike. Thus every stamp is its own unique variety. The differences can be detected just by looking through a microscope, but there are many other variables such as the precise stamp dimensions, the composition of the paper, the thickness, the weight, the density and depth of inking, the spectrographic analysis of ink and gum, the exact shade of colour and fluorescence (both plotted by the same technique of measuring light wavelengths), the position of phosphor bands, and several other characteristics which a scientist can measure and record. Even then the variables often change with time; for example, every piece of paper changes in thickness and weight, and almost always in its linear dimensions, depending on the ambient humidity. I strongly believe philately will become more and more scientific, and already the keen student takes for granted the need for scientific tools. Three centuries ago a simple convex lens (magnifying glass) was an item of advanced technology, found only in the savant's laboratory. Ten years ago philatelists began to accept the need for an ultra-violet lamp. Today it helps enormously to have access to a spectrometer of some kind, and I predict that by the end of the century every serious philatelist will use a miniature ultra-violet lamp, spectrometer, and travelling microscope as routine tools.

Using such tools, it might be possible to separate out quite new sorts of varieties. Out of the thousands of millions of examples printed of the most common modern stamps, it might be found that a very small number differed sharply in some important respect. For example, they might be printed on paper distinctly thinner than normal, yet of a kind which was not obvious to the touch. In the old days of hand-made paper this would have meant little, but today the existence of a very small printing on 'thin paper' would certainly get into the catalogues and become eagerly sought at a high price. But I am sure most philatelists will agree that the term 'variety' ought to be reserved for stamps which can be seen to be different when touched or looked at by a person with normal eyesight, without the need for any equipment at all – the only permissible aids would be a perforation gauge or a colour guide, which are meant to help verify these two factors by comparing the stamp against standards that can be carried in the pocket. In my experience, the expert philatelist prefers his own judgement to any colour guide, and he can usually 'see' the gauge of perforation (or know how to count the projecting teeth).

To take a good example from British stamps, the issues of

Edward VII differ greatly in printer, paper, ink, and perforation. It is possible to bring to bear all sorts of tools to measure these variations, but the expert requires none of them. He does not need to deface a chalky-surfaced stamp by touching it with a piece of silver (the traditional test, the chalky coating reacting chemically with the silver to leave a black mark); nor does he need scientific devices to measure the light wavelengths of the ink, or its fluorescence; nor does he need to whip out a gauge to measure the perforations. With experience each stamp is instantly identifiable, just as we can recognise a friend from among city crowds without going up and measuring his face.

It is important to emphasise this point. A philatelist specialising in stamps from Great Britain could sort a huge pile of Edward VII unused 6d stamps (a particularly 'difficult' value) into at least twenty distinct printings, distinguished by the paper, gum, ink, and change of printer. The casual collector would notice that they were not all quite the same colour, but would be helpless to go much further even if he was given scientific tools. On the other hand, he might well be sidetracked into trying to separate them according to trivial differences in the printing, by noticing tiny blobs of colour or microscopic differences caused by die wear or variations in inking. Such differences are not of philatelic importance. They do not prove anything beyond the fact that no two stamps are alike. Many modern collectors have devoted much of their spare time looking for 'varieties' distinguished by details that can be seen only by someone with excellent eyesight. They ought perhaps to ask themselves the true importance of such varieties. Can they be assigned to particular stamps from known positions printed by known plates or cylinders? Are they 'constant', so that a number of identical examples can be collected? Perhaps most important of all, can a non-collector see them at arm's length?

The main part of this chapter discusses different types of variety under a number of clear subheadings. Usually there is no room for argument — either the stamp *is* the variety or it is a more common 'ordinary' one — but the subject is full of pitfalls.

Varieties are invariably priced well above the normal level. There may be a common green stamp priced in the catalogue at a few pence and a rare deep-green variety priced at a few pounds; here is an obvious source of speculation and argument. There may be a common stamp priced at a few pence; but in the course of time diligent study by specialists may separate the issue into a score of shades and other printing differences which suddenly mean that the 'common' stamp has vanished, being replaced by a lot of more expensive subgroups. This is discussed in Chapter 7, where it is argued how far varieties can be equated with money, and how far the prices paid for stamps can be influenced by the detailed subdivision in a specialised catalogue.

Plating It is usually characteristic of a security printer that he discloses little or nothing of his work. When the public first began to use adhesive postage stamps in 1840, there is no record of anyone bothering about the technical details of their printing. It was not until almost sixty years later that the new pastime of serious philately eventually brought to light that the penny black had been printed from eleven plates, each containing twenty rows of twelve impressions, and that most of these plates had been subjected to various repairs, hardening treatments, and other improvements in the course of their lives. The pioneer philatelists also discovered that seven of these plates were used at different times to print the red-brown penny that replaced the black stamp, and they went on to work out details of more than 270 other plates used to print 'penny red' stamps issued prior to 1864 – when a new series of plates was made that had the plate number helpfully written on each stamp, making subsequent 'plating' no problem at all.

It was soon apparent that some of the plates had been used to make millions of stamps, while others were much rarer. Even when a plate was found to have been at press for many months, or even years, so that its stamps were not rare, it was discovered that modifications to the plate resulted in some of its stamps changing their appearance slightly, depending on when they were printed. The concept of a plate existing in 'State I', 'State II' and so on arose, and gradually the specialists unearthed states that cannot have lasted more than a few days; they found varieties among the red-brown stamps which had no counterpart in the black printings from the same plate, and then they might find a single – priceless – example of the variety in a black printing. It was all very exciting, and it was made possible because the position of each stamp could be identified by its corner letters. In other countries the task of plating was made far harder by the absence of such letters, though diligent research has gone far to 'plate' the best early issues of most of the early stamp-issuing nations.

Plating is not so much a search for the abnormal type of variety as the assignment of every stamp of an issue to a particular plate. Such a task is very difficult when it is first begun, even seventy years ago when classic early stamps were easier and cheaper to come by in large quantities. Fast progress was possible only from the discovery of strips or blocks, which showed which varieties came from the same plate. The task had a great deal in common with a very difficult jigsaw puzzle. Finally, around 1910, just a few gaps remained to be filled in and a few plate modifications remained to be put into chronological order and approximately dated by working backwards from the dates on covers on which the stamps appeared.

Modern stamps – indeed, most issues of the twentieth century – cannot be plated. Their numbers are too great, the visible differences between stamps too slight, the number of printing plates or cylinders too large, and the incentive insufficient. It is conceivable that, in the course of time, increasing use of precision instruments will make it worth while for specialists to start trying to plate stamps of this century, but the task would appear formidable. The would-be plater sorts each stamp according to all the variables, which I have already mentioned. Often a date or place of use can help, but in general it is easier to plate mint stamps. But, whatever plating task is attempted, it seems impossible – or impossibly slow, which is almost the same – until one has been at it for a long time, always concentrating on the same issue or group of stamps. The real expert on a particular classic issue can plate stamps very much faster and more surely than the ordinary collector trying to do the job using detailed catalogues. Fortunately the number of real experts does not seem to be falling off, because the total number of serious philatelists is strongly on the increase and a major proportion of them have chosen to concentrate on early classic stamps.

Plating is a major part of the great philatelic objective of creating order out of chaos. It is rather like a beautifully kept garden, where everything has a neat name-tag. If such a garden is left untended, or put in the hands of someone who knows nothing about gardening, it will gradually become overgrown with weeds, and the name-tags will fall off or become mixed, which is far worse! Then a fresh expert will be needed to separate the good things from the bad, clean them up and put on fresh names. It is very important never to try to be too clever, and succeed only in plating stamps incorrectly; and it is equally important never to let a properly plated stamp become separated from its identification. I am strongly against writing on the backs of stamps, even in pencil; a plated stamp ought to be mounted in an album and 'written up' or put in a stock-book with a pencilled note in the book.

Re-entries As described in Chapter 4, it often happened in early stamp manufacture that the impression entered on the printing plate had to be re-done. If this was necessary before the plate had been used, it is strictly called a 'fresh entry', but it is often difficult to ascertain when the second entry was made unless stamps are available both without and with the betraying marks. Where every copy has the marks, the term 'fresh entry' ought strictly to be applied, but this suggestion is pedantic and doomed to failure. 'Re-entry' is the term used in practice to describe all second entries of an impression.

In modern stamp manufacture the whole procedure is, as far as possible, mechanised, and it is automated to a considerable degree. The opportunities for mistakes and irregularities are reduced as far as possible, hence the modern collector's delight at finding even small flaws. But in early stamps the opportunities were there in profusion. Indeed in early hand-engraved issues

117

there are sometimes no normal stamps at all, only varieties! Where the printing plate was made by successive impressions of a carefully engraved hardened steel die, the only major possibility of trouble lay in pressing the die in the wrong place or pressing it down at a slight angle so that the impression was not uniform all over. Sometimes the impression would be entered again without trying to erase the first, especially if the original entry was in the right place. It sometimes happens that stamps printed from a particular impression on a particular plate were originally pale and weak and then, in later printings, were clear and in rich colour. This is evidence of a 'coincident re-entry'. The original die had been pressed into the printing plate a second time, exactly on top of the first, giving a deeper and clearer impression. But there is nothing odd about the stamp, and the only way of discovering a coincident re-entry is to have weak early stamps and strongly printed later ones.

Fig 37   Re-entries are often prominent in old stamps printed by line engraving. The British 2d, plate 5 contains many fine examples, two of the best being at the top of stamp DB, plate 5 (issued perforated, a), and at the top of TH, plate 4 (issued imperforate, b). Re-entries are rare in modern stamps, but a fine one can be found in the British 10s printed by De La Rue in 1960 (c).

It is much more common for the term re-entry to mean the non-coincident type, in which the second impression is not exactly on top of the first one. Where the original entry was clearly in the wrong place – and sometimes most of an entire column or row was considered thus – it was obviously preferable to try to restore the surface of the plate to its original flat level before entering a second time. This was very difficult. If the plate was thin or especially malleable, it could be 'knocked up' from below and then filed or ground flat, but most early plates were of mild steel and about three-quarters of an inch thick. The British printings were restored by 'burnishing'; the incorrect impression was rubbed smooth by a hand tool having a very hard, smooth, rounded surface which slowly pushed down the raised parts of the impression and used the metal in these parts to fill the hollows. But the difficulties are obvious. Today it would be possible to build up the surface and grind it flush, but burnishing merely flattened out the original entry without completely removing it. When the image was re-entered there were often traces of the original entry left which could hold ink and print, and this unwanted portion of the original design was almost impossible to eliminate. In fact it often became increasingly prominent as the cyclic stress of using the plate gradu-ally opened out the pattern that the burnisher had tried to rub smooth.

There are many hundreds of really fine re-entries among the world's line-engraved or recess-printed stamps. Sometimes the first and second entries of the impression are separated so widely that there seems to be no immediate connection between the two, but in most re-entries the separation is a millimetre or less and so the design appears to be doubled. It often shows best on frame lines and lettering, though on many keenly sought re-entries in modern stamps the most obvious areas are in the pictorial parts of the design. Frequently the original entry is largely erased, and the parts that print are those that show through printed parts of the second entry where erasure would have been very difficult with-out spoiling the new entry as well. In early British stamps all re-entries have been recorded in great detail in standard reference books, but many other early stamps exhibit excellent re-entries that are recorded only in specialised books or not at all.

The student will soon learn the characteristics of an obvious re-entry, where the design is slightly doubled in one or more places, having the effect of filling in part of the white areas with inked lines or shapes parallel to the boundaries. But one often meets marks which may be a re-entry, a doubled letter (on a stamp with check-letters inserted by hand), a guideline to help in laying down the plate, a recut frame line, or just a burr mark or a mistake by the engraver. In early stamps a good re-entry may double the value. For example, the first Canadian stamp in the Gibbons part 1 catalogue, SG 1, is listed at £50; the same stamp with an excellent re-entry (the best of many known on this issue, the imperforate 3d 'beaver') is listed at £80 as SG 1a, assuming identical margins and general quality. Later and more common stamps are even more inflated by a re-entry. The 1841 imperforate penny red of Great Britain is listed at 25p in fine used condition, but in this printing there are re-entries that change hands at upwards of £10. In many modern stamps a good re-entry can multiply the value more than two hundredfold.

Constant flaws Re-entries are especially interesting members of the large class called 'constant flaws'. The term explains itself, apart from the fact that the flaw need not be truly constant. What often happened in the early days of stamp printing was that the plate would develop a crack, or other fault, which would become progressively worse. Thus the stamp(s) affected might at first be issued in perfect condition and would then appear with the flaw in successively more pronounced states. In modern stamp manufacture this is extremely rare. Instead the gravure cylinder, or whatever is used to print the stamps, may start its active life with a small flaw which will remain unvarying throughout the printing (though there are some famous examples of 'progressive' flaws). Alternatively, individual stamps may be marred by transient flaws caused by specks of foreign matter which become interposed between the inked cylinder and the paper.

It will at once be seen there is some difficulty in defining a constant flaw. The essence of the phenomenon is that it should be seen in a number of stamps, all of which should have what any objective observer would say was the same characteristic flaw. If this is due to damage to the printing plate it will affect every stamp from that part of the plate, but what about the case where a piece of thread – or a hair from the machine-minder – or other extraneous material becomes stuck to the plate? It may leave a distinctive irregular line on a thousand impressions; then it may shift, and leave a different line on a few more, and then fall off. In modern litho printing, where the plate cylinder is essentially smooth-surfaced, even a pinpoint of solid matter can cause a visible flaw. Such a flaw is invariably in the form of a white ring, because the tiny projection pushes the blanket cylinder away at that point and prevents that part from being inked. Here again the flaw may suddenly appear, last for many impressions, and then vanish.

By this time the reader will have a 'feel' for the different ways in which stamps have been made. There is obviously a world of difference between them. Over a century ago stamps were printed by flat plates in hand presses, and making the plate was a matter of skilled work with engraving tools, chisels, punches, burnishers, mallets and hammers, steel wool, emery paper, flickering gas jets, and constant attention to annoying faults – attention which might involve placing the plate face-down on a pile of sheets of leather and beating one point with a heavy ball-hammer. Today the business involves advanced optics, advanced photography, precision machine tools, constant chemical concentrations and temperatures, clean atmospheres, accurate control of time, and virtually no hand-working of metal except through the medium of acid. Opportunities for flaws are fewer, and if a bad one does occur it is usually possible to return immediately to the preceding stage and continue afresh. When a gravure cylinder or litho plate has been finished, small flaws have sometimes been corrected by 'retouching', described in the next subheading.

A philatelist can usually say with some assurance what probably caused any significant constant flaw. In the days of line engraving

121

the trouble often lay in the die itself, so that the same flaw was impressed into a large number of the positions on the printing plate. Wherever the die had a narrow upstanding ridge there was an obvious source of weakness; the narrow edge could be locally depressed by a blow (by accidentally dropping the die, for example), resulting in the stamps from the plate all having a broken border or other line. One of the most instructive flaws in all philately is the 'O flaw' of the British 1840 penny black, which affected four printing plates (nos 7 to 10). It began as a small break in the black edge of the stamp under the letter O of ONE PENNY, indicating that the recess in the plate at this point had either never been made or had become bridged. The flaw spread to become a large white area, which later was blurred or removed by attempts to repair or re-enter the offending impressions. A white area on an engraved stamp means that that part of the plate is not recessed and so cannot receive ink. It could be caused on a single impression by the groove or recess becoming filled with solid matter, but for a similar flaw to be seen on almost every impression in the plate means that the fault obviously lay with the die. So the

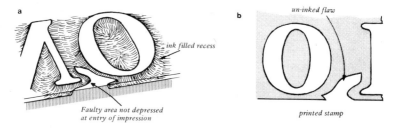

Fig 38   A 'constant flaw' is a characteristic mistake which can be seen on many copies of otherwise correctly printed stamps. Sometimes the flaw is not truly constant but progresses through different 'states' (usually getting worse). The first major example in history was the O-flaw on the British penny black of 1840. This appeared, in gradually worsening form, on many impressions on four of the last plates used to print this stamp. It sometimes made the O of ONE look like a Q.

die must have been dented, chipped or corroded at this point, and the fault must have been progressive. Thus, instead of pressing into the plate, that part of the design was left at the original plate level and so was wiped dry of ink on each printing of a sheet of stamps. Remarkably, the flaw never spread right into the O but was always separated by a thin black line, so a corresponding narrow ridge of metal must always have survived in the damaged die.

Elsewhere, narrow ridges of metal have caused much trouble. In the British stamps of Edward VII, made by typography, the frame lines often tended to break. These stamps were printed on paper watermarked with a bold imperial crown, and in an endeavour to obtain a good printing impression, despite the uneven water-marked paper surface, the pressure of the press was increased. By this time the printing plate for each colour was surrounded by a heavy border, often called a Jubilee line because it was first added to plates in Queen Victoria's Golden Jubilee year of 1887, intended to ease the blow of the inking roller striking the stamp impressions around the edge of the plate. Even this bold line often cracked and broke (it was often deliberately also filed or sawn to leave a char-acteristic printed image to identify the plate used or date of print-ing), and in some cases pieces fell completely away. The same thing sometimes happened with the frames and borders of indi-vidual stamps. In one or two cases, extra pieces of strip metal were soldered on as a crude repair; alternatively, a completely fresh stamp impression was made, the old one sawn off the plate, and the new one welded or brazed in place. Such 'repaired clichés' can be identified whenever they were inserted slightly out of alignment.

Every country that issued stamps prior to World War II prob-ably has examples of good constant flaws. Many are known in their first ('constant') state and also in a repaired form which may be far from perfect. Some of the latter are discussed in the next section.

Retouches There is no clear definition of how a retouch differs from other ways of correcting flaws. In the case of typographed or recess-printed stamps, a retouch can be made only by mechanically repairing the plate, whereas the term is much more often applied to the kind of retouching possible by an artist or process worker in the photographic stages of modern stamp printing. I consider the word should be used only for local improvements or fault-rectification that do not involve metal dies, plates, or cylinders. Where actual mechanical changes are made the word surely ought to be 'repair'?

Despite this, there are many well-known corrections that have been called 'retouches' even when they involved mechanical repairs. In British stamps one example is the 1½d (three-halfpenny) of 1912–24. Between 1918–21 one stamp on each of two plates bore the clear inscription THREE HALFPENCF. Had this been a die fault it would have affected all the impressions in the plate, but it affected only the stamp at the right-hand end of row fifteen. Clearly the fault lay in the block of lead in this position from which the electrotype printing plate was given its images in the bath of acid. This offending lead was in position for plates 12 and 29, another odd fact because the intervening plates were perfect! Many examples are known of the 'PENCF' stamp, but a rarer variety is the same stamp after the error had been repaired or retouched. The final E on PENCE is then found to have a longer stroke, even longer than usual, with a prominent serif. This is typical of the cases where the error, which is obvious, multiplies the value of the stamp more than a hundredfold, while the corrected error, which is far from obvious, multiplies its worth about a thousand times.

Values reflect rarity. In the Australian 4d stamps of 1915–23, one of the impressions on the printing plate cracked to give the variety 'line through FOUR PENCE'. In the original printing in various shades of orange or yellow, this is not too difficult to find, and it was not corrected. In 1921, just after the colour was changed to violet the line was repaired but at the cost of the two words appearing in thinner letters which show up markedly under a magnifying glass. The corrected stamp is difficult enough to find, but the uncorrected violet is so extremely rare that copies command prices well over £100, whereas the ordinary violet 4d is worth only a few pence. In the third printing, in 1922, the stamp was again changed in colour to pale shades of blue. The uncorrected version is of course unknown here, but with difficulty one can find the retouch with thin letters. A much easier example of a 'mechanical' type of retouch is seen in the 17c Canadian special-delivery stamp of 1946–7. In the original printing, every stamp had the French translation of special delivery rendered as EXPRÊS, with a circumflex accent. It is amazing that this was not noticed, but it was not rectified until the following year when the word appeared with the correct grave accent. Both forms are common.

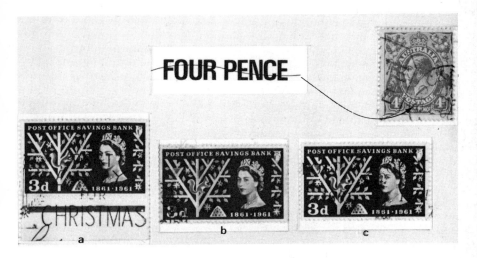

Fig 39 Retouches are attempts to cure faults in stamp printing. The ideal retouch restores the stamp printing to a perfect state, but many retouches still leave a characteristic fault. For example, in Australia in 1919 a plate used to print 4d stamps was damaged so that one impression had a white line through FOUR PENCE. In 1921 this was retouched by filling in with metal and re-engraving the letters, but the new letters were thinner than before. A modern example with gravure printing is seen in the British Post Office Savings Centenary 3d stamp of 1961 (a). One impression was damaged so that a nick appeared in the S of SAVINGS (b). Later this was retouched to leave a modified S (c).

The real world of the retouch is found in modern gravure and litho stamps. Here the automated and almost untouched-by-hand methods which are used to make the stamps theoretically result in a perfect product. Certainly fewer than one stamp in a million reaches the public with any really significant error or flaw. On the other hand, the idea that the stamps are made by a foolproof computerised process is so far a pipe-dream. A very large number of the impressions are doctored by skilful hands to try to erase flaws and correct or improve the resulting stamps. A successful retouch is one that cannot be seen and so remains unknown, but there are countless examples that are anything but invisible. The reader probably knows of many retouches which are worse than the flaw. Thin scratches can be retouched into broad messy stripes, small nicks into larger blobs, and slightly pale areas made more obvious than before by bold cross-hatching.

Errors of colour Modern inks are extremely resistant to chemical change, and errors of colour are almost non-existent (and therefore, when they do occur, they are extremely valuable). Early stamps were sometimes printed in ink of entirely the wrong colour, and even when correctly printed the ink often changed its colour in the course of a long period. Probably the outstanding example of a 'changeling' is the British $\frac{1}{2}$d of April 1900. Although the ink was meant to be a bluish-green the pigment often had a tendency to turn bright blue, and it is possible to find superb mint copies which have no trace of green. These are of no special value and are not errors, but it shows that one has to be on one's guard where inks can be so readily changeable.

The classic British 'penny blue' of December 1840 has been mentioned, and there are several other very early stamps in the same class. This blue penny was not an error, but nearly all the others are. One of the finest varieties in all philately is the Swedish '3 skilling' (inscribed TRE SKILL. Bco.) of 1855. Printed correctly in green, this is a fine classic rarity in its own right, good copies seldom failing to fetch well over £100 and sometimes over £300, and much more on cover. Late in the last century a Swedish

126

schoolboy walked into a stamp dealer's with a fine copy of what looked like the yellow-orange 8 skilling value; but it was a 3 skilling printed in error in 8 skilling ink. The suspicious dealer at once soaked it in water (!); when it stayed the same colour he paid the delighted boy the 7 kroner for which he had asked. Today I do not know what this unique stamp would fetch, but in kroner the sum would exceed one million. Another stamp in the same class is the Uruguay 1858 with a face value of 180 centésimos, printed not in green but in red of the 240c value. For many years experts considered this must somehow be a changeling, but they finally accepted it as genuine.

Among the 'Cape triangulars' issued by the Cape of Good Hope in 1853–65 the best are the locally produced 'woodblocks' of 1861. In laying down the impressions to form the stereotyped plate, one of the 1d blocks became transposed with one of the 4d ones, with the result that stamps of both values came off the press printed in the colour of the other. Put another way, one stamp in each freshly printed sheet bore the wrong inscription. In 1860 the Italian kingdom of Sicily issued by mistake the ½g (mezzo grano) value in blue

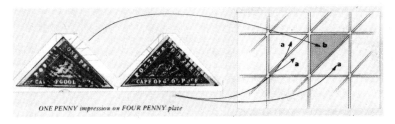

ONE PENNY *impression on* FOUR PENNY *plate*

Fig 40   In 1861 the Cape of Good Hope (in what is now the Republic of South Africa) made some 1d and 4d stamps themselves. They engraved their own steel printing plates, but the result was not as fine as the original stamps with British-made plates, and they soon became called the 'woodblock' issue. It was not at first realised that one impression of the 4d and one of the 1d had become transposed. So collectors discovered what looked like a wonderful error of colour. But it was not a case of using the wrong ink: it was just that each plate contained one impression of the wrong value.

instead of the usual orange. In the famous USA Columbian issue of 1893 the 4c, normally printed in ultramarine, once appeared in the totally different deep blue of the 1c value. The New Zealand 'commemorative series of 1906' originally was to have had the 1d value printed in deep-claret ink; this was judged unsatisfactory, but one sheet was sold in this colour (the regular printing being vermilion).

Shades of colour No branch of philately is so characterised by hope and uncertainty as shades. The ideal situation is a common stamp that was printed in one unvarying colour except for a very small part of the printing that appeared in a quite distinct shade, and is therefore of much greater value. Unfortunately it is seldom like this. There are two things to consider. One is that most stamps are printed in vast quantities and that the shades of ink used may vary slightly all the time. The second factor is the way a catalogue publisher interprets the shades he sees. No listing of shades can be better than the opinion of an expert, and nobody but that expert himself can always guarantee to have interpreted the list correctly. Usually there is a clear distinction between a common stamp and a rare shade, but when the stamp appears in a host of catalogued shades there can be problems.

In most simplified, or 'all-world' catalogues, the British 1d stamp of 1912–24 is described as just 'red'. Several catalogues list 'red' and 'vermilion'. The Gibbons part 1 lists 'bright scarlet, scarlet, pale rose-red, carmine-red, scarlet-vermilion'. The Gibbons Specialised volume 2 lists 'bright scarlet, deep bright scarlet, scarlet, deep scarlet, brick-red, deep brick-red, vermilion, pale red, pale rose-red, pink, carmine-red, bright carmine-red, deep carmine-red, scarlet-vermilion, orange-vermilion (1917–19), deep orange-vermilion (1918)'! The expert will unfailingly identify any copy of this stamp according to this list. Most people know the difference between, say, carmine, scarlet, and vermilion, but it takes experience to know what is deep, what is bright and what is both deep and bright. It also takes good eyes, and an ability not to be distracted by a stamp seen against a coloured background (take some ½d stamps from the same issue and look at them against backgrounds of bright blues, yellows and yellow-greens and the results can be most misleading).

Skill comes with long experience, but what about the collector who cannot wait? There are various published colour reference cards, but my comment here is that I do not possess one. There are various reference collections where the true shades are marked, but these cannot be consulted by the millions, nor can the overworked experts. In the long term there seem to be two answers. One is to use modern printing methods to try to produce a shade card having hundreds of reliable and unvarying shades which can infallibly be matched against shades as described in catalogues; the other is to bring science to the rescue and try to express each shade in precise numerical terms. I have long believed that philately will benefit from the increasing acceptance and availability of scientific methods and equipment. Almost everyone today who has to sort, classify or identify things resorts to some form of measurement. For example, in interpreting an infra-red aerial photograph of the Earth one can do much by merely studying the picture with expert eyes, but even an unskilled person can do better by spectral analysis of the different colours. In the same way anyone with a spectrometer can identify any shade of stamp with absolute precision, and without needing experience or being put off by the background colour, once an expert has written down the results or plotted a curve for the wavelengths of each listed shade. This seems to me the method that will be used in the future to establish unvarying standards, and which will come to be used by the various national expert committees who give their opinions and certificates on such matters.

An alternative is for the philatelic world to adopt one of the long-established world-wide colour standards, such as that of Munsell, and list every shade in numerical terms corresponding to that standard. Then all that the unskilled collector will have to do is carry a set of colour standards (which should fit the pocket) and know how to match any one of them with what may be only a small portion of the stamp. Colour matching does have one possible advantage that both the stamp and the standard may be equally affected by the lighting. Many inks look quite different colours in daylight, under tungsten-filament lighting and under different kinds of fluorescent lighting, and it is hazardous to buy expensive shades in conditions of misleading lighting.

Whatever method may be used in future to establish the identity of shades in numerical terms, a stamp is worth what a buyer will give for it. It may be unhelpful to apply advanced scientific methods merely to show that something is not a rare shade after all; the owner might prefer not to know. Personally, I do like to know what I have, and if possible to gather as many rare shades as possible. To me an album page of superb shades can be far more beautiful than a page of JFK or space flight, even though the young collector might find a page of 'the same stamps' quite uninteresting. To others with the same inclination my best advice is 'try to become familiar with the really rare shades'. These sometimes come up in auctions, or in good dealer's shops complete with a certificate. Then when a dealer says 'Look at this, a real copy of the Cyprus green, catalogue £100, you can have it for £25, much less than it would fetch in auction', you will know if it is, even in a dimly lit shop.

Missing colours Most early stamps were printed in only one colour, so this variety did not arise. One of the earliest examples concerned the French 5-franc lilac-coloured stamp of 1869. This, a good stamp in its own right, had the value printed in a separate operation, and copies are known with this important inscription missing. From then until the present day, stamps have come on to the market with one colour totally missing. Often the variety is found over a whole sheet, or part of a sheet, and it can often be seen to have been due to a second sheet of paper becoming partially interposed (when one might expect to find the missing ink printed on the gum of the interfering sheet). There are many instances of gross faults in gravure printing resulting in the printed design (which may be of a single-colour stamp) suddenly going 'off focus', becoming increasingly blurred and weak and then, in extreme cases, fading out altogether, leaving the rest of the sheet blank (often called 'albino').

Dozens of modern commemorative stamps are known with crucial parts missing, often including the name of the country or the face value. Britain has produced some startling commemoratives with large oval spaces which were intended to have been filled by the queen's head. A businessman found he had a strip of such stamps – in this case the red 2½d Post Office Savings Bank issue of 1961 – and put one in his wallet, telling his secretary to file the rest in a safe place. A year or two later he found the 'safe' file had been cleared out, in a routine housekeeping operation, so the only copy of this superb error is now a creased and grubby single stamp!

Error of design The proper interpretation of this is for the design of a stamp, or one impression of it, to have been executed in an incorrect way. It could be argued that the Cape woodblock 'error of colour' was really an error of design. Anyone lucky enough to see the whole sheet would realise at once that this was true, though to see the single stamp is to suggest an error of colour. Some of the other early 'errors of colour' may also really have been errors of design. In other words, instead of using the wrong ink the fault

Fig 41   Some of the most startling printing errors are those in which an obvious frame or border has been left empty. This can be because one sheet has completely missed one colour, but in this case (from the British NPY issue of 1962) it can be seen that the blue ink that printed the queen's head suddenly faded out on one sheet leaving a horizontal row with oval frames almost empty.

131

may have been due to an incorrect impression, for a different value of stamp, inserted into a correctly inked sheet.

One of the fertile sources of mistakes ought to have been the British policy of identifying each stamp in the plate with corner letters. In fact there are only three such errors known. The rarest and best occurs on the imperforate 1d red. Plate 77, registered in April 1847, had the first stamp in the second row, normally bearing letters B-A, with a blank square at lower right. Months later this was noticed and the missing A was punched in. The so-called 'B-blank' is a superb variety – I have once seen a used copy, but never expect to possess one. Much more common are the 1½d from plate 1 lettered in error O-P, P-C, when it should have been C-P, P-C, and the 2½d from plate 2 lettered L-H, F-L, instead of L-H, H-L; but even these fetch £25 to £70 in used condition, and much more mint. If you cannot afford such sums you can, for a few pence, buy the recent Guernsey 1d and 1s 6d definitives bearing a map of the Channel Islands. In the first printing the parallel of latitude appears as 40° 30'N, and in the later printing it was corrected to 49° 30'N (the original location would be somewhere in the middle of Spain).

Inverts Some of the best of all varieties involve part of the design

Fig 42   Early British stamps had corner letters inserted by a skilled platemaker using a hand punch. On the 1½d plate 1 of 1870 stamp PC (third from the left in the sixteenth row from the top) should have had the same letters in the reverse order in the top corners. But instead of a C the platemaker used an O, giving rise to the famed error OP-PC. Nobody noticed until an American collector spotted the mistake in 1894.

being inverted. This is not the same as an error of design, because it results from one particular colour, or an overprint, being inverted in an otherwise correct stamp. Such rarities are often of startling appearance, though this is not the case when the inverted part fits perfectly into the remainder. For example, the Gibbons 'Elizabethan' catalogue lists under Kenya, Uganda and Tanganyika the 1954 brown 5c stamp with the black vignette of Owen Falls dam inverted, and laconically comments that 'only one used copy is known'. This variety of a worthless common stamp thus joins the roll of supreme rarities where only one copy exists. An inverted rectangular picture correctly located in its frame could well be missed, yet if the whole sheet was thus printed how did the other ninety-nine come to get away? A second copy may yet be found. Another stamp of immense rarity where undoubtedly one whole sheet was affected is the Canadian St Lawrence Seaway commemorative of June 1959. A number of copies have been found in which the entire blue print, the whole centre of the stamp, is upside-down in relation to the red inscription. It is far from obvious, and I suspect there may be other copies of this basically very common stamp that have not yet been noticed.

But the most classic inverts are often very obvious. One that I would have thought nobody could miss is the India 1854 printing of the 4 annas in which the vermilion frame is upside-down in relation to the blue queen's head, yet I found what looked like one in an auction lot that I bought, unseen, with a postal bid. If anyone else had noticed it I should certainly never have succeeded with my small bid. This particular copy turned out, on expert scrutiny, to be 'probably a forgery', but there are about two dozen authentic copies – and one cover of priceless value bearing two affixed to it! These 4 annas were among the first stamps printed in inks of two colours. Another early two-colour series were the top four values, 15 to 90 cents, in a set of ten definitives issued in the USA in 1869; except for the top value all are known with the centre inverted, multiplying the value of what is in any case a rare and valuable stamp. America has some excellent inverts apart from these. In 1901 a customer who bought ten of the 2c value of the Pan American Exhibition issue used three and then noticed that the centre, the 'Empire State Express' train, was inverted. He complained to the Bureau of Engraving and Printing, wanting to know if they were valid for postage! Fortunately he told his companions and one of them suggested he should sell the other seven at a large profit, which he did. A similar case occurred with the 1918 air mails, but in this case the buyer was a collector, and unlikely to complain! The stamp was the 24c, and the Curtiss mail plane on the copy bought by the collector, on the day of issue, was inverted. He managed to borrow $24 and bought the rest of the sheet. The Post Office tried to get it back, by a variety of methods, but the buyer held out and eventually sold it for $15,000. The profit of $14,976 looks good, but today this split-up sheet fetches about $35,000 a stamp. So if the original owner still had these 100 stamps his profit could be $3,499,976!

Among overprints there is a vast range of varieties. Overprints are applied, in a contrasting ink, to a sheet of previously printed stamps. The overprint plate is usually not made with the care lavished in regular stamp printing, and there are countless examples of missing full stops, mis-spelt words, and incorrect dates, but inverted overprints are among the better varieties. Often the sheet is overprinted once correctly and once inverted (such as the Canadian 'one-line' 2 cents overprint on the carmine 3c of

Fig 43   One of the first stamps to be printed in two colours was the Indian 4 annas of 1854. A very few of these stamps exist with the blue printing of the head upside-down in relation to the frame. One original cover is known bearing two copies of this famous invert.

1926), and there are cases where just one overprint is inverted while those on the rest of the sheet are correct. Few British stamps have been overprinted, but one very important series is the 'official' stamps of 1882–1904. These are often basically good stamps in any case, especially in mint condition, and only a millionaire could aim to buy a complete mint set. Several of the overprints are known inverted. The 'GOVERNMENT PARCELS' on the 1900 green and carmine 1s was discovered inverted, and in 1915 five copies were put up for certification by the Royal Philatelic Society expert committee. A vital member of the committee was Charles Nissen, who was able to say that the setting of the letters differed from all those he had seen in the correct overprint; so the five inverts were rejected as forgeries. It so happened that Charles's son, Harry, was the man who, in 1947, found further examples of the inverted overprint well tied by postmarks to the original wrappers! The stamp is back in the catalogue.

Wrong paper Only expert philatelists might be expected to notice such trivia, but in fact stamps printed on incorrect paper are an especially good example of the kind of material that the expert can 'win out on'. Ideally the expert ought to try to find such items well away from the country of issue, where the seller is less likely to be well informed. Often the use of unusual paper is not an error but merely an authorised using up of waste or left-overs. For example, the British 1961 'CEPT' commemorative printing did not quite use up its allocation of coated (so-called 'chalky') paper, and in 1963 this was used to print a few of the Isle of Man 3d value. These naturally look much finer and brighter than the ordinary printing, and their value has risen meteorically, as anyone could have predicted. Another example from modern Great Britain is the phosphor-graphite 2d value printed on 'St Edward's Crown' watermarked paper, and in this case the paper was officially admitted to be erroneous. A friend of mine at first used to sell this stamp at 25p; today a copy seldom changes hands under £20.

In classic British stamps erroneous watermarks abound, despite the extreme care of the printers. The 1867 red-brown 10d was in error printed on 'emblems' paper, and about eleven used copies are known, seven of them posted in Constantinople (no mint copy is known). When the brown-lilac £1 of 1884 was in production on Imperial Crown paper – the long stamps lying across three watermarks each – someone at Somerset House sent De La Rue 505 sheets of the orbs paper by mistake, and these were duly printed and issued to give a stamp of even greater value. But this pales into insignificance beside the 1880 surface-printed 1d. Although it was only in use for eighteen months, this 'Venetian red' stamp is common and of no particular value. To the astonishment of the philatelic world a collector found a copy a few years ago printed not on Imperial Crown paper but on orb watermark paper! Since then I must have hopefully looked at a few thousand but I do not expect to find the second copy.

6
Fakes and Forgeries

This is not a wholly unsavoury subject. Indeed another of the quirks of the philatelist is that, just as he often jumps with delight at finding a stamp containing an error or flaw, so does he eagerly seek forgeries worth much more than the real thing. The subject raises a host of questions. What is meant by a fake, or a forgery? How is it done? Who does it, and why? What determines the value of a fake or forgery? Is it against the law? The number of ways in which a stamp can be not quite what it seems are many indeed.

The meaning of 'forgery' is quite obvious. It is a stamp which looks to an inexpert eye the same as a properly issued stamp but which has been manufactured by other hands at a later date. It may have been manufactured to defraud the revenue by being used postally instead of genuine stamps, or it may have been done 'for kicks' to satisfy the whim of a skilled craftsman, or its primary purpose may have been to defraud the inexperienced stamp collector. A special category of forgery is the imitation of an enemy's stamps produced in wartime, and in some cases these officially manufactured copies were cunningly altered – or, in a few cases, rather crudely – to serve as vehicles of propaganda. There is also a wide range of different types of facsimile, some of them produced officially (some indeed, proper postage stamps in their own right), and some merely copies of valuable stamps which could fool nobody and are merely fun objects for stamp collectors. A fake is yet another category, comprising a genuine stamp doctored to make it look like a rarer or better genuine stamp (in particular, to make it appear to be a valuable variety). Yet another category is the bogus issue: there are many cases of people printing stamps that the country in question never issued, and even of printing sets of stamps for countries that never existed!

In 1840 there were no collectors to defraud, but the Board of Inland Revenue in London was most anxious that nobody should try to print his own postage stamps to stick on letters. After looking at one of the early line-engraved stamps, few people today would think forgery even worth considering, but in 1840 there were more than 10,000 skilled engravers in Britain and they might have judged differently. After all, between 1797 and 1817 there were 309 convictions in Britain for forging banknotes, and in those days this sent a man to the gallows. Forgery had ceased to be a capital offence in 1832, and the authorities were concerned lest this should open the floodgates and find penny blacks and twopenny blues pouring out of every back room in the nation. Perhaps it is a remarkable testimony to the design of these stamps that no postal forgery of them has ever been discovered. If anyone should try to make new copies today it would be for much more return than one or two pence a time, and perhaps a major explanation of the forger's timidity here is that so many collectors are experts on these issues and so unlikely to be deceived.

While on the subject of these classic stamps, I will recall the 'official forgery' mentioned earlier. In 1856 the Board of Inland Revenue, perhaps intrigued at the absence of the expected stamp forgers, organised an 'official forgery' of the current 1d stamp, then printed in various red or red-brown shades with a re-engraved head from die II. Few details have been recorded of the tools and facilities that were made available to the official forger, and I believe the specimen in HM The Queen's collection (two 'stamps', one clipped off diagonally) is the only one in existence.

But the general inference at the time was that a convincing forgery is exceedingly difficult; this is largely because of the singular ability of human beings to detect trivial differences in human faces.

So far there is only one known instance of British postage stamps being forged to defraud the revenue. It is an oft-told story. In 1898 Charles Nissen, one of the first and greatest expert philatelists, studied 1s (one shilling) stamps on old telegraph forms which should have been destroyed soon after use in 1872 but instead found their way from a derelict papermill to the stamp trade. He realised some were forgeries, skilfully printed by lithography on unwatermarked paper. All were cancelled at the London Stock Exchange, and it seemed obvious that one of the counter clerks must have been 'in' on the racket (he may have worked alone, but if so he was a remarkable man). He fixed the stamps to the forms and cancelled them, and the public never handled them. His stock of real stamps did not diminish, and pocketing the shillings is estimated to have brought in £15,000 a year for much of 1872 and

Fig 44   So successful were the attempts of the British Post Office to prevent stamp forgery that only one case is known of a forger defrauding the revenue (though there are plenty of cases of forgers defrauding collectors!). Stamp PF is a genuine 1s plate 5 used at the London Stock Exchange in July 1872. Stamp KM is a complete forgery, used at the same place in the same month. Nobody discovered the fraud until a philatelist spotted one of the forgeries many years later. This is remarkable because some of the stamps, such as KM, bore corner letters that are impossible. There are only twelve stamps in a row, so the one at the right-hand end has letter L (the twelfth letter in the alphabet) in the lower right corner. An M in the lower right corner was impossible, but the forger did not realise this.

1873. The forgeries have many combinations of corner letters, some of which – an almost unbelievable mistake – are impossible, because in the genuine sheets the horizontal rows ran from A to L (there being twelve stamps in a row) whereas the forgeries go beyond L (Fig 44).

This case is unique in 'GB', and it was also one of the scores of world-wide cases in which the plot was uncovered not by a government official but by a philatelist. In recent years there have been famous cases of postal forgery in the USA, Australia, France, Germany, Italy, most South American countries and many countries in the Far East. One or two of these forgeries were for stamps of high face value, but nearly all were for quite trivial amounts – a cent, a penny or pfennig or two. In almost every case the true stamp was not printed on watermarked paper, and this undoubtedly made it more difficult to come to the conclusion that the stamp was indeed a forgery. To me the chief lesson of these dozens of cases is that the expert philatelist can 'see' a forgery, whereas the unskilled observer cannot see it even when it is explained in detail. In a high proportion of postal forgeries in this century the gauge of perforation has been wrong, though I suspect the main reason for detection was the general aura of 'wrongness' that an expert could sense but perhaps not explain.

Most of these postal forgeries are recorded only in specialised catalogues. In any case they are usually rare in relation to the corresponding genuine items, and are usually of greater value. For example, I collect Australian stamps and have scores of 1932 George V and Sydney Harbour Bridge 2d stamps, but I have yet to come across one of the forgeries. These were produced so that the organisers of a lottery (itself illegal) could save heavy postage bills, so there was no problem of distributing or selling the stamps. Yet these very common stamps, stuck on envelopes so that absence of a watermark was hidden, were still detected almost at once by expert collectors, who can hardly have been expecting to find such a thing.

Forged stamps used in the post are obviously criminal; in any case, from the philatelic viewpoint they are good rather than bad.

Unfortunately most of the efforts currently being made to forge stamps are aimed at defrauding not the revenue but the collector, and it is very difficult to bring a criminal charge. Merely to make your own copy of a rare stamp is no offence. To tell someone what you have done and invite him to buy it is no offence, and you can take his money. But you must tell the purchaser what you are selling is a forgery; it is a felony merely to say 'I cannot vouch for it as genuine.' In any case such niceties are academic; the man who would forge a rare stamp might not shrink at telling a lie. But he must pass the goods off privately – if he puts them into an auction or takes them to a top-class dealer he will almost certainly be discovered very quickly indeed.

To me it seems rather self-defeating to forge rare stamps. Rare stamps are valuable because they are rare. To print a few hundred would at once debase their value. In any case, with real rarities any collector likely to buy would already know where the existing copies were, and would want to know in some detail where any new and unknown copy had come from. I doubt if any forger of rare stamps has ever been able to sell them through proper channels, but has had to rely on 'bent' dealers, or collectors prepared to buy something they strongly suspect of being what it is.

During much of this century, the world of philately has been kept at fever-pitch by a series of brilliant forgers who often did their work quite openly. Probably the most famous of all these

Fig 45   One of the wiles of the faker is to make a tête-bêche pair, usually by taking a genuine pair and turning one stamp upside-down. This pair of French stamps of 1870 looks convincing, even to an expert, but a grenz-ray (X-ray) photograph gives the game away.

names is that of Sperati, actually a whole family, who operated from France and from Pisa. They made copies of very many valuable stamps, and the few I have handled would certainly fool me. Most of the forgeries – certainly in the case of British stamps, on watermarked paper – began life as a genuine stamp in the same series, usually a used copy. For example I have seen a Sperati copy of the British 2s brown of 1880 which is thought to have originally been a genuine 3d on the same 'spray of rose' paper. The forging process resulted in the printed image of the genuine stamp being faded or dissolved out and a new stamp being printed over the cancellation (and I, at least, could not tell it was not under it). Many of Sperati's productions were lightly pencilled on the back, with a signature or date or other details, but this just invited erasure. Jean de Sperati, the patriarch of the clan, operated until 1953. He scattered his beautiful creations far and wide, describing them openly as 'facsimiles'. He had a very close rival in the Swiss, Fournier, who called himself an 'art publisher'. Both men had a fantastic array of counterfeiting equipment, and huge stocks of apparently priceless stamps of their own manufacture. Fortunately the British Philatelic Association acquired the whole stock of Sperati, and the tons of Fournier hardware were secured by the Union Philatelique de Genève, and except for special albums for the guidance of collectors, the spurious rarities were destroyed.

No account of famous stamp forgers would be complete without mentioning the comic-opera world of Benjamin and Sarpy. They were really a trio, Alfred Benjamin, Julian Hippolyte Sarpy and George Kirk Jeffryes. They traded as stamp dealers at 1 Cullum Street, in the City of London (a street where you can still buy stamps). Back in the 1880s they would make you a fine fake or double overprint or any other rarity while you waited. At home – and philatelists will enjoy the fact that Benjamin called his house 'Sydney View Villa' – the forgeries proper were executed. Eventually the 'London Gang' became such a menace that proceedings were taken, at the instance of the Philatelic Protection Association. At their trial in 1891 it took a long time for the prosecution to establish that a stamp is a 'document' for the purposes of the law. Once this had been done their sentences of six and four months' hard labour were foregone conclusions. This is one of very, very few cases where successful prosecutions have been brought against stamp forgers who had no intention of defrauding the revenue.

To show what a small world it is, it was a bona fide dealer, W. Foster, of Cullum Street, who in 1949 became the expert who told the world about postally used forgeries of Singapore. These Singapore stamps probably fall into a slightly different category of official or political forgeries. In 1948–9 the George VI definitives of Singapore were coming on to the market in a flood from sources outside the British Military Administration or Singapore Post Office. This was a time of political upheaval in the Malay Peninsula, and it was announced at the time that these forgeries emanated from Chinese sources. But they were intended to be as much like the genuine stamp as possible, unlike the majority of political forgeries undertaken for propaganda purposes. World War II produced a great crop of these, including rather crude German printings of the British George VI definitives and 1937 coronation stamp with the UK emblems replaced by Stars of David or

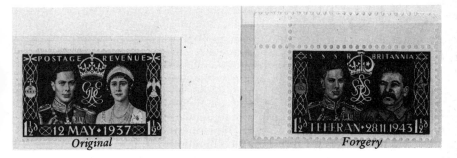

Original   *Forgery*

Fig 46 One of the better-known wartime propaganda forgeries is the British 1937 coronation commemorative (left) suitably doctored and printed in Germany in 1944 (right). The forgery bristles with communist and zionist symbols and is not really meant to deceive anyone. It has line perforation gauge 11 instead of comb 15 × 14, and the watermark is totally dissimilar.

hammer-and-sickle designs, and in the case of the coronation stamp with Queen Elizabeth replaced by Stalin, who also replaced George V in a similar copy of the 1935 Silver Jubilee stamps. Britain and the USA retorted with cunningly reworded German definitives, with skull-like teeth showing through Hitler's cheek. Only a few years ago such things were given away with cheap stamp packets; today they are worth pounds!

These issues were just propaganda labels. A second type of political postage stamp is the true forgery printed to disrupt an enemy's economy, or to do real postal service after conquest and occupation. Yet a third type is the new design of stamp prepared either to subvert enemy influence or to serve as a postage stamp when an enemy-occupied territory has been conquered or liberated. One of the best-known of these is the set printed in Nazi Germany for use in India after the British had been defeated by the Axis forces.

The question of the difficulty of forging postage stamps revolves around the circumstances. National propaganda forgeries are no special problem, whereas the lone forger in his den may be faced with very great difficulties. The technique of mass-production of a common stamp to defraud the revenue is usually entirely different from the forgery of a valuable rarity. As for values, this again varies enormously. In general it can be said that no good forgery is without philatelic value, provided there are very few in circulation and that they are always clearly marked or in 'known' places. Even when the genuine stamp is valuable, a forgery is frequently worth even more. For example, the 'Lowden forgery' of the British Edward VII £1 almost at once began to change hands at prices higher than the genuine used stamp; and, despite the immense appreciation of the latter, the forgery has moved ahead even faster, largely because when Lowden was prosecuted almost all his forgeries were destroyed.

Forgeries are of immense interest, but fakes are invariably just cheap and nasty, and leave an unpleasant taste in the mouth. Here there is no object at all but the defraud of collectors (many people undoubtedly make their own rare varieties just 'for kicks' or so that they can pretend they have a rarity, but if they have any sense they will destroy or unfake them when they want to sell their stamps). I cannot immediately think of any possible subject for faking that I have not already found: blued paper, white paper, perforated stamps made imperforate and imperforate stamps given rare perforations or rouletting, re-perforated cut-off wing margins, filled-in perfins, rare shades of colour, errors, rare over-prints, rare watermarks, rare kinds of paper, rare plate numbers, re-entries, missing or incorrect colours, shifts of colour or phosphor bands, rare combinations of phosphor band and water-mark, graphite lines (often in rare places), offsets, mirror images, double prints and printing flaws by the score.

As in almost all of philately the best answer is to be an expert; if you are not, then leave the rarity alone until someone can vouch for it. If there were no market, there would soon be no fakes.

Of course, one often simply has to buy something on trust. If you buy a home freezer you take it on trust it freezes properly. You buy this book on trust, without being able to read it first. When you buy from a reputable stamp dealer or auction you can, usually very safely indeed, take it on trust that all the important material is exactly as described in the catalogue, because the cata-logue is written by an expert. For example, I once asked a British auctioneer, Frank Stott, if he could show me the 'repaired tear' his catalogue mentioned in a seemingly superb British 1878 £1, be-cause my close examination had failed to find it. I have never met anyone who had ever heard of a valuable stamp sold at a reputable auction afterwards turning out to be a fake.

One of the saddest aspects of the faking business is that every fake means the loss, probably irreparably, of a genuine stamp. There is no stamp so common that a perfect copy does not deserve to go on living. Even seemingly insignificant stamps may one day turn out to be worth many times face. For example, one of the best examples of the British 1½d stamp of 1918 in the rare 'brown' shade that I ever saw had been faked to look like the PENCF variety. At the time, probably long before World War II, the faker ignored such a common stamp and cannot have known anything about shades. Almost the only faking that may do no positive harm is adding super-broad margins to an imperforate stamp, because when these are soaked off, the thing in the centre is no worse than it was before the fake margins were added.

Another faking operation that may not actually harm the stamp

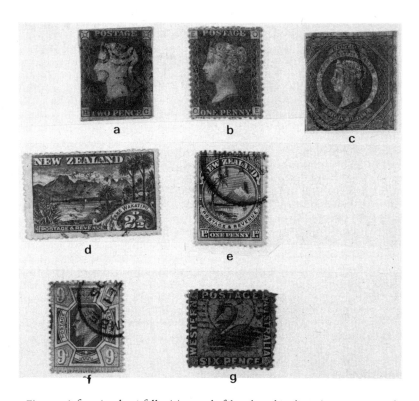

Fig 47　A few simple pitfalls: (a) a crude fake, the white lines (see Fig 37 a and b) having been filled in with blue ink to make the stamp look like the more valuable 1840 issue; (b) a re-gummed stamp in which the modern gum has soaked through the watermark at upper left; (c) a case of clipping off the perforations to fake the much rarer imperf New South Wales 8d (which unfortunately comes on paper with a different watermark!); (d) a typical thin (invisible from front); (e) marginal tear (invisible from front); (f) repaired corner (upper left); (g) crudely repaired margins (right and bottom).

very much is re-gumming. This is probably the most common fake of all. Somewhere in the world, large numbers of stamps are re-gummed every day, to make them look like perfect mint copies. Before being thus treated they looked good from the front but on the back either had no gum or else were covered with old hinges, ink or pencil writing, and grubbiness. No very great skill is required to make such a stamp look as if it had just come from the post office, and superficially it seems a rewarding operation. Unfortunately a fake is a fake is a fake, and a re-gummed stamp invariably can be spotted by an expert a mile off. He will at once sense the wrong feel, the wrong type of gum, the wrong colour and surface finish, and often the fact that the new gum has soaked into the torn tips of the teeth of the perforations. A re-gummed stamp can usually be restored to a genuine condition with a clean, ungummed back. This may have the incidental benefit of prolonging the stamp's life, as outlined in Chapter 8.

To detect fakes, by far one's greatest asset is familiarity with the real thing. This familiarity is often elusive. The expert committees of the various national philatelic organisations are constantly called upon to judge stamps submitted to them, and despite their profound collective experience and familiarity they very seldom pronounce a rare variety genuine without closely comparing it with a copy known to be genuine. Where there is the slightest doubt, they will use an ultra-violet lamp, a microscope or any other tools needed to find the answer. Sometimes they will merely decline to issue any certificate, but almost always they soon have no doubt whatever whether the stamp is genuine or false. Any serious philatelist should become as familiar as possible with the ultra-violet lamp. (Forensic scientists use them to examine cheques, documents and other things of legal interest.) Such lamps come in many forms, some of them easily portable. With practice they enable one to detect a very wide range of fakes, repairs and 'improvements' that would be very much less easy to see by daylight or ordinary artificial lighting.

In addition to familiarity with the real thing, one needs to ask definite questions. A pilot would be a bad insurance risk if he just settled into his cockpit and asked himself 'Does everything seem all right?' He has to run through a detailed check-list, without missing one item. In the same way, you are unlikely to spot the work of the clever faker merely by holding the stamp with tweezers and vaguely looking at it. Ask yourself such positive questions as: have any perforation teeth been stuck on; has a corner been repaired; is there a repaired tear anywhere round the edge; is the back wholly original or has some paper (or other material) been added to cover a thin; has the surface been touched-up or 'improved'; has anything been rubbed out; was there a pinhole, which has been disguised by working the paper inwards towards it to fill it in; was the stamp a perfin, with the holes filled in and inked over; could there be anything wrong with the cancellation; could the stamp have been re-gummed, and so forth. Life is too short to follow such a routine with anything but valuable stamps, but with such material it ought to become second-nature.

7

Stamp Values

A stamp is worth what you can get for it. But this supreme truth has countless provisos. You, as the seller, may not recognise the stamp for what it really is. You may need some cash immediately, and not be in a position to find the best deal. The buyer may or may not identify the stamp correctly, and may or may not be sufficiently honest to point out good points as well as bad. Most of this chapter is concerned to point out home-truths and common sense which may not be immediately apparent. The most fundamental fact of all is that stamp values depend on the circumstances, on what is fashionable, and on the environment, and thus they change with time. The price a stamp will realise on any particular occasion is the result of the interplay of all these factors.

Normally the trend of values is upwards. When a stamp is off-sale, the total world stock can only dwindle. Each year, except for classic rarities, a few copies, or perhaps millions, will be destroyed by accident or design. Almost everywhere people tend to have more money and more leisure time, and are increasingly prepared to pay higher prices for good properties that seem certain to appreciate in the course of time. Of course, in terms of any given currency, there is usually a strong process of inflation at work which makes a unit of that currency worth less and less, but this does not really enter into the argument, because it is self-cancelling. For example, a stamp might have been worth £1 in 1940 and might fetch £5 today simply as a result of inflation; but today's £5 is actually 'worth' no more than the £1 was in 1940. One must remember this when looking at old catalogue prices. Some of the most costly rarities have not changed very much in catalogue value over the past fifty years, yet the buying power of the sum listed may have fallen by 90 per cent over this period. In fact, the answer is often that the catalogue is out of date.

Obviously, catalogue prices exert a strong influence on the actual values of stamps, but one must remember what these figures mean and interpret them with common sense. The catalogue is usually a dealer's list of stamps together with the prices at which he is prepared to sell them. The general and simplified catalogues are always based on the most common variety of some issue. Frequently these give no clue at all to the rich wealth of variations that exist, most of them worth more than the figure given in a simple catalogue and some worth many hundreds of times more. Whether or not these values are realised depends on the circumstances. Children and casual collectors seldom have any catalogue at all, and have no idea of what stamps they possess beyond their superficial appearance. Pages from their collections generally look tatty and most dealers or auctioneers would not consider them worth detailed examination, but if you have time you can pick up material at far below its 'value' from such collections. Again, a lot depends on the type of material. Most dealers in Britain are well-informed on British stamps and many are specialised experts, and you will not normally be able to buy a British stamp from them except at a price higher than you could sell it for; on the other hand you might do very well if the dealer happens to have a big lot of Nicaragua, which is almost a closed book to him, and you happen to be an expert on that country. In the same way I know dealers in the USA who are experts on their own country and on such places as Germany, Israel, and The Vatican. If I ask them about Great Britain they will probably pass over a haphazard stock-book and say 'Here, see if you can find anything' – and then look up the price in some simplified catalogue. This obviously exerts a profound effect on what is meant by 'value'. In general the stamps of country X are most highly priced in country X and cheaper everywhere else.

There are many other major influences. One of the most obvious and important is condition, discussed in detail later in this chapter. A second – bearing in mind that the true value is what you can get – is how well the material fits the needs of a buyer. If it happens to be precisely the thing he needs to complete a major part of his collection, he will invariably grit his teeth and buy it even at an elevated price. One often finds two equally determined buyers in an auction. They have both set their heart on a particular lot which happens to be precisely what they most need. For example, British stamps used to be printed with a 'control', a letter/number combination printed in the margin of the sheet. One of the rarest is the 1914 control E14 on the 1s value. It was my only gap in the controls of the 1912–24 issues of stamps, and I was determined to buy the copy that came up in an auction. At that time the catalogue value was £30, and I was prepared to go at least as high as this. At £35 I sat back to watch two other bidders fight it out. The lot was knocked down to one for £92! The answer is that that was the true value of that stamp at that place and time. It could be that, when the buyer later wanted to sell, nobody would happen to be around prepared to pay more than, say, £5. This again would be the true value at that later place and time, and the vendor should ask himself whether he ought not to wait for another place and time.

Value is obviously linked to scarcity. The more a stamp is divided up according to watermark, paper, shade, perforation and other factors, the scarcer each listing must be and the higher the price. Sometimes the influence of this factor is not great. For example, the British 1912–24 definitives were originally listed by Stanley Gibbons as a straight list with one entry for each value. But almost immediately obvious shades of colour were considered worthy of inclusion and the set was renumbered and greatly expanded. Yet the prices for the more common shades remained unchanged. Even today the bottom six values of this set are still listed by Gibbons in fine used condition at the nominal 5p which is the figure chosen by this company as the minimum to cover overheads. This is despite the fact that all six values are shown in specialised catalogues in a tremendous variety of fine colour shades, and the answer is that the common shades are still common and the subdivision merely picks off the rarities.

Yet it is possible to exert a marked effect on catalogue prices, and thus on 'values', by splitting up the main body of a printing. When Gibbons first listed stamps of Edward VII, the British issues were again treated as a plain set, one of each value. In 1905 it was necessary to list a quite different shade of the ½d value, and before long the simple set had become a long list of sixty items, to which a further sixty-two were added when the printers were changed. Apart from the original printing of the ½d and 1d, there is no such thing as a common British Edward VII stamp, because each specimen falls into a quite small subgroup according to its paper or shade. Yet the preceding issue of Queen Victoria remains a relatively simple list even though most of the values could likewise be subdivided into numerous distinct shades. This would at once tend to push up the catalogue price, because there would be only a fraction as many of each type. Of course, this effect is permanent and universal; when Gibbons wish to produce a simple catalogue or check-list they just take the cheapest printing of each stamp, and if the whole of an issue is divided into highly priced subgroups there will not be any 'cheap' type left.

Today there is usually much less scope for such subdivision, although in the course of time, when they are better understood and appreciated, many of the most common modern stamps are certain to appear in the more specialised catalogues divided up according to paper, ink and other variables. Some stamps, such as a high-face 'commemorative', are regarded from the very start as things of interest and value, and they are studied and if possible divided into subgroups. The most common definitives are almost ignored, and it is usually years later that it is realised that they exist in a host of variations which, in the course of time, come to be equated with considerable monetary values.

Mint stamps generally have a value which tends to vary more or less in proportion to their face value, which is usually what one would expect. Used stamps are invariably likewise priced according to face value, but this is often nonsense. Any collector who has any experience at all will be able to think of countless cases where the price written in the catalogue bears no relation to the price he is prepared to pay. For example, my current basic catalogue of Canadian stamps lists the present definitive 15c stamp, fine used, at twice the price of the 3c, 4c and 5c coil stamps. The latter are really difficult to come by, and I will buy them anytime, yet if anybody wants a hundred copies of the 15c they are welcome because I am ankle-deep in them. In the same way I am inundated with Australian 25c 'scarlet robins', which are listed at three times the fine-used price of the elusive Australian coil stamps. In such cases the catalogue editor ought to use his head. It is very easy to discover which stamps are easy and which difficult to obtain. I do not object to the company thinking up an inflated price for common used stamps of fairly high face value, because there are many collectors who do not receive mail from distant countries which they collect; but I do object to scarce and elusive stamps being priced at a much lower level just because their face value is low.

It is in such cases that the catalogue ceases to be a guide to a stamp's value. Eventually a catalogue will reluctantly catch up, and accept the apparently unpalatable fact that a low-value definitive can be elusive and that customers will pay a substantial sum for it. In the case of modern British stamps, this fact has been driven home swiftly by fantastic demand, so that a few very rare low-value definitives of the present reign are priced at several pounds. Yet the catalogue often takes many years to realise the situation with stamps of other lands, unless that other country is fully covered by an up-to-date specialised catalogue. Thousands of stamp dealers are often being asked such questions as 'Have you got a fine-used Kenya 25c of the 1960 issue?' This is in the catalogue at a few pence. He will not have it on ninety-nine occasions, but on the hundredth he will actually have a copy. What does he do? Sell it for a few pence or put a price on it nearer to its true value? There is an old story about the collector who asked a dealer for a very elusive little stamp catalogued at a few pence. The dealer offered him one, at ten times the catalogue price. The collector angrily refused, saying he could get it cheaper from a rival down the road. 'Why don't you go to him then?' asked the dealer. 'Well, just at the moment he hasn't got a copy in stock.' 'I know,' said the dealer. 'When he does have a copy he sells it at twenty times catalogue.'

This tale has been told a thousand times, and something like it happens every day in real life, but it emphasises that the price in a catalogue may be far below a stamp's true value. There are also occasions when it may be unreasonably high, and in this case it should be possible to buy the stamp more cheaply elsewhere. In the case of modern issues it often requires fine judgement to assess how the price is likely to move. Often the catalogue price is clearly nonsense, and can be confidently predicted to move firmly up or down in the course of time. It helps enormously if the quantities printed or sold are published, because these probably give a reliable indication of the number of stamps in circulation.

It will probably be helpful to run briefly through the careers of some contrasting stamps to see how their price has reflected the supply and demand. I have again chosen British stamps, because these bring out the major types of history particularly well, but the same general characteristics can be found in the stamps of any 'good' philatelic country.

1840 1d The penny black, the first and most classic of all adhesive postage stamps, was recognised as a collectable item within a year or two of the colour being changed in February 1841. Yet fine-used copies could still be bought at face value up to about 1875, by which time stamp-collecting was very widespread. In 1900 a typical fine-used price was 3d, and this rose to 1s in 1910, 2s in 1920, 3s in 1930, 5s in 1940, 10s in 1950, 30s in 1960, and £5 in 1970. At present, the catalogue price is £14, and it will not be long before this will be the lowest price at which most sound copies will change hands. The firm trend of the graph is self-evident. At any recent point on the curve, the general view of collectors has been 'It's a rather inflated price at present; it's unlikely to go any higher for a long time.' This is what they are saying today. Of course, there is no evident reason for any change in the slope of this curve, which just reflects what people are prepared to pay. Wistfully I have just seen a 1935 newspaper clipping of a London sale consisting entirely of these stamps; 'prices ranged from a few shillings to £2 for single specimens', the £2 being paid for re-entries on plate 11! Today I never expect to see a four-margined copy of this plate sold at under £50, and a re-entry in good condition would certainly fetch £100.

1873 3d plate 11 This is typical of the attractive surface-printed (typographed) issues by De La Rue that covered all values over 2d until 1880, and every value thereafter. This threepenny stamp was sold in fine-used condition for face value until about 1910, so early in its life it was valued at about the same level as a penny black. By 1920 it was changing hands at 6d to 1s, in 1930 a typical value was 2s 6d, and in 1940 outstanding copies were sometimes fetching 5s. The 1950 price was 10s and in 1960 the catalogue value was £1. It is still £1. Like so many surface-printed stamps, the catalogue value has hardly changed in twenty years, during which time inflation alone should have resulted in a rise of more than 100 per cent. In practice what this means is that in 1963 I could buy these stamps at quarter-catalogue, whereas today I think I am doing well at half-catalogue. The real value of these stamps is far above catalogue; they are fewer in number than the penny blacks, but they lack the same glamour and esteem.

1882 £1 The £1 on anchor-watermarked paper was on sale for just fifteen months. In the early days few top collectors kept mint copies, and very few collections even boasted a single fine-used copy, though there was certainly a much larger number of mutilated and otherwise damaged specimens. By 1910 mint copies were invariably fetching £50 on either blued or white paper. By 1930 it was common for one to fetch £100, especially on true

155

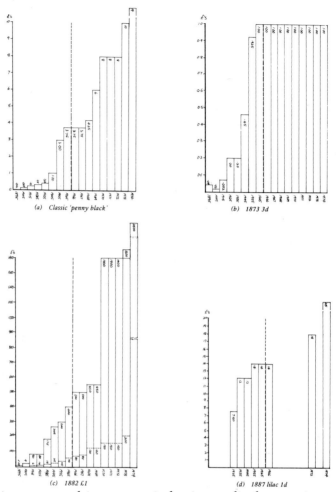

(a) Classic 'penny black'

(b) 1873 3d

(c) 1882 £1

(d) 1887 lilac 1d

white paper, and in 1950 typical prices realised at auction were £225 on blued paper and £300 on white. Since then this rarest of all Great Britain issued definitives has seldom been seen mint, but Gibbons has listed it at £400 (blued) in 1963, at £500 in 1967, £850 in 1969 and £1,400 in 1971. In 1974 the catalogue price was £2,250. At any time in its career, this stamp has been considered far too expensive for anyone outside the millionaire class, and certainly too expensive to be a sound investment. I do not possess a

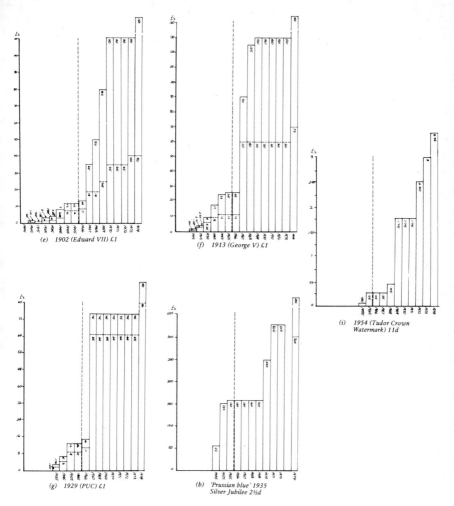

Fig 48   Simple bar charts giving a dramatic indication of the growth in value of
some 'good' British stamps. In each case the monetary unit is the £ Sterling of
the year, and the value is plotted every ten years to 1965 and every year thereafter. (a) The classic penny black (typical fine used from common plate); (b)
fine used 1873 3d plate 11 (a forgotten value?); (c) 1882 (anchor watermark)
£1; (d) 1887 lilac 1d with marginal control letter A; (e) 1902 (Edward VII) £1;
(f) 1913 (George V) £1; (g) 1929 (PUC) £1; (h) Prussian blue 1935 Silver
Jubilee 2½d; (i) 1954 (Tudor crown watermark) 11d (mint).

mint one, but if I had the money I would buy one like a shot. If you can guarantee to keep it in the condition in which you bought it, there could not possibly be a finer investment.

1902 £1 Taking the 1902 and 1911 printings of the Edward VII £1 together, this stamp is about a hundred times as common as the 1882 stamp mentioned above. Either mint or used it was relatively cheap for years. Until the mid-1920s it could be bought mint at not much over twice face, and after World War II it could still be bought, with luck, for £5. By 1948 the figure had climbed to about £8, and the figure in the 1963 Gibbons was still only £12 for either printing. Then there came a very firm and dramatic rise, largely because Gibbons's new managing director realised the firm could take the lead very strongly and that the market would accept it. In the 1967 part I catalogue, the two printings were listed at £35 and £40, mint. The Specialised Catalogue for the same year, put to press a few months later, shows £45 and £40 respectively (an odd reversal), and the price then went swiftly to £110 in 1969. In 1974 it was £150. I would not expect to see the slope of this curve maintained, but it will probably be a £200 stamp by 1980, despite the fact that there are plenty of copies about.

1913 £1 This was on sale for just under thirty months, and the number printed or used is approximately one-quarter that of the Edward VII £1 stamp. This means that it really is a rare stamp; big 'GB' auctions may contain a dozen mint copies but there are probably fewer than 500 in existence. Quite early in the 1930s it became difficult to buy a good mint copy, and ten times face was commonly asked within twenty years of the stamp going off-sale (a rare thing in those days). By 1940 the price was usually around £15, and this rose to £18 in 1950, both these figures being quite close to the Gibbons catalogue figure. Realisations continued to climb slowly, and in the 1966 part I the cheapest (blue-green) shade was still only valued at £25. But by 1967 this had shot up to £90, the following year it was £125, in 1969 it reached £130 and its present level is £140. This stamp is certain to continue to appreciate firmly.

1929 PUC £1 This high-value commemorative shows a very interesting history in fine-used condition. From very early days, even while it was still on sale in the mid-1930s, it fetched 5s. During World War II fine-used copies could still be bought at this price, but when collecting picked up again in 1946 the price shot up and levelled off at £5. Here it stayed until about 1960, when it climbed gently, reflecting the Gibbons figure of £9. But in 1967 the part 1 figure was suddenly fixed at £75 mint and £65 used. At the time, this was much higher than the prices realised in auctions, but the strong demand for this stamp brought it up to the catalogue level, which is now sharply rising (£150). Although it is a common stamp, held by almost every GB dealer, I know one man of sound judgement who buys a fine-used copy whenever he can get it for £80 or less. Who can say the stamp is not worth it, if people are prepared to pay such a price?

1935 'Prussian blue' 2½d The 2½d Silver Jubilee stamp was printed as a colour trial in a shade quite unlike the common ultramarine (and also unlike the so-called Prussian blue of the 1921 definitive of the same denomination). Three sheets were accidentally perforated and issued at Edmonton, North London, 41 having been sold when a collector noticed the odd shade and, with one other person, bought the other 319 stamps. At first these stamps sold for £5 each, but the price rose fast as wealthy collectors tried to invest in what looked 'a good thing'. I know a man who says he bought one in 1940 for £10, and I have also been told he must be a liar! Before the war H. & A. Wallace reckoned their half-sheet of 60, with W35 control in the right margin (which had a perforated edge), to be 'worth £5,000'. Today it would fetch considerably more. The Gibbons price has more than doubled in the past five years to £400, and I have seen one copy fetch more than this. In 1947 a great authority, Robson Lowe, wrote 'The current market value of this variety is far in excess of its true worth . . .' I am doubtful that such an assertion can have much meaning. When the statement was made, the average price realised in Robson Lowe auctions was £55 mint and £90 used, yet he obviously considered

159

there was some 'proper' value at a much lower level, which had been exceeded only because of the rash bidding of rich speculators. Those speculators had the last laugh. A price level in the £300–£400 range is very high for a stamp of which at least 319 copies are in the hands of collectors, or investors, but this reflects the fact that the stamp is fashionable, well-known and glamorous. There are many other stamps that change hands at around £300 of which fewer than 25 copies are known.

1954 definitive 11d This stamp was on sale on Tudor Crown watermarked paper for barely eighteen months, and it is very much an odd postal value (it paid for the minimum-weight registered parcel). Its rise in price is interesting in showing the growth possible with a regular issue of quite low face value. I recently saw a cylinder block of six fetch a price of £24 – about ninety-five times face – less than seventeen years after it could have been bought over the post-office counter.

1884 lilac 1d with control A The use of marginal control letters began in 1884, and the letter A on the lilac 1d is one of the least common. The emergence of serious philatelists in the early years of this century is obvious, because I have a dealer's magazine advertisement of 1908 pricing this stamp at £2, which was then a remarkably high figure. Like so many specialist rarities, its appreciation has been rather slow, for the simple reason that it cost pounds when penny blacks cost a few pence. At the same time I could not imagine a surer investment.

A glance at Fig 48 will show the way in which prices, and thus values, have moved for a range of better stamps of a 'good' philatelic country. Somewhat similar curves could be plotted for good stamps of most of the 'better' countries (a term discussed in Chapter 9). Most of the cheaper or more common stamps ultimately appreciate along some sort of curve, though in the case of many commemorative stamps issued since 1965, in most of the bigger countries at least, it is difficult to think of anything that cannot be bought in auction at face, or even below. The value of a stamp depends very much on supply and demand, and the factors determining each side of this vital equation are often complex and hard to predict. One seldom knows just what the supply will be. In the case of some recent sets of the British Commonwealth issued for small islands by the Crown Agents the total quantity amounted to 30,000 sets, which, at the equivalent of 25p face, means that for £7,500 one could have bought the entire issue! This would obviously exert a profound influence on the prices at which stray copies changed hands. There have been many cases of syndicates trying to buy up enough current or off-sale copies to 'corner' the market and then sell them at a large profit. In 1936 a gang (so they were described) was silly enough to try this with the Edward VIII 2½d stamp; they thought they could buy so many it would be out of stock at almost all post offices and that the public would then be glad to buy their big stock at a shilling or more each. The Post Office merely brought out a few million more, making the racket collapse early in 1937. In February of that year an official of Stanley Gibbons pointed out 'The stamps will never be worth more than their face value.' In fact his firm now sells this stamp at ten times face, but Edward VIII stamps are typical of issues that the non-collector supposes must be scarce and therefore valuable, when in fact they are just the opposite.

The other side of the equation, demand, can be capricious. The true classics, such as the penny black, are rock solid, but there are many examples of classes of stamp which variously ought to be sought after at high prices but are not, or which have suddenly come into fashion and have shot upwards in price, or which started in a blaze of publicity and then fell into disrepute. Slightly off-beat items such as 'officials' and postage-due labels tended for many years to stay at prices well below the levels that their scarcity might have suggested, and in some countries they still do so; but in Britain these two classes have come very strongly into favour and now fetch extremely high prices. On the other hand, British stamps overprinted for use in other countries are in general not yet fashionable. Definitive and some commemorative stamps from Queen Victoria to Queen Elizabeth were overprinted in often

161

very small quantities for postal administrations throughout the Middle East, North Africa and other territories. Except in the case of the Irish Free State (as it was then called) these overprints are usually worth only a fraction as much as the original stamp, especially in mint condition, yet they are invariably much scarcer.

There is a very great deal of the element of fashion in stamp-collecting. It is fashion that makes these overprints relatively low-valued, and it is fashion that inflates the values of many other issues. Many modern collectors have been bitten by the bug of thematic collecting. This is poles apart from philately. Instead of being concerned with the stamp itself as a piece of hardware, with its method of use, and the history of the posts, the thematic collector is concerned solely with the subject of the picture (if any) printed on the stamp. If one wished to take thematic collecting to its logical but absurd end, one could build up a vast collection of stamps bearing pictures of people whose surnames began with the letter A, or of stamps whose design contained precisely thirty letters. This is not really any more pointless than collecting nothing but stamps bearing pictures of cathedrals, coats of arms, or fish. But the popularity of thematic collecting has exerted a marked influence on several sets of stamps, especially good early examples of issues bearing popular themes. For example, the set issued in Angola in 1951 bearing pictures of birds – today a very popular theme – has appreciated in the past twenty years from £3 to well in excess of £60 in fine mint condition. This is undoubtedly much better than it would have done if each value had merely borne a picture of the Portuguese president. It takes both skill and luck to pick out new issues likely to appreciate sharply on thematic grounds. Postal administrations, of course, are not interested in appreciation, but merely in securing the maximum philatelic sale at face. There are thus pressures not to start a new and possibly unsuccessful theme.

It is impossible to discuss stamp values without mentioning the subject of condition. Everyone who stops to think about it must know that the value of a stamp depends upon its condition, but non-collectors usually cannot be bothered to think much about the matter. A non-collector who knows someone who collects stamps takes it for granted that the object of interest is the adhesive stamp. Indeed the record shows that many of the early collectors thought likewise. In fact, any serious collector must be interested in both the stamp and its surroundings. I must explain in some detail what this means, because it is central to the value of one's possessions.

Years ago, and unfortunately sometimes today, interest in stamps centred upon the printed design. It was considered quite in order to snip off the useless margins and perforations; indeed often it seems that the object of interest was the central part only of the design. I have more than 400 British stamps of the pre-1880 period in which all that is left is the central portion bearing the queen's portrait. Anyone who gave me a single perfect copy of any of these stamps in exchange for all these sad victims would be foolish. Indeed in an average week I probably see a hundred or more classic

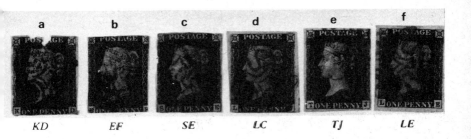

| a | b | c | d | e | f |
| KD | EF | SE | LC | TJ | LE |

Fig 49   The penny black is catalogued at £10 in good used condition. Disregarding such things as rare plates, re-entries, and special cancellations, it is possible to assign a value to all these examples just on the basis of one vital factor: condition. (a) This ought to be rated zero, and only a very young collector would use it as a space-filler; (b) cut into on all four sides, but possibly worth a few pence; (c) slightly cut into at left, probably worth £1; (d) three good margins, not cut into, about £5; (e) four good margins, what the catalogue editor had in mind; (f) superb copy, could easily fetch twice catalogue value.

and potentially valuable stamps that would have been perfectly all right if only they had been left alone, but which unfortunately fell into the hands of a collector.

A particularly shattering story concerns a Canadian friend. When a boy, he was allowed to pick over sacks of old mail being cleared from a Montreal office. He found several hundred covers bearing imperforate 'pence type' stamps of the early 1850s. If he had merely kept them, he could today put these covers into an auction and with the proceeds buy himself an estate with all the swimming pools and private golf courses he wanted. What he actually did was what seems to be an instinctive act by non-collectors: he tried to get the stamps off the covers. If he had lifted the stamps in a skilled way he would merely have reduced the value of his property by at least one-third, for reasons I will explain later. What he actually did was peel off the top layer of each stamp, leaving the securely stuck back of the stamp still on the cover. This he regarded as only a slight nuisance, and he gleefully stuffed the flimsy upper layers into his pocket. Today he is an expert collector but he has never quite got over this tragic destruction of material of fabulous value. Few of us get the chance to wreak such havoc, but the peeling and tearing of a stamp from a cover seems to be a primeval animal instinct ingrained at birth.

To return to the notion of 'the stamp and its surroundings', it is a good general rule that the collector should 'always maximise the size of the unbroken piece of paper that finds its way into your collection'. (Read that again if you like.) One has to use common sense, and there are many ifs and buts, but this gets across the basic message. Yet it needs much elaboration.

If you have any 'entires' a hundred or more years old, leave them strictly alone. Do not think of cutting anything off, or of throwing anything away. If it is a cover containing a separate letter, keep the letter. If you have an early picture postcard, keep it, even if the message is written in a messy childish hand. If you have large numbers of used envelopes and cards of the first half of this century, you will probably not reduce the value if you neatly cut off the stamp(s) and complete postal cancellation. If there are two or more cancels of different kinds, or any transit or arrival marks, keep the entire. With modern material, cut off the cancellation as a strip if it seems of any interest; if you are certain it is of no special interest, and you can see no reason to preserve the place and date of use, lift the stamp if that is worth having. If it is a large block of stamps, cut neatly all round the block. If you are certain you can lift the block without it falling apart, do so; this may make it easier to iron it flat (see Chapter 8). If you have two different denominations of stamp se-tenant, or a stamp used se-tenant with a booklet-pane slogan or advertisement, never think of separating them. They are likely to

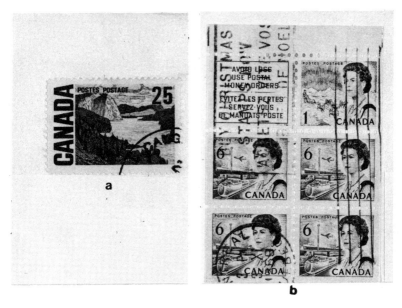

Fig 50   Every time you post a letter you have a choice of making up the postal rate either in the common way or in an unusual (and thus philatelically inter-esting) way. Most Canadians faced with postage of 25c would either use five 5c stamps or a single 25c (a). This 25c copy is superb, but in thirty years' time it will still be practically unsaleable. But the complete se-tenant booklet pane (b) will be a very rare item, and will probably one day change hands at more than twenty times face value.

be common stamps, worth nothing at all, once they are separated. Obviously, it holds that if you are about to stick stamps on mail to a collector (or to yourself), try to use a complete booklet pane (with stitched or stapled selvedge if there is one), or a stamp with advertisement attached, or a se-tenant pair, or a strip from a coil-dispensing machine. Always try to use something unusual, off-beat or in some way likely to appeal to a future collector (for example in every country there are many ways of obtaining an interesting postal cancellation). Never, never separate a stamp from its neighbour, or from a bit of sheet margin, or from an advertisement if it can possibly be avoided.

Merely leaving a piece of sheet margin on a common modern stamp, mint or used, may not do much for its value, though it certainly will not depreciate it. If you have an early imperforate stamp, or better still a perforated one, with a complete piece of

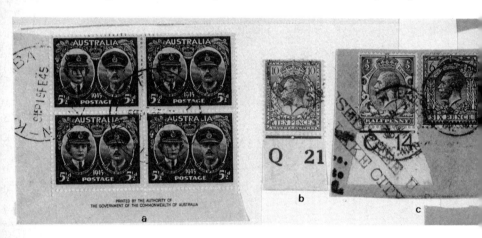

Fig 51   Three more examples of stamps obviously posted by philatelists: (a) a fine corner block, with marginal imprint (the non-philatelist would tear the margin off as 'unwanted'); (b) a stamp with marginal control (year 1921) and also plate marking on the 'jubilee line'; (c) a ½d in a rare shade, with marginal control, used with a 6d with a rare perforation (gauge 14 all round). Item (c) is just the sort of thing that, had it fallen into the hands of a non-collector, would have been thrown away as common and worthless.

sheet margin it will be greatly enhanced in value, particularly when the margin contains an inscription or other interesting printing. With modern stamps, added margin can help where there is any question of unusual paper, or watermark, or phosphor or other 'tagging', or with a stamp printed on the gummed side. Many modern margins contain the printer's imprint, a cylinder number, colour-registration 'check dots' or other markings, and these certainly enhance the value. In any case, nine collectors out of ten, given the choice of a mint or used stamp with or without margin, would pick the marginal copy. Obviously an old imperforate stamp should be as big as possible, but a collector may feel he can improve such a stamp by neatly cutting off a ragged or damaged edge (Fig 52), provided he leaves as much neat margin as possible. Frequently one finds a perforated stamp to which adheres a piece of the next stamp, either on one side or above or below. Most experienced collectors would consider it preferable to remove this excrescence, although they might leave it if it showed a small portion of a se-tenant stamp of different face value. This may seem a trivial consideration, but it is likely to be equated in cash terms a century hence.

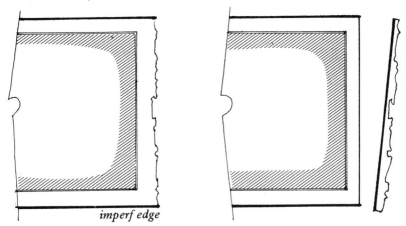

imperf edge

Fig 52   The one occasion when one may perhaps improve a stamp by cutting it: if one has really sharp scissors it is possible to trim a ragged imperf margin and improve the appearance.

The stamp's surroundings are one facet of the vastly important topic of condition, which exerts a profound influence on the value of stamps of all kinds. Apart from special trials undertaken by the postal authorities, stamps can basically be divided into two categories: mint and used. There is a perfect condition associated with each, and any other condition falls short of perfection. The perfect condition for a mint stamp can be described very easily: it is precisely as issued by the post office, assuming that no damage was incurred at the hands of a clumsy post-office clerk! Even then there are some ifs and buts. Early imperforate stamps were cut up by hand. It is possible to find an imperf mint stamp in perfect condition, with full original gum (og), yet its value would be much reduced if it had no margins. An unused copy with four large, even margins would command a higher price even if it had no gum. Indeed the subject of gum, especially on very old stamps, is discussed in Chapter 8. In the context of stamp values, gum deserves a paragraph to itself.

Obviously, as 'mint condition' means exactly that, any stamp that shows gum disturbance cannot be called mint, but must suffer the lower rank of 'unused' or 'part og'. But many experts would say that the importance of having undisturbed gum has tended to get a little out of hand. It is worth considering for a moment what the catalogue editor means when he writes in a price for an unused stamp. Suppose the stamp is a common one of the past ten years: the price quoted will be that for a true mint copy; indeed it will probably be torn from a post-office sheet under the eyes of the customer. If the stamp is considerably more than ten years old – say, prior to 1950 – the catalogue assumes the stamp will be a good copy, with original gum, but possibly bearing a light hinge. If the stamp was heavily hinged it might be sold at a discount. For stamps issued before 1900, the catalogue price assumes only that it is a structurally perfect copy, of good colour, clearly unused; the back may be heavily hinged and may have little gum left. In this case a true mint (unhinged) copy would certainly command a substantial premium, for in many cases it would be a very rare thing. It is worth bearing in mind two facts: it is simple, with the aid of a sweat box (see Chapter 8), to remove the heaviest mass of hinges and still leave the back looking unhinged, except to the expert; and it is not too difficult to re-gum an old stamp, again making it look unhinged, except to the expert.

To show, in terms of hard cash, how the condition of the back may affect the price, I can cite the case of three unused copies of quite a rare British stamp, the 2½d printed in the winter 1875–6 on 'orb' paper from plate 3. At the time (1970) this was catalogued at £20 unused. A copy that looked perfect and fresh, but had virtually no gum, was sold in auction at £18. Another copy that looked fine but had clearly been re-gummed was sold in another auction at £14.50 (the buyer told me he would probably clean the gum off). Very soon afterwards a superb unhinged mint copy fetched £32. All these stamps were perfect in every way apart from their gum. So if you acquire any material in mint condition that is already of considerable value – and this can happen to a rare stamp within a year or two of it being withdrawn from post-office sale – it is well worth taking care to leave the back in its original condition. But when buying old unused stamps, try as soon as possible to judge what the back ought to be like, and always take a stamp with little gum in preference to the one with an obvious coat of phoney gum – and remember the dealer (see Chapter 1) who stuck a hinge on deliberately!

Many old stamps have gum creases, which are creases that have been ironed or pressed out from the face but which cannot be eradicated from the back. This comes into the category of damage, and to most expert collectors damage of most kinds results in a very sharp reduction in the price they would pay. Obviously it is impossible to set down any meaningful hard-and-fast figures for kinds of damage and the resulting degradation in value, but my own view (which is pretty general among serious collectors) is that you just don't buy a damaged stamp. The only possible exception is that a collector may have a good and comprehensive collection of a country which is complete except for one extremely rare stamp that he cannot afford. I am in this position with a collection of used Canadian stamps; my gap, and it is a fairly obvious one, is the 'twelve penny' first issued in June 1851. To fill this gap I would consider buying a damaged copy – even then it might cost several hundred pounds – although I do not even know if one exists. But if I or my executors were to sell my Canadian collection I should leave clear instructions to remove such a stamp or ensure that the damage was made known. It is of the first importance, if you have a good collection of stamps in perfect condition, to remove any damaged material before you sell. Never try to pass off imperfect material – unless you want the entire collection to be downgraded *in toto*.

This notion of the 'gap filler' is a valid one. The young or impecunious collector can soon build up a comprehensive collection of poor copies which, had they been perfect, would have cost thousands of times as much. The collector who can afford to spend a substantial sum on his stamps can still, if he wishes, buy a poor copy to plug an otherwise impossible gap. But the value of a stamp never ceases to be wholly dependent upon its condition. Condition is determined by many factors, of which the main ones are: (a) structural damage (a tear, a thin, a surface rub, a crease, a piece missing from the border, especially at the corner, a pinhole etc); (b) chemical damage (oxidation, 'rust', mould, exposure to water or other solvents, exposure to strong acids or alkalis, exposure to heat sufficient to cause browning or charring, and exposure to strong sunlight); (c) the quality of cancellation, in the case of a used stamp. Some collectors also take into account the 'centering'. Machine-perforated stamps, especially in the early days when line-engraved printing was done on damp paper which subsequently shrank, are often found where the design is way off-centre. Even with surface-prints cases are known of ridiculously large errors. Different collectors have different views on how this affects the value. Gibbons probably set a fashion in pricing some of their catalogues for 'average' copies and adding a note, adjacent to the entry for each major issue, saying something like 'for well-centred, lightly cancelled copies add 25 per cent'. One could plot a curve of how bad centering affects the value of a stamp (Fig 53). Such a curve could not be more than a personal opinion, but unless one has odd ideas it should be realisable in hard cash. Obviously a degree of off-centering that would have been common in 1855 would be extremely rare in modern stamps and thus much more valuable.

Most stamp manufacturers generate a fair amount of 'printer's waste' which, in all security printing, is extremely carefully supervised and destroyed at the earliest opportunity. Hardly any of it escapes to reach the stamp trade, and this is why such material is often valuable. In some cases there is no doubt that somebody deliberately smuggled the item out, but usually a gross shift of colour

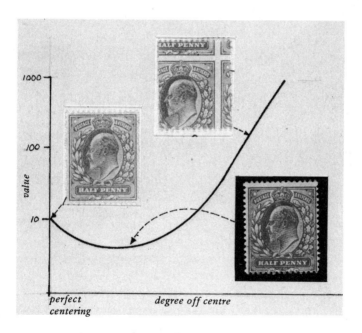

Fig 53 Most modern stamps are perforated almost exactly along the inter-stamp gutters. A common stamp (the example here is the British ½d of 1911 printed by Harrison) probably has its value slightly depressed by being perforated slightly off centre, but a copy showing a gross shift in perforations is worth real money. This example, with large parts of four stamps visible, is probably worth as many pounds as the perfectly centred copy is worth pence.

or perforations, or a case of missing perforations, is accidental and results from the almost superhuman checkers being for once defeated. It is a testimony to the work of these checkers that the value of gross mistakes is relatively enormous. For example, a block of six very common Great Britain George VI stamps has just fetched £850 simply because it was imperforate except along the bottom edge. It sometimes happens that stamps are deliberately issued 'imperf between' (for example, a 1964 booklet issue of 5d stamps in Australia), but in general anyone who finds incomplete or faulty perforation today is on to a very good thing indeed.

The biggest premium Gibbons quote for above-average used stamps is 75 per cent, in the case of the Great Britain lilac/green issue of 1883–4. These stamps were printed in doubly fugitive ink, were often somewhat off-centre, and were generally cancelled by 'killer' obliterators which smothered the surface with heavy black bars. Any Great Britain collector will know what a good and valuable set this is, but it serves as an outstanding example of the importance of condition. For many years the Gibbons part 1 has said of it: 'stamps which have been soaked, causing the colour to run, are almost valueless'. (Indeed in some recent catalogues the word 'almost' is omitted.) A friend proudly showed me his collection of used stamps of this set, in which there were 31 green copies. To him there were 28 in the true 'deep, dull green' colour and 3 that were slightly pale. In fact he had 28 slightly washed-out copies and 3 that were even worse. He had never seen a copy in the true colour, and when he did he was surprised and saddened. So before any collector of any country spends money on stamps, especially used classical copies, he must become familiar with the genuine colours. In the case of the 31 green stamps, I suppose they would fetch £10 to £15 in an auction, whereas perfect copies would have fetched well over £50.

The subject of cancellations is far too involved for me to lay down slick, valid and universally applicable rules. Any student of postal history of any country will soon become aware of the types of obliterators used and of the ones that are valuable. The student of Great Britain will probably spend his first few months keeping his eyes open for a penny black cancelled with a yellow maltese cross or a penny red bearing a red one. After a few years he finds too many other more likely things to think about, but would like to feel if ever such an extreme rarity did come along unheralded that he would not fail to notice it. Obviously in such cases any thought of aesthetic appeal flies out of the window. So do questions of four wide margins. There are no rigid mathematical equations relating the factors that determine stamp values, but I would pay more for a penny black with hardly any margins and a genuine yellow cross, than I would for a four-margined copy with a black one. There are countless other cases where the expert would at once spot a rare cancellation that would instantly outweigh considerations of mere appearance. But one should remember that in his classic *Encyclopaedia of British Empire Postage Stamps* in 1947 Robson Lowe wrote, 'It must be good looking. This is a visual hobby and an offence to the eye is an offence to the hobby.' Today, material is scarcer and much more costly, and there is a strong tendency to buy something second-rate. Certainly, many stamps with very heavy cancels are today fetching high prices, whereas twenty years ago they would have gone for next to nothing. Value is a matter of supply and demand, and any collector who disbelieved Robson Lowe and bought piles of 'offences to the eye' at rock-bottom prices in 1947, could today make a killing. There are now far more collectors, and they are prepared to pay large sums for any sound material, heavy cancel and all.

Some are even prepared to pay large sums for stamps that are not structurally perfect. Twenty years ago it was almost unheard of for any dealer to offer a damaged stamp, unless it was an acknowledged outstanding rarity. Yet today I have only to pick up the first stamp magazine that comes to hand to find an advertisement such as '£1 green, SG.212, mint, fine colour, few short perfs, vertical creases (not really visible from front), small thin, tiny marks on face, superb appearance, £40.' A few years ago no dealer of quality would have been interested in such a stamp, yet today I have no doubt it will be sold at the price asked. There is no doubt that the rigid yardsticks of condition have been relaxed, just because of the interplay of supply and demand, so that now Robson Lowe might well say 'This damaged rubbish is fetching far more than it is worth.' Such an assertion – reasonable though it may sound to an expert who for a lifetime has either given such 'rubbish' away or (more likely) torn it up – can no longer be sustained. A stamp is worth what people will pay for it. If, in perfect condition, they are very costly and elusive, from now on even damaged stamps are going to be saleable.

On the other hand, some of the most valuable and perfect of all stamps are not saleable. If a burglar was so ill-informed about the stamp business as to steal a priceless rarity, he would soon regret it (unless he had previously reached an agreement with a crooked collector, who in turn would have to keep the stamp hidden). In February 1965 thieves stole the splendid Great Britain collection of Major C. E. Raphael, and with it many items of fantastic 'value', one of them being a superb mint penny red printed from plate 77. This stamp alone would have had a value of around £5,000 had Major Raphael chosen to sell it. What is its value today? Apart from its present keeper, nobody knows where it is, but hopefully it is in some album of a collector whose enthusiasm overcame his honesty. He cannot sell it, because it would be recognised at once. Probably the true value of this stamp at this moment in time is negative, because to try to sell it would swiftly bring the police.

To avoid ending on a sour note, here are some brief stories of how values of some rarities that *were* saleable have appreciated over the years. The Swedish '3 skilling banco' error of colour, mentioned earlier, was sold by the dealer who bought it (for 7 kroner) for the equivalent of £120; it then changed hands at the equivalents of £700, £1,500, £5,000 and finally, together with other stamps, £27,000. If it came on to the market today it could well reach £100,000, which is a price only one or two stamps have ever commanded. The early 'POST OFFICE' stamps of Mauritius are so few they always fetch enormous prices. A superb cover bearing two of the 1d value was once discovered in a sack of old postal items in a bazaar in Bombay; the last time it came on to the market, in 1968, it fetched £158,000. The only other comparable cover, bearing a 1d and a 2d, was discovered by a schoolboy in Bordeaux in 1902. The subsequent prices realised by this cover were £1,800, £5,000 and £28,000. It would undoubtedly fetch more than the last figure today. The best-known of all valuable stamps, the British Guiana 1856 1c black on magenta (printed locally because of a sudden shortage of British supplies), has always had a spark of fame and romance surpassing that of any other tiny bit of paper. Found in an attic by another schoolboy, it changed hands for 35p, then went to one Ferrary for £150, then to Arthur Hind for £7,343, then in 1940 it was sold by his widow for about £10,000, and finally in 1970 it was auctioned for £116,000.

8
The Care of Stamps

Many things which seem outwardly to stay the same are usually undergoing a process of change. Almost all the hardware of philately is deteriorating. Stamps, hinges, album pages, old postal covers, even catalogues, all are undergoing a slow and invariably irreversible process of change. The deterioration is sudden and violent at times, when unskilled or tired hands get to work; at other times it is slow – much slower, in most cases, than the deterioration of our own bodies – so we do not notice it. This means that proper philately, with an eye on our grandchildren's children, is really a considerable challenge.

The stamp bought across the post-office counter is a fragile and almost ephemeral thing. Looking after it is very much like walking a tightrope. One has a choice of precisely one good and correct line of progress, which reduces the deterioration to a minimum value. If this line is followed, there is every chance a stamp will last several centuries (and I would be very surprised if philately did not do the same). As an alternative, the collector has a choice of an infinite variety of bad actions. Any one of these will immediately and irreversibly hustle the stamp a lesser or greater distance along the path that leads away from perfect mint or perfect used condition.

176

Having stepped off the tightrope with such an act, there is not much one can do about it. If the stamp is, or was, of any value I strongly advocate leaving it in the damaged condition. If you have caused a cut, a tear, a crease, a pulled perforation or any other deterioration, you will be wasting your time if you try to repair or hide it, and you will at once make any purchaser doubt all your other possessions.

Care of stamps is an attitude of mind. Admittedly it involves such elements as some manual skill, reasonably good eyesight, and the use of proper philatelic tools, but none of these is of any use if the basic approach is wrong. Pilots ought to make good stamp-collectors because they have to follow proper procedures scrupulously and can never, never say 'I can't be bothered.' Once a collector says 'It's only a common stamp' he is on the edge of a precipice. There are countless stamps which today fetch high prices which not long ago were so common they were despised. Even if you are going to use a stamp for postage to a non-collector, take care to tear it through the perforations neatly and affix it, and any others used with it, with a spot of care (don't, for example, follow a common practice in Spanish territories of sticking stamps round the edge of an envelope so that half is on each side). If the stamp is to be used on an envelope, always leave a good margin between the stamp and the edge of the envelope. If you cannot see why, the finest printing variety I ever discovered for myself, a complete missing colour, was on a stamp which had been carefully stuck at the very top of an envelope which arrived in my office and passed smartly through a letter-opening machine working like a bacon-slicer. If your mail is going overseas, remember to try and make up the postal rate in an unusual way; stamps common in one country are very seldom those used on overseas mail, and I recently had a request from a New Zealand friend for a fine-used British $2\frac{1}{2}$p!

Obviously there is not time in one lifetime to treat every postal item like gold-dust, nor to scan every cover and stamp for possible philatelic interest. But it takes no longer to do things correctly, and in fact with experience you can soon pick out items of philatelic interest without seeming to notice the rest. With the correct attitude of mind you ought to be able to practise your hobby for many years without once departing from the tightrope of good procedure. Once you take care of stamps as a matter of course, the only thing to watch is letting stamps come into your life at a time when you are grossly overtired. I still believe philately is a splendidly restful way of 'unwinding' after a long and arduous period of effort, but at such times one's judgement and skill can be impaired, with disastrous results. If you are very tired, keep away from valuable material!

The rest of this chapter is a collection of information on the processes of degradation suffered by philatelic material, and a list of dos and don'ts. Unfortunately I am cynical enough to believe that only a few readers will go away and at once be better collectors of fragile stamps. Some readers will already know how to look after their possessions, and there is little point in preaching to the converted. The rest will either read and forget or else think they know better. As I said, it is all based on an attitude of mind. I see masses of large 'junk lots' which must often contain pages put together by children. Unused stamps are stuck fast by clumsy hingeing, stamps are present with pieces of them missing, and one has an overwhelming desire to ask 'Did you notice these things?' and 'If you did, are you interested?' When I am able to ask, the results vary. A lady collector told me she always very carefully mounted mint stamps on a light hinge and then, as an extra precaution, licked the corner of the stamp and stuck that to the album leaf; and a juvenile enthusiast, told he had a corner missing, retorted, 'It's only a cheap stamp.' This chapter is not for them. (Or is it?)

On the other hand, there are people who really would welcome some guidance. There was a tale going round the London trade about a very wealthy man who, widowed late in life, turned to stamp-collecting. Unlike most of us, he was able to buy practically whatever he wanted. He was, like all successful businessmen, alert and intelligent, and he took expert advice on his buying. After a while one of the experts said 'You must have a really fine collection now; I'd love to see it.' When he saw it he could hardly believe his eyes; priceless mint and used material had all been beautifully mounted with Sellotape (for North American readers, Scotch tape is similar). Nobody had told him the correct procedure. So what should he do about it? Opinions vary. I have had a lot of experience removing adhesive materials from philatelic items, and the last thing he should do is just pull the tape off. He could use a suitable solvent (and one cannot prescribe without knowing both the stamp and the type of tape) or, in certain circumstances, it is possible to remove such adhesive tape by applying heat, either with a hot flat-iron or by holding the item in front of a fire. I must also record that some experts would consider this error irrevocable, and tell him to leave things alone. Certainly, if you want to send a valuable stamp by mail to get it postally used, do not try to protect the edges by covering them with adhesive tape unless you know from experience you can strip the tape off without delaminating the stamp (pulling off the top surface of the stamp with the tape).

For all stamps, mint and used: never cause physical damage, such as a surface rub, a torn perforation, a thin, a cut, a missing corner, or a crease; never allow them to stay loose in the spine of an album, collection of papers, wallet, pocket or any other hazardous place unless they are inside a properly arranged stiff folder or envelope (as described later); never put them where they can come into contact with a substance containing any kind of oil, such as tanned animal skin (but if a wallet is plastic 'imitation leather' it should do no harm); never expose them to strong sunlight, or any other radiation with a high ultra-violet content, except for the briefest periods; keep the surface as clean as possible, and especially avoid marking them (if you want to test for a chalky coating, read on); keep the reverse side (the back) scrupulously clean, and never, never write on it; try to acquire the habit of handling stamps only with tweezers of a philatelic type.

For mint stamps: never allow a mint stamp to become the slightest bit moist, and if you are living in a steamy tropical environment with close to 100 per cent humidity, then give up philately or send the material to a drier place for attention later; take the greatest possible care that the back never comes into contact with anything under high pressure, or with anything that is even the slightest bit damp (a substrate, such as paper or blotter, will stick fast to a mint stamp even if it feels almost dry); and never separate the advertisement or selvedge from a booklet pane, a portion of sheet margin, or any group of stamps forming a strip or block.

For used stamps: always pay extreme attention to condition, and if the stamp is off cover examine it carefully, as described later; if it is on an interesting cover or piece, keep it there; if it is well tied to an original piece, keep it there even if the piece does not seem to add much; if you ever doubt your ability to lift a single, a pair, strip or block, without causing the slightest damage, then leave it alone; if it is off cover, keep the back absolutely clean, with no gum, hinge or paper residues, writing, or anything else that cannot be removed without any risk of harming the stamp; in general, keep the stamp as dry as possible, especially if it is known to be fugitive.

Having listed all these generally negative rules, it will help to give an outline of some reasonable positive ways of practising the art of collecting. Ultimately most material will probably end up in an album. There are countless kinds of stamp album, and other albums for covers, miniature sheets and other kinds of material. Albums for stamps are often printed to contain particular sets of stamps, but these would be of little use to the expert philatelist who may wish to fill several volumes with stamps which all look more or less alike. In my own case I use one type of large-capacity, peg-fitting, loose-leaf album, with white leaves quadrille-ruled (ie like graph paper) so that everything can be exactly positioned and aligned. I do not use leaves incorporating linen hinges or tissue overlays. I have nothing against these, but they are very expensive indeed when the number of leaves runs into thousands. Some albums have black paper. Many people think stamps look good against such a background, but I have spent many hours removing black fibres and even complete black chunks from the backs of carelessly mounted mint stamps, and like black leaves only when the contents are mounted with proper care.

180

If one collects only newly issued stamps in mint condition, then there should be no great problem, because the stamps themselves should need no attention at all. The material when bought should be perfect (check for torn perforations and, especially, for missing corners), and to keep it perfect it should be mounted in the album in Hawid or similar transparent folder-type mounts, which grip the stamp adequately without affecting it in any way. But before you do anything else, plan ahead what you are going to collect, in what quantities, and where it is going to be mounted. There are plenty of guides, many of them special books, to how one should arrange a collection. Much of it is common sense, and in my view there are not many rules that cannot be bent if there is a good reason.

My Great Britain collection, for example, is arranged in chrono-logical catalogue order. One has to have a master-plan and mine is the basic SG part 1 catalogue list. Here, for example, stamps of Edward VII printed by De La Rue form an unbroken list dealing with each value fully at a time; then the printings by Harrison and Somerset House form second and third lists. This is the order I have followed, and most Great Britain collectors do the same, but if desired, an alternative scheme could be adopted. For example, each value could be dealt with completely, beginning with a full treatment of the halfpenny from the first De La Rue to the last Harrison, and then on through the equally long and complicated set of penny stamps. Another alternative would be to put everything in strict chronological order. This would appear to jump about all over the place, but would in fact be a thoroughly practical and sensible idea. In general, mint and used stamps do not appear on the same page, but I make an exception in the case of varieties and certain other items. Each page is carefully planned and very fully written up using a fine pen and black ink. The writing up is done last of all, when everything is in place.

Album pages are invariably sized (ie the paper has a coating of size), so that ink does not run on the surface or soak through the depth of the paper. But it is unsafe to use a strong chemical bleach. A friend made a mistake in his writing up and used a powerful household bleaching agent, applied with a brush from a small bottle, to erase the ink. When I know it is safe, I do this myself and it is very effective, but in this case the bleach soaked straight through the paper and spoilt a valuable stamp on the page below. This is a typical example of being wise after the event; try always to take precautions beforehand. Most expert collectors would probably say you simply do not let powerful bleach anywhere near a valuable album. Obviously, when writing up it is desirable to protect the stamps on the page, and to slip a thin but rigid sheet of such material as polystyrene or aluminium, or a copy of a magazine, under the leaf you are writing on to protect anything on the page below. Even if you are filling a virgin album from front to back it is a good idea to do this, to avoid the writing impressing itself on the next sheet.

My protective sheet is usually a page-size piece of tough, but slightly flexible, transparent plastic. This is perforated with a pattern of very small holes with coloured rings round them, and took about twenty minutes to make. It takes only a few seconds to line up the sheet on each album page and then make tiny marks with a

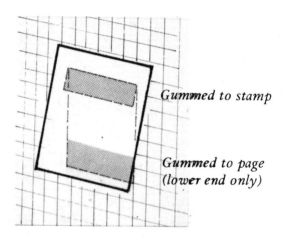

Gummed to stamp

Gummed to page (lower end only)

Fig 54 How to mount a used stamp, or a mint copy that has been previously hinged. It is remarkable how many people stick the large part of the hinge to the stamp and the small part to the page!

182

sharp pencil through, say, all the red-ringed holes. This shows the positions of the 'north-west' (top left) corners of the printed part of the stamps for that page. Different-coloured rings pick out the hole-patterns for different numbers of stamps on the leaf, from five to a maximum of twenty-seven. The more valuable the stamp, the fewer there are on a page (to allow more room for comment in writing up). There are countless ways of arranging and writing up pages, but I recommend the use of a transparent template of this kind because it means that the page layout can be done with un-failing precision in a matter of a few seconds, and there is no possi-bility of error. But try to avoid having exactly the same layout on every page: it will make the album too fat and burst at the spine!

I happen to write-up beneath each stamp, but one can do it alongside or in any other way that is immediately clear, unam-biguous and legible. Some people can write neatly, some can print neatly, and others ought to try to use a typewriter or, if they have ample spare time, a stencil. In my own case, I discuss the stamp issue itself, in the fullest possible detail, on the page(s) containing mint copies; the writing on the pages of used examples is con-cerned with corner-letters, shade, place and date of use, anything odd about the stamp or its usage, and in a few cases a note on the excellence of the copy or on the existence of some small short-coming that might not be evident. The last bit may seem like fal-ling over backwards to be honest. In fact it is common sense. One day the collection will be sold and such comments will help both the auctioneer and his customers, and will probably improve the prices realised rather than depress them.

At this point, I am going to suggest ways in which you treat stamps both before and after they come into your possession. Too many keen collectors seem to notice the faults in their stamps only after they have got home. Buying stamps ideally involves the provision of, (a) daylight, or a true 'daylight' lamp, for judging shades; and (b) a bright Anglepoise or similar lamp for intense il-lumination. The bright light is a vast help with watermarked stamps, because watermarks can usually be seen clearly through a stamp held for a second or two in front of such illumination. It is not really practical to use a bottle of benzine at an auction. Benzine is a volatile petroleum distillate (very widely used as a solvent and thus as a household and industrial cleaner) which when dropped on a stamp immediately penetrates the depth of the paper and shows up any watermark. It does not harm the gum on mint stamps, but can dissolve the inks in some photogravure printings and so should be used with caution. The best practice is to place the stamp face-down in a shallow black tray (a small black, or black-painted, lid will do) and put one drop of benzine on the back. The watermark will probably be seen immediately. Then the stamp can be left to dry in a second or two: benzine evaporates rapidly. There are also various electro-optical watermark detectors which cannot harm the stamp at all but are expensive and even less portable than benzine. I seldom fail to find a bright light adequate, but it is surprising how many auction rooms and dealer's shops have nothing but a weak suffused glow which is useless for water-mark detection.

Discovering watermarks in stamps on cover is very difficult unless a bright light can shine through all the layers of paper. If you have a really important case worth a great deal of trouble, there is a photographic method in which a piece of Du Pont Dylux 503 photosensitive paper is placed behind the stamp inside the envel-ope and is illuminated first with a studio photoflood (or, prefer-ably, a blue fluorescent tube, which generates less heat) and then, taking care to keep everything in exact registry, with powerful ultra-violet light. This works well with classical stamps, but many modern phosphor-tagged stamps soak up the ultra-violet energy and give poor results.

Stamps with graphite lines are obvious even on cover because the lines show clearly from the front, especially at the margins. Chalky stamps ought to be obvious to anyone really familiar with stamp printings. The surface is denser, smoother and whiter, the printing of brighter and sharper quality, and the stamp often feels heavier and stiffer. In the case of used stamps, most early 'normal' (ie not chalky) issues curl − sometimes almost into a drum − if damped and left to dry, the curl having the printed design outwards. Chalky stamps, on the other hand, arch strongly the other way (concave seen from the front), because as it dries the chalky coating contracts even more than the paper. The coated surface looks shiny, feels quite different, and must be treated with care. Heavily coated paper often gives a fugitive impression, and will invariably be irreparably damaged by being creased. If you have a really doubtful stamp with sheet margin attached, you are welcome to see if a piece of silver (the precious metal) will leave a black line, indicating chalk. I strongly dislike leaving black lines on the surface of good stamps, even on the margin. In any case, there are several kinds of coating not based on chalk or china clay that do not react visibly to silver.

One of the most difficult problems, both to the stamp-maker and the stamp-collector, is the gum. Early gums were impure, being made to a loose specification and often with very lax or non-existent quality control, and they were brushed on by hand. The coating was distinctly uneven, and in places was very thick – especially when, after complaints that the stamps would not stick, gumming was done twice. One has only to think for a moment of a pre-1860 stamp of almost any country that still has its original gum, to picture something with a back coated thickly with hard, yellowish glue that has cracked and crazed and is practically cracking the stamp as well. There are a few very early stamps in true mint condition, with perfectly smooth original gum, but these are exceptional (often closer inspection shows that the gum has been put on quite recently). There are many experts who are seriously worried at the chemical and physical reaction between gum and paper in early stamps. This problem will not prevail around the year 2100 with today's stamps, because one of the advantages of PVA gum is that it does not crack or craze, and it is applied thinly and evenly by machine. Good, refined gum arabic should give no trouble either. The problem arises from the poor quality of both the gum and the gumming operation in early stamps.

One of the worst things that can happen to a stamp is for oily or other penetrating fluids to work their way through the depth of the paper. In some cases, good solvents are known which can leach

185

out such stains without harming the stamp. In other cases, including most varnishes, ballpoint inks, and early gum, I know of no safe and effective solvent once the stain has fully dried. Constituents of early gums very frequently cause a chemical reaction, basically an oxidation, which discolours the printed surface and the whole depth of the paper. Apart from this, the gum often reacts with fillers in the paper (alums and resinous additives in particular) to yield acids and other harmful products which slowly break down the paper. A third hazard is the microbiological one, in that there are several, if not many, species of bacteria, fungus and other micro-organisms that can live and even multiply on gummed stamps under adequate conditions of temperature and humidity. But the most immediately apparent problem of all is that thick, old gum can craze and warp badly enough to damage the stamp itself. I have experimented with using a warm (not hot) iron to flatten early gummed stamps, pressing the iron at about 100°C firmly on to paper, with the stamp under the paper between two layers of thin aluminium foil or polythene. It seems to work well, but I would not challenge the view of some experts that, eventually, most of the oldest unused stamps must be scraped clean of gum and carefully washed. So much for the cult of 'unhinged mint'. Original gum is today often worth a lot of money, so it would be tough if we find that, to preserve the stamp, we have to soak it off.

If a mint stamp has been hinged, no harm can be done by hingeing it again. I use pre-folded hinges. The fold is made close to one end; it has to be 2mm (0.08in) away to grip properly, but anything much over 3mm is too broad. The whole point of these pre-folded hinges is that they are ready-made with a narrow portion just big enough to adhere to the stamp yet not so big that they spoil a large area of the back of a mint stamp. Yet time after time I find such hinges stuck on the other way round, with the big, broad part stuck to the stamp and a tiny strip just managing to adhere to the album page! So I will repeat the proper drill: pick up the main part of the hinge in the tweezers; lick or otherwise lightly moisten the *narrow* portion; place this in position on the stamp, properly aligned and close to the top, but not overlapping the perf holes;

either leave to dry or else press gently in place, taking care to keep the hinge wide open; when quite dry, moisten only the lower part of the large side of the hinge, pick up the stamp and hinge in the tweezers and place it accurately on the album page, using tweezers to keep the hinge pressed against the stamp until it is on the page; at once, open the stamp so that the moisture squeezed out from under the hinge cannot stick the back of the stamp to the page. When the hinge is dry the result is a fine copy that can easily be turned up with tweezers so that the reverse side can be inspected.

When expert collectors are buying or examining stamps, they will usually spend more time looking at the backs than at the

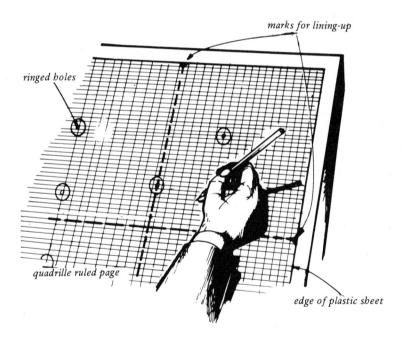

Fig 55   Use of a 'template' for swift and accurate marking-out of an album page. Any collector can make his own template from any handy piece of transparent plastic of suitable thickness (flexible but not flimsy), with carefully drilled or punched holes for different arrangements of stamps.

fronts. With an 'honest' collection of good material it will be possible to turn up every stamp easily, and verify that it contains no flaws. All the backs, mint and used, will be at once accessible, either on neat hinges or in Hawid mounts (never take a stamp from a Hawid mount without using tweezers; fingers will open the mount so wide it will be unable to grip again). If a stamp is still on a piece of original cover, and is well tied by the cancel, well and good; in this case it is the piece that is hinged. All other used stamps have perfectly clean backs. What a contrast from the type of page I so often see, where stamps seen from behind are revolting! Bits of original cover or parcel wrapper are overlain by countless pieces of stamp margin, hinges and other rubbish, so that the whole thing stands quite high above the paper. I have kept one stamp as a memento together with the 23 different things (14 whole or part hinges and 9 other bits of paper) that were stuck to the back when I acquired it! One of the upper layers of strata had a catalogue number written on it in ink; it was wrong.

Proper pre-folded hinges can be attached to any used stamp, no matter how priceless; there is absolutely no point in putting used stamps in expensive Hawid mounts. At the same time, there is not very much point in putting even unused stamps in Hawid mounts if they have already been hinged, provided the album pages will never become the slightest bit damp and never pressed together. When I acquire a mounted unused stamp, unless the hinge is extremely neat, I put it in a sweat box and sweat the hinge off. A sweat box can be bought or made, and is simply a box in which one can keep the relative humidity at 100 per cent. I have made several from suitably sized plastic boxes with lids. Metal boxes can rust or give other undesirable trouble. Most plastics are chemically and physically inert. All you need do is find a strong plastic box that is big enough to take a cylinder or plate block, or the largest block of stamps you expect to handle, and that has a close-fitting lid. Put a few layers of blotting-paper in the bottom, make them sodden with water, and then rest on top of the wet blotter a layer of thick plastic-covered wire mesh or other support that will let vapour through but will not allow water to climb up by capillary action. Then rest the stamp(s) on this, gum upwards. Experience will show how long different kinds of material need. Fugitive stamps need to be looked at after quite a short time; they ought to come to no harm, but I would take a peep after five minutes, and again after half an hour, to make sure nothing bad has happened. Ideally, material needs to stay in the sweat box for upwards of two hours for everything to separate cleanly, especially in the case of items covered in thick layers of old hinges. Then, when the stamp is removed and placed face-down on clean blotter, the unwanted hinges and other matter can easily be removed from the rear using two pairs of tweezers. In the case of a mint or unused stamp, take the greatest care not to cause fresh gum disturbance. Really badly clogged stamps, with a dozen or more layers of strata on the back, may need two or more periods in the sweat box before they are completely clean.

I merely soak off the bulk of ordinary used material by floating the stamps on cool water. I put an inch or two of water in a large white or transparent container, wait until the water is still, and then place items *face-upwards* on the surface. They will not sink, even if they start by curling up into a cylinder. Old and dirty line-engraved stamps, with the backs covered in old hinges and bits of paper, may be pushed under the surface; water cannot hurt this kind of printing and it helps give the stamps a wash. Other stamps should be kept floating on the water's surface tension. Again, it

Fig 56   Unless a stamp is highly 'fugitive', a used copy is best cleaned up by floating in cool water. The surface tension will keep it afloat even if it temporarily curls up.

needs a bit of experience to judge how long is safe, because there are some stamps so fugitive that they need to be taken out after less than a minute. Such stamps are placed face-down on clean blotter, squeezed into the blotter with a soft, clean forefinger (or the 'karate edge' of the hand), moved to a dry bit of blotter, and then gently attacked with a suitably shaped pair of tweezers or a plastic scraper with a fine blade. With fugitive stamps, one has to work very fast, yet it may be impossible to finish the job in one operation. Keeping a close watch on the stamp, it is again floated face-up for ten seconds or less, brought out, dried on to the blotter again and at once cleaned a second time until the back is a perfect sheet of clean paper. Then it is pressed between two layers of blotter to dry. The blotters are uniformly weighted all over to iron everything flat from the wet condition. Non-fugitive stamps can then be dealt with in the order that leaves the least fugitive, or dirtiest, until last. I normally get 35 to 45 definitive-size stamps floating at once, and I work through that lot before putting in the next load. Loading the water surface a second time takes long enough for the first of that batch to be ready when all are afloat. Last in are the fugitives – never more than two – and these are dealt with immediately. Any really tricky item, such as a fine-used block of highly fugitive stamps, needs a sweat box. Never, never leave a fugitive stamp floating or even the least bit damp while you answer the telephone or any other summons.

Paper, gum, hinges, and other rubbish scraped off each stamp can be wiped off on an old album page or other piece of paper. Never let the water get visibly dirty or yellowed by dissolved gum; when it is, change it. Wash your hands as well. Do not go on using blotting paper covered in gum and dirt. It is possible in an evening, say between 8 and 11 pm, to deal with 200 dirty old stamps off tatty pages and restore each to a perfect fine-used state. It usually takes longer than that time to mount them and write them up. Most serious collectors usually have a large number of stamps still waiting to be put into an album or in some other way disposed of. They must be kept in an ordered way and in a dry place, safe from water, pets, young children and other menaces. So at this point I must add something about how stamps deteriorate and how the process can be slowed to a near-zero level.

The subject is one of enormous complexity, and though it has troubled museums, libraries, art galleries, and archives for centuries, most of the research that will provide complete answers has yet to be funded. After all, it is difficult to combat a process if the process itself is largely unknown. Certainly there are many quite different ills, and the collector must try to guard against them all.

One goes under the general title of oxidation. Literally this means chemically combining with oxygen, present in all ordinary Earth atmosphere. Oxidised paper looks brownish or straw coloured, loses its strength and becomes very brittle and fragile. The process is quite irreversible, and a stamp or cover in this state can only be protected but cannot be restored. The symptoms are very similar to those of scorching, and the cause is in many respects similar also. Strong light rapidly accelerates oxidation. It is often seen round the edge of old album leaves, but stamps deep in an album should not oxidise rapidly.

Another form of oxidation is rust. This term is normally applied to oxidation of ferrous metals, and certainly stamps ought to be kept away from staples, steel binding or any other rust inducer. At the same time the red-brown speckling often seen round the edges of old stamps, colloquially called 'foxing', is in my view not due mainly to metallic rusting as has often been suggested. I believe most of it is due to microbiological attack, by fungus and other micro-organisms, many species of which find an existence on paper containing the least traces of moisture. You can see them at about × 200 magnification. They may die if the paper subsequently dries out, but will leave indelible 'rust' marks where their colonies were sited. Fungicides are legion, but their use is often hazardous. The best is probably orthophenyl phenol, but some authorities in museums and archives have used orthocaptan, thymol, and various alkaline sodium salts, with which they have soaked interleaving sheets sandwiched when dry between the sheets of valuable material. One expert (Robert Fellows, writing in *Stamp Collecting*) recommends keeping paper fairly alkaline, and suggests readings of 7 to 9.2 on a Gardner's pH meter.

Such scientific mumbo-jumbo (as it may seem to be to some readers) is really evidence of the way serious philately is bound to involve greater scientific knowledge, and increasing use of scientific tools and techniques. Many will simply say 'Life is too short' and carry on as before, but they are pushing their luck. In my work I am often in various kinds of laboratory and I once met an engineer-philatelist who said 'You mean to tell me you actually *lick* your hinges!' He told me to lick a microscope slide; then he showed me the bacteria which could clearly be seen with the microscope he had nearby. He always used distilled water and a camel-hair brush. I did not argue at the time, but I think this is overdoing it. There are countless bacteria in the air around us, and it is extremely unlikely they could cause any harm to a stamp-collection; they would probably not find it an environment where they could multiply.

Attempts to clean or improve stamps and covers should always be undertaken in an atmosphere of 'think first, act afterwards', and not the other way round. This is absolutely vital, and plain common sense, yet how often do we ignore it! With experience one can judge immediately if a cover is sound and strong, or whether it is oxidised, or liable to split at a filing crease, or just too thin. If it is obviously sound it should not be hazardous to clean it with powdered art gum, soft breadcrumbs, or even with an indiarubber eraser if this is new (old, perished indiarubber is a menace). Erasing marks from stamps, on or off cover, is something that an expert would not do nine times out of ten, and on the tenth occasion he might regret it. When you come to own a rare and valuable stamp that is perfect except for a livid blue or red crayon mark, the inclination to try to make the mark a little less blatant will be well-nigh irresistible. Indeed the impetuous collector might actually think he could erase it as if it had never been. My solemn advice is don't. If the wish to disregard this advice is still almost overpowering, try to agree with yourself to put off doing it for a few months. In those few months, ask a few experts. If after that you still try to rub out the mark, go ahead and add to the long, long procession of sad stamps I have seen where the erasure is worse than the mark. (I have lately seen a Great Britain £5 orange where the sequence was obviously: crayon mark; vigorous rubbing out; replacement of the eroded design with orange water-colour paint!)

In any attempt to improve or restore a stamp or cover, it is very important to know what the true colour ought to be. Ancient documents are never bleached, but are left oxidised. In contrast, old prints and stamps are often supposed to be white, and are frequently gently bleached. But one must try to remember what colour old hand-made paper really was. In some exceptional collections you can see beautiful examples of very old mint stamps, and even specimens of the unprinted paper. Put a piece of modern white paper beside them and the contrast is startling. Modern papers are made quite differently and contain special whiteners, and it would be very mistaken to try to make early stamps the same colour. In the same way, definitely blued or toned papers must be left alone; and in my view fraudulently blued fakes ought to be left alone also, and in this case expert opinion should be sought, because they might just prove genuine! I do not believe in too much usage of chemicals, even though various bleaching agents such as hydrogen peroxide, calcium hypochlorite, chloramine, and potassium permanganate have been used by stamp collectors for generations. In the case of early (say pre-1940) stamps, it is extremely unlikely you will discover something not in the specialised catalogues. So if you find a stamp that is blued, toned or on any other tinted paper, look diligently in a detailed or specialised catalogue. If it is not there you should seek advice before trying a bleaching operation; I think the answer would usually be 'leave it alone'.

What are the best conditions for the long-term storage of stamps and the hardware of paper, gum, and ink generally? A fair answer is 'not too hot, not too cold, not too damp, not too dry'. The ideal temperature is within the range 15 to 25°C, or 60 to 75°F. The ideal humidity is 45 to 60 per cent. Below 45 per cent will dry out the paper until it becomes dehydrated and brittle; anything much over 60 per cent will promote the growth of mould. And beyond doubt it helps if air can circulate around the material. In a large collection this is practically impossible; in this case, it helps if the proud owner gets a volume down every now and then to gloat over it and examine the condition, because the act of turning the pages is beneficial. Central heating is a great benefit, because it not only helps maintain the temperature in the right range but in winter it promotes circulation of the air. The ideal is for each album to stand upright and opened. This is invariably impractical, but do try not to squeeze albums together too tightly, nor stack them in a pile.

Obviously it is difficult to have a big collection of many volumes with air circulating round each page. In my view there is something to be said for putting each volume into a sealed polythene envelope. I have a philatelic friend in Alaska whose reply to the question at the start of the preceding paragraph would be 'Somewhere where you won't get flooded!' His valuable collection was practically destroyed in a catastrophic flood at Anchorage a few years ago. He salvaged what he could – I need hardly say he resisted the temptation to spend many hours painting the gum back on valuable mint material – and is now building it up again. He has enclosed his albums in the way I have described. Not only are they waterproof but the impervious film seems to keep the contents in perfect condition, even though the air motion around the leaves must be zero. I might add in this context that, though I have yet to meet a collector who has lost everything in a fire, I have met several who have lost practically everything because of the water used to put out a fire. Here again there is a good reason to use polythene bags – and make them stout ones. Ask at a freezer supplies shop if you cannot get them from a stationery store. Obviously each envelope should be filled with the album, or whatever the material may comprise, and ordinary air; do not include any drying agent, moistening agent, or chemical. On the other hand, it may be a good idea to keep a fungicide nearby, perhaps as a coating on a cupboard wall or wherever the collection is kept, to discourage any mould growth even if the humidity does not rise beyond 60 per cent. Obviously, such ills as dry rot, persistently damp walls, or steam from the kitchen are potentially lethal.

The most valuable collections of all are normally kept at

least partly in a bank vault. I cannot imagine a bank manager who would not allow a customer to inspect the vault. I have never seen one that was not scrupulously clean and suitable in all respects for philatelic material, because banks are continually being asked to store valuable pieces of paper which may have to be kept in perfect condition for very long periods. Despite this, if you are in this class of collector, have a few words with the manager to emphasise the importance of the stamp environment. He knows his bank and its own environment best, and may be able to forestall any future disaster.

There are many companies throughout the world that either specialise in philatelic insurance or else have a very experienced philatelic department. Premiums are generally very modest, of the order of 0.25 per cent (so that a collection valued at £1,000 will need a premium of £2.50 per year), but the premium naturally varies according to how the material is kept. For a collection below this value the insurer will normally just take the owner's word, but for really big risks he will probably send an expert to visit the owner, inspect the material in some detail to confirm its value and also have a keen look at how it is stored. The insurer will be interested in every kind of hazard, from theft to accidents, that could result in a claim. Obviously it takes a lot of expert time to value a large and high-quality collection, and this in turn costs a considerable sum – typically, 1 per cent of the valuation total. On the other hand, if you ask an auctioneer to sell a collection he will value it for nothing, because it is obviously in his own interest to realise the highest possible price and miss nothing that ought to appear as an extra attraction in the catalogue. Valuable collections are an important part of one's property, and every owner of such a collection must make up his mind as early as possible how he intends the asset to be disposed of in the event of his death. As this is related to the question of insurance I will deal with it here.

It is doubtful that the reader could build up a valuable collection without coming to possess firm views on these matters, but my own opinion is that unless you wish to bequeath it to named people in your will, such a property should be placed in the hands of a reputable auctioneer. No matter how old or young a collector may be, he should take this particular bull by the horns and make arrangements as soon as his collection builds up to a really large sum. He should tell his nearest relatives or friends which auction-eer he has chosen and write instructions into his will (this is vital), and also discuss the matter with the auctioneer. In this way it will all happen as he intended, unlike the fine Swiss collection – worth many thousands of pounds – of a friend which saw its owner pass away very unexpectedly and was not even mentioned in his will (because when he drew up his will years before, the collection was not worth mentioning). So, my strong advice is: *do it now*. Go and see the auctioneer of your choice, and ask him to sell the whole lot in the event of your sudden loss of life or interest. He will be able to have it valued, but unless you want to sell straight away he will make a charge for this service. He will probably work in part-nership with a philatelic insurer, or at least recommend one who will unquestioningly accept the auctioneer's valuation. So at one stroke you have sewn up the future of the collection (don't forget to tell the auctioneer who to send the cheque to) and placed it under full insurance cover at the price of detailed valuation and a modest annual premium. Questions of death duty and valuation for probate vary with each country, but in general stamp-collections are very good properties in this regard and may be pen-alised only if particular items (individual stamps, blocks, covers etc) are worth a large sum by themselves.

I need hardly add that the task of valuation will be eased if everything is beautifully written up in albums. It seems to me that too many people around the world, who lead busy lives, have built up valuable stocks which are hidden away in envelopes, stock-books and old tobacco tins. This is not the right way to care for good material, and these people ought to remember that the 'spare time' they are perpetually waiting for is likely to prove a pipe-dream unless they make some.

Indeed, although this is a slight digression, many collectors who have been buying hard for many years as an investment, have been far too busy to do anything but collect. I know some who have stamps of enormous total value yet do not possess an album, though they are always meaning to. Moreover, they have little idea of what they actually possess, not because they are not sufficiently expert but because their lives are crowded. A fellow-collector of Great Britain has a vast wealth of stuff all neatly arranged in cigarette tins, shoe-boxes full of envelopes and other containers, but is far too busy to get it into albums. I found he had a pristine mint copy of the 1962 National Productivity Year 3d with 'Queen's head omitted' (similar to that shown in Fig 41). I asked him what he had paid for it. He stared in utter astonishment. It took him the best part of a minute to remember that he had bought it at a stamp exhibition on the day the variety was first sold to the public at £85 each. Today it is priced by Gibbons at £350. But this is the point: he had tucked it away as soon as it was bought, and completely forgotten he had it. Anyone could have walked off with it. There is surely a moral here for all collectors who are short of spare time.

If you have anything in this class, either pull yourself together and get everything into albums, nicely written up and insured, or else pull out all the most valuable items, put them into a good stock-book and leave it at your bank, while keeping a very detailed inventory of each item. Pets, young children, firemen's hoses, damp and mildew, excessive dry heat, and – perhaps worse than all the rest – inadequate philatelic knowledge and sheer carelessness combine to cause considerable loss of value of the world's stamp heritage each year. Yet with knowledge, care and a little thought in advance, practically all of it can be avoided. So I ask the reader to ponder the question 'What could possibly happen to my collection, and how can I protect it?' I would take a bet you will think of something – so do it *now*.

9

The Business of Stamps

Stamps sustain a large volume of business of quite different kinds, quite apart from the businesses of charity stamps, trading stamps, revenue stamps, and the dozens of other non-postal kinds of adhesive label. On the one hand there is the 'stamp trade' made up of whole- or part-time professional stamp dealers, auctioneers, publishers, and the makers and retailers of the great wealth of philatelic publications and accessories. On the other, there are the postal administrations, and although the Universal Postal Union has at least 144 members – in every case, the sole authority of a national government empowered to run the postal services of that country – I doubt if there is one that has not come round to the view that philately is much too important to be ignored. Indeed, many postal administrations exist primarily to serve philatelic needs, and look on the national posts as a relatively small part of their business!

For example, the tiny principality of Liechtenstein, between Austria and Switzerland, has been so successful in its philatelic marketing that it claims to have 100,000 credit-account subscribers who receive mint copies of all new issues and/or cto (cancelled to order) copies and first-day covers. This is pretty good for a country with a population of about 18,000. At a rough guess only about 20 per cent of Liechtenstein's stamps are postally used, the remaining 80 per cent serving a valuable export role as a commodity eagerly bought by collectors all over the world. In fact, as outlined in Chapter 10, philatelic material bought in large quantities does not usually appreciate rapidly in value; but this is of little concern to the postal administration. Almost every postal administration is very interested in its philatelic marketing. Bearing in mind that some of the most obvious policies defeat their own ends, in ways I shall explain, there are a number of important things an administration can do to increase its philatelic business.

At the start it is important never to forget that the objectives of the postal authority are in general quite different from those of the collector. The postal authority is interested only in its current and future operations, and in keeping expenditure low and revenue high. Obsolete stamps are of interest only to the extent that if they show marked appreciation in value they will tend to make the country famed as a 'good' one philatelically. A 'good' country is one whose past stamps are proven sound investments, and whose present stamp-issuing policy is sensible and carefully planned. The best policy probably benefits both the national revenue and the world's stamp collectors, and it is possible to lay down a few broad guidelines.

I commented earlier that some obvious policies are self-defeating. Too many new stamp issues are as bad as too few, from the point of view of the postal administration (though either course can make the country of interest to serious philatelists). Suppose a country never issues new stamps. Today this is an impossible policy, because no nation is immune to inflation or to changes in postal rates, but in theory it is possible to make the issue of a new stamp a very rare event indeed. Such a country would be of intense interest to serious philatelists, and serious investors, for the basic reason that it would be of very little interest to the great mass of the world's stamp collectors. The casual collector would either ignore the country entirely or else quite easily put together a 'complete' collection of its all-too-familiar stamps. The serious student would be attracted by the fact that these stamps were really far from identical. He would realise that, though the basic design had not changed, there were actually many minor variations in size or design, differences in paper, in perforation, and perhaps even in the printing process. There would thus be many rare and difficult varieties, made all the better by the fact that most people ignored them. This is fine for the serious student, but it is bad for the country that issues the stamps. After World War II, Britain was in this position. Although very much a 'good' country to the serious collector, it hardly ever issued a commemorative or feature stamp and so the world's millions of collectors either ignored Britain or else collected a simple straight set of definitives and thought there was nothing more to do. Although it is impossible to measure philatelic sales, it is very unlikely that Britain had an income as high as £50,000 per year from philatelic sales at any time before 1955, and probably 80 per cent of this was to collectors inside Britain.

The opposite extreme is just as bad for philatelic sales. Imagine a former colonial country newly granted independence. At last it can run its own postal services and decide on its own philatelic policy. Quite apart from a natural wish to issue highly nationalistic stamps as a reaction to a rather boring and foreign-managed administration, an 'emergent nation' will immediately wish to cash in on the extra revenue derived from philatelic sales. Suppose it decided to bring out a major new set of stamps every week. Obviously, collectors would soon decide they were being 'taken' and would drop the new country like a hot potato. Collectors would be equally deterred by a spate of changes in colour, changes in perforation, or unnecessary overprints. Anything that makes it appear that stamps are being deliberately issued, or altered, merely in order to extract money from unsuspecting collectors has the effect of killing a country stone-dead in the philatelic world. So obviously the best policy is somewhere in the middle. But where?

One answer is that the biggest philatelic revenue is gained when the face value of new issues in a year is the maximum that does not deter more than a few collectors. But there are many other requirements that must also be met. The stamps must be attractive,

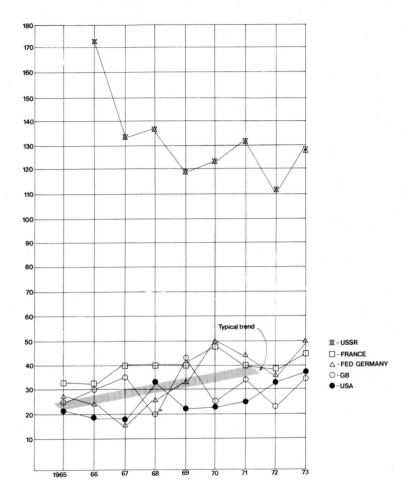

Fig 57   What is the correct number of new issues per year? Too many puts people off and debases the currency; too few and the nation may lose both revenue and collectors. Here are the broad statistics for five major countries, France, Great Britain, Federal (West) Germany, the USA, and USSR. The 'number of issues' ignores minor variations, different printings, miniature sheets and so forth.

interesting, easily understood, and likely to appeal to collectors everywhere – and, as businessmen will appreciate, you cannot just wait for collectors to acquire an awareness or an interest. The most successful philatelic countries treat philatelic sales as a business commodity that must be properly marketed like any other product. But here again there is obviously a point where the extra marketing costs begin to exceed the extra sales gained.

The accompanying graph shows the number of new issues per year in recent years from some important philatelic countries. World-wide, the Soviet Union is not one of the top philatelic countries. One problem it faces is that few people get much mail from Russians, so they have to pay for almost every Soviet stamp they get. Another problem the collector faces is the sheer profusion of Soviet issues, but of course the USSR is a great agglomeration of different 'Soviet Socialist Republics' and many of the issues are used just in one or a few of these republics and not throughout the Soviet Union. (In the same way even little Britain issues regional stamps intended for use in only one of the countries forming the United Kingdom.) But the graph does show that the most successful countries issue about the same number of new stamps per year, and – including definitives – this number is usually not very far removed from 30, lying in the range 15 to 45. In most cases, at least some of the subjects for feature issues are regular annual ones, such as Christmas, or basic themes decided in advance by groups of nations. But most of the subjects are usually the free choice of the issuing country.

I have already discussed stamp design and manufacture, but a few words here are needed on how the subject and design of a feature issue are related to philatelic revenue. Long experience has shown that the design has to be easily understood. This frequently means that the stamp designer, who has read-up the subject deeply, has to abandon neat and clever ideas and instead produce a stamp he might consider terribly ordinary, and perhaps even second-rate. As an example of the designer's problems I can cite the British Post Office Technology issue of 1 October 1969. This was in my view a fine and unusually interesting quartet of stamps, but the Post

Office found that they were rather unpopular with collectors because hardly anybody could understand them. One value, for example, was based on the way PCM (pulse-code modulation) can turn a continuous sine-wave into a succession of discrete values. The majority of collectors are technology illiterates and they found these stamps much too clever. On the other hand they would have understood a picture of a modern telephone. One lapse into the technology of telecommunications would not noticeably affect a nation's philatelic revenue, but a succession of 'difficult' stamp designs certainly would.

So the ideal is fifteen to forty-five bright, attractive and immediately understandable and interesting stamps which, if they are not definitives, depict themes related to the national history, habitat or image, issued individually or in groups at intervals through each year. Their appearance is all-important. Printing must be of the highest quality, and there is no doubt that a special appeal is exerted by multicolour gravure or by really fine recess printing. Recently a delegation from another European country visited the postal authorities in London and Paris because they had received continual complaints from their public and philatelic customers, who invariably asked 'Why can't we have stamps as good as the British or French?' It so happens that the French image is one of recess printing and the British one of multicolour gravure, but both nations have managed to build a strong reputation for attractive and nationally characteristic stamps. Again, both nations issue their feature stamps with various face values. Some countries, notably the USA and USSR, concentrate upon their inland letter rate(s) because their feature stamps are aimed primarily at their own population. Britain and many other countries take the view that a feature stamp can serve as an ambassador of national culture to other nations, and most special issues have face values appropriate to the main letter rates not only within the country but also overseas. At least, this is the official policy; a cynic might think the main reason was that this considerably increases the philatelic revenue.

In the dark ages, which in Britain extended up to 1960 or even

later, postal authorities existed solely for postal purposes; philatelists (or anyone who showed an interest in stamps beyond merely
buying and using them) were merely a nuisance. Whilst never for-
getting that their prime purpose is, or ought to be, something else,
almost all the world's postal services now run a philatelic department. Most of them have one or more special bureaux or sales
counters (in Britain there are eighteen philatelic sales points,
despite the small size of the country), special philatelic posting
boxes, a wide range of services for collectors (such as new issues
sent to postal subscribers, serviced first-day covers and presentation packs in various languages), and possibly a philatelic news
sheet. In Britain and many other countries there is a high-quality
Philatelic Bulletin printed on art paper and giving news of current
and forthcoming issues, changes in definitives, special cancellations, stories behind feature stamps, and even examples of unac-
cepted designs. In some countries there are philatelic posting
boxes, the mail from which is always given a neat and clear cds
cancel (or a first day of issue cancel if appropriate), even if the
mailed item happens to be a large package or parcel. In ordinary
post offices in many countries there is no way of being sure of a
neat cancellation, and parcels are impressed with coarse rubber
obliterators which ruin the appearance of stamps and almost kill
their value. Even today there are occasions when, due to im-
patience, ignorance or, sometimes, sheer wilful destruction,
obvious philatelic items are mistreated. In the early 1960s, before
collectors had any service or facilities in Britain, I was silly
enough to send a packet of magazines by air to Kenya with postage paid by thirteen stamps each of which was a valuable variety
on a different commemorative. The only way to secure a neat
cancellation was to register it, but this allowed vandals to draw
thick blue crayon lines (which were already marked on the packet
under the stamps) and scribble over the stamps with a ballpoint
pen so that all but four were badly damaged and two were actually torn in half. Today this sort of thing is very rare, and if it does
happen and the customer complains, a full-scale inquiry is likely
to follow.

The reason for the change is simply that most postal administrations either run on a knife-edge or lose money, and philately is one area where it is possible to show a sure profit. A typical stamp has a total manufacturing cost of about 0.125p and its face value may be anything upwards of ten times this. Even though the manufacturing costs are trivial compared with the overheads of running a postal or philatelic service, it is still possible to show a substantial profit. The scale of philatelic operations is in most countries small compared with the postal service (except in such places as Liechtenstein and small Arab sheikhdoms!). In Britain, philatelic sales amounted to a little over £2.4 million in 1972–3 (the last year for which figures were available as this book went to press) whereas the revenue from the posts was over £561 million. On the other hand, philately showed a profit and the posts showed a large loss, so philately is a thing to encourage.

Philatelic sales are very difficult to judge. Some of the stamps bought at a philatelic counter undoubtedly do service through the post, perhaps on the mail from a stamp dealer, and so cannot be judged philatelic revenue. On the other hand, a vast amount of material is bought over the counters of post offices throughout the land, and there is no way of guessing what proportion of sales by a local office may be philatelic. More than 90 per cent of my purchases, of cylinder blocks and similar items, are from ordinary post offices at periods when they are least busy. In most other countries, too, practically all the philatelic sales are made across the counters of ordinary local offices. My own view is that the UK figure of £2.4 million is a very large underestimate, but the shape of the curve of philatelic sales since 1963 is probably not inaccurate. It shows a peak in 1969 and a present revenue that is static. Obviously this revenue can be increased, but only at a cost.

Countries anxious to increase their philatelic revenue have on the one hand tried to provide more services to collectors, and on the other have advertised their wares more extensively. Probably most of the world's postal administrations supply cto stamps, but Britain is one of the diehards that insists a stamp should be either mint or else genuinely postally used. A few administrations with no reputation to lose print – or, rather, get somebody else to print – hundreds of millions of 'stamps' without gum and with a neat corner cancellation printed at the same time as the stamp! These labels find their way into countless cheap packets, and it just could be that, because they are so lowly and despised, they might one day be of value (see Chapter 10). Frankly, I doubt it.

In almost every country the first choice of collectors is their own country. So, where philatelic exports are concerned, postal administrations are in general competing for second place. Perhaps surprisingly, the main barrier to philatelic exports is bad communications. There are still millions of collectors who think British stamps are all the same – a hangover from forty years ago – because the ones they see on envelopes all look alike and they never look at a catalogue with Great Britain in it. Even collectors who are aware of a particular overseas country, and try to collect its stamps, usually have little or no idea what stamps that country has just issued, or is about to issue, and only the vaguest notion of the stamps issued by that country in the past. This is because they probably have an out-of-date catalogue that gives a broad-brush treatment totally ignoring the wealth of booklet panes, advertisement or slogan labels, se-tenant issues, coil strips, and all the other items that could greatly increase the philatelic revenue of the issuing country if they were better known.

How do collectors acquire their stamps? In the case of used stamps, they may receive them on their mail, or get them from someone who does, or they may purchase them from a friend, a club or exchange circle, or from the trade. None of this helps the issuing country. I have valuable used collections of several countries that have not brought a penny of extra revenue to the countries concerned. Postal administrations are interested in things they can sell, and in the case of stamps this means mint, cto or fdc. Such things generally have to be bought. The administration does its utmost to build up a list of clients who buy such material direct, either by requesting what they want or by paying an annual subscription and receiving new issues, fdcs and other items as they appear. From some countries, collectors can request particular

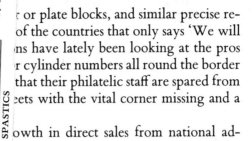

…r or plate blocks, and similar precise re-
…of the countries that only says 'We will
…ns have lately been looking at the pros
…r cylinder numbers all round the border
…that their philatelic staff are spared from
…eets with the vital corner missing and a

…owth in direct sales from national ad-
…0 per cent of the foreign sales of the
…ilatelic material is bought through the
…housands of stamp dealers, discounting
…nge operators, and probably about one-
…ssionals. The rest combine the activity
…n with an utterly different job which is
…n. All of them have to choose very care-
…nd which national administrations supply
their stocks of new material. The national administrations therefore take a keen interest in the dealers and try to make as many of
them as possible their regular customers. I do not know any dealer
who does not have to pay at least face for his newly issued stocks.
In fact, most of them will buy saleable foreign material at a sufficient percentage over face to pay for someone's air-mail postage
in sending it. Many collectors buy sheets of their own country's
new issues, remove any nice varieties that happen to be discovered
immediately upon issue, and air mail the rest to a distant dealer
who pays them 10–20 per cent over face, or credits them with a
like sum which the collector can work off from the dealer's stock
of the collector's chosen country. This is convenient to the collector and the dealer likes it too, because he feels his foreign friend is a
firm and reliable link who will keep him instantly fed not only
with the obvious new issues but also with other interesting items
such as new booklets and coils, and minor changes in definitives.

Ultimately these things would appear in specialised catalogues,
but few dealers have time to read such catalogues except those
covering their very small prime range of countries that usually
make up the bulk of their business. The other countries have to

look after themselves, and increased trade comes the way of an administration that can find a way to get its news across, easily and quickly, to the largest number of dealers. Despite the profusion of stamp magazines and philatelic newspapers throughout the world, the average dealer finds it hard to maintain anything but superficial knowledge on stamp issues except from his chosen group of nations. In any case, the dealer is limited in the amount he can spend on new issues because he needs large amounts of capital to run his trade in expensive classical stamps (unless he deals only in modern issues), and he cannot afford to build up huge stocks that will take a long time to sell. Many administrations have agents in the more important countries from whom dealers in that country can obtain supplies of current and recent issues. Care must be taken not to show favouritism. It is very tempting to try to build up one's overseas business by direct-mail 'shots' of literature, or by sending out free copies of the national philatelic bulletin, or a presentation pack of a new issue. This is likely to draw an instant angry response from dealers and collectors elsewhere who remind the administration they have to pay for such things. Indeed some collectors are so sensitive that they complain to an administration whose stamps have suddenly appeared with, say, a missing colour, if the prized variety is not on sale from their own local dealer or agent!

Behind all the effort is the knowledge of the potential market. For example, in Japan there are probably at least 40 million people who are potential collectors. Of these, probably 5 million actually are collectors, and of these again, probably fewer than 100,000 make any serious attempt to collect British stamps – probably fewer than a tenth of this number buy new British material as it appears. I doubt if as many as 1,000 buy British material in any depth, including all the available manufacturing variations. Thus with careful promotion the British Post Office could multiply its philatelic sales in Japan tenfold, a hundredfold, or a thousandfold. In the same way, the US Post Office might do the same in India or the USSR or any other potentially enormous market that is at present almost untapped. But trying to penetrate the market calls for shrewd judgement, and for money to be spent only where it will have an effect.

Most philatelic departments around the world are already engaged in carefully controlled experiments in selected markets to discover what actions on their part seem to bring the most cost/effective returns. Each administration tends to play things close to its chest, and not many even disclose what they think their annual philatelic sales revenue might be. Some have tried television spots, both in their own country and abroad, because about half the population could be regarded as potential collectors. But why should any particular person collect stamps? More to the point, why should that person spend money in *purchasing* stamps to collect? This is what the postal administration and the stamp trade are interested in. In the case of the stamp trade some of the material could undoubtedly be properly described as a good investment, but the newly issued material from the Post Office could not be thus described. Some new stamps undoubtedly are splendid investments, but out of each 1,000 new stamps bought by the world's collectors at least 995, and probably 999, are destined to appreciate in value not much faster than the cost of living. This is because most of them are of very common issues which always will be common and almost unsaleable. Britain and many other countries have 'trade descriptions acts' which would make it an offence for a postal administration to claim that one cannot fail to make money from stamp-collecting. In fact one can make money (see Chapter 10), but it is possible only with knowledge and foresight which many post-office customers do not possess.

So the post-office philatelic marketing staff in at least a hundred countries play it fairly cool, try their best to give good service and to avoid offending anyone, and cash in on the fact that they sell items at face value. Most of the public attraction to stamps around the world comes from the efforts of the philatelic trade, from fantastic prices realised by great rarities, and by the sustained mild interest caused by continual new issues. Every day many people become collectors, and a small proportion later develop into serious philatelists who devote to their hobby a great deal of time and money. Ultimately they may become so expert that they concentrate on a narrower and narrower front; some of my friends with the deepest knowledge of early British stamps have only a hazy idea of what is currently on sale, and are very poor philatelic customers of the Post Office. The Post Office is much more interested in the little Johnnies who spend their pennies on new stamps.

To close this chapter, it is worth examining in broad outline the growth in the mails and the growth in numbers of stamps. Most countries show a continued strong growth in numbers of postal items, but a less-strong growth in usage of stamps. In the USA, Britain, and other highly developed countries there has been only a modest growth in the numbers of stamps used during the past forty years. This is due partly to the enormous growth in telecommunications, which has largely replaced the post as a means of social and business communication (except where there are particular reasons for a written document or 'hard copy'), and by the fact that in these countries the business world has almost given up using adhesive stamps in favour of postal meters or franking machines. For at least thirty years the philatelic literature has speculated on when and where the last stamp will be used. Like so many predicted terminal events, this one seems to get further and further away. Many organisations handling vast quantities of mail, which might appear ideal customers for franking machines, have found that they get better results if the cover bears an attractive stamp. This is especially the case with direct-mail advertising, both to home and overseas recipients, who (it has been found) are much more likely to read the message if the envelope has a nicely cancelled feature stamp than if it has been metered by a dull franking machine. Of course, philately and even simple stamp-collecting would continue indefinitely even if stamps were as obsolete as whalebone in corsets. But that situation is not in the foreseeable future. I think there is little doubt that most of the world's stamps have yet to be printed.

10
Stamps as an Investment

Throughout this book I have repeated the fact that buying newly issued stamps and then keeping them does not necessarily show a profit. Indeed, the people who stick recent commemorative stamps on their direct-mail circulars, mentioned at the end of the previous chapter, could make use of this fact by buying these stamps at well under face in an auction instead of from an intermediate dealer who charges a premium. The vendor in the auction is likely to be someone who hoped that the material would sharply appreciate in value and then suddenly needs to sell.

Some collectors claim that they are disinterested in any notion of 'investment'. Like the old-time hobo who in 1932 proudly claimed 'I ain't one of your common depression tramps; I was a tramp way back in the boom!', their attitude is 'I collect stamps for love, not money, and I despise these upstarts who do it for gain.' I still regard this attitude as a deliberate posture, because I am sure such people take some interest in the price they pay and in the price at which they sell. In any case, stamp-collecting is undoubtedly the greatest and most widely practised hobby that is capable of showing a net profit. But whether or not any one collector does come out at the end of the day 'ahead of the game' depends on many things. In this

211

chapter I will range over what these factors are, and will conclude with a look at stamp-collecting in comparison with other ways of using one's money.

What makes the process interesting is that it contains a feedback mechanism that tends to make it self-defeating. The only way one can make money with modern stamps is to invest in items that later on will be desirable and scarce, so that the basic law of supply and demand will work to advantage. But if millions all pick these 'best choices', they will hardly appreciate in value at all but will instead flood the market. I cannot think of any form of investment that does not rest on the supply and demand of a commodity at one point in time, and the supply and demand of it at a different, later, point in time. The general idea is to try to buy cheaply and sell at a high price. In the case of stamps, the interplay of supply and demand is such that, as described above, one can usually buy fairly recent stamps (in bulk) at well under face, both outside and inside the issuing country. But material that can be bought under face (and, of course, I am referring to perfect mint items) is available so cheaply because it is common, and nobody wants to buy it. In general, common items are not likely to prove good investments because they are likely to be common for as far into the future as one can look. So the best things to do seem to be, first, to become a real expert on your chosen stamps, and then to buy carefully selected items at face (if they are modern) or as cheaply as possible (if they are not). But there is a bit more to it than this!

If you ask a philatelist 'What is the best way I can invest in stamps?' he is likely to reply 'By carefully buying valuable classics in the finest condition.' This is obviously sound. Superb early issues are certain to be good investments no matter how far ahead you look. Stamp-collecting is so world-wide and enormous a hobby that it is inconceivable that it should suddenly go out of fashion and die away. I have already insisted that the adhesive postage stamp is not likely to become an obsolete thing in the next several decades; and, even if at some future time new technologies did enable every human to receive instant hard-copy letters at the same moment that they were transmitted by someone 10,000 miles away

212

(and we can do this now, of course, but at a price), the postage stamp would undoubtedly remain the centre of a vast international hobby and an industry based on that hobby. So the man who has a large sum to invest, and has the expertise to know which stamps to buy, need never fear that they will one day become just worthless pieces of paper. All he need worry about is the precise environment in which the precious items are stored.

For the investor who wants to make money with stamps, yet does not wish to devote any time and effort to gaining philatelic knowledge, or to his buying and selling, the obvious answer is to become friendly with an expert you can trust and get him to buy material for you. If one can see snags here, an alternative recommendation is to pick the soundest investment you can find and buy it whenever you can at the best price you can. But here again there are obvious pitfalls. There could not be a better investment than the penny black, which has such renown and glamour that it has for many years fetched prices higher than its degree of rarity would appear to warrant, but the element of scarcity does not actually enter into it. A stamp is worth what people will give for it, and in the case of fine penny blacks the supply is quite large but the demand insatiable. The hesitant investor can remind himself that the supply is not getting larger, but smaller (because every year a few copies are lost through carelessness or ignorance), while the world population of collectors grows at least in proportion to the world population. But how can the non-expert investor buy such items at the best price? The catalogue will not help him.

Suppose the would-be investor decides to walk into a good GB dealer's shop. The price he will pay will not be the lowest but the highest the dealer can reasonably charge. The dealer has to make a living and he does so by fine judgement of what the market will bear. The dealer exists to serve his customers. Most of these customers are concerned mainly to collect as a hobby, and they are happy to buy from the dealer and trust his pricing. Very often the dealer's prices are rather lower than those quoted by the publishers of major catalogues, because the dealer may not suffer such massive overheads and have certain other advantages, but it is only common sense to appreciate that to walk into a dealer's shop and buy large numbers of classical stamps each at the dealer's price is probably not the best form of 'investment'. If a dealer has any nice penny blacks, he will price them individually and will expect to sell most of them individually. In the case of valuable items, the dealer performs an essential service in very many ways. He can sell stamps singly. He can sell just what you want. I often buy from dealers who happen to have just what I do not have. Every collector knows the joy of filling a long-standing gap, and without dealers this would be much more difficult. But for the man whose main objective is to put a lot of money into buying good material purely as an investment, a better choice is to attend a suitable auction. Here he will find himself surrounded not only by collectors but also by dealers. And the odds are that he will find that the dealers, who must later sell at a profit, are the strongest bidders.

Our non-expert friend is likely to feel like a lamb among wolves. Even though he will have examined each lot closely, how will he know how high to bid? One lot may be an album page of good-looking penny blacks, but all suffering from minor faults. The catalogue says £14 for a used copy. There are twelve on the page. Is the lot worth £20 or £168, or somewhere in between; or should he give it a wide berth? Another lot may be an album page of twelve superb copies, all with four very large, even margins, and light cancels. Are these worth less than £168, or more? He may bid for the superb lot and find the bidding getting way out of hand, going up towards £200. Is it because this is a fair price, or because one or more of the stamps are great rarities (the catalogue would say so), or because the bidding is between non-experts who do not know when to stop and go on because the other one is doing likewise? Without expert knowledge our investor is likely to buy at a high price. In the long term he will do much better than just recover his money, but his return on capital will be as bad as the man who buys equities when the market is at its peak.

I doubt if anyone totally disinterested in stamps will have reached this point in the book, but if they have they will by now

214

be sure of the following facts: (a) walking into a post office and buying one copy, or one sheet, of a newly issued stamp is not likely to prove any better an investment than buying a can of baked beans; (b) there are modern stamps that will appreciate firmly in value, but the more these are collected the lower the appreciation will be; (c) fine classical stamps are sure-fire winners, but without being an expert on them one can buy badly and in effect lose a lot of investment appreciation; (d) with expert knowledge one can not only derive immense and enduring pleasure from good stamps but also show an excellent return on capital; (e) provided they are properly cared for, stamps are as safe an investment as any other commodity, and probably better than most.

In practically every country there is a lesser or greater degree of inflation. This means that one has to 'run to stay in the same place'. If you have £100 or $100, this must be made to turn into at least 120 by this time next year just to hold its real value constant. Put another way, if you just hide the money in an old sock it will steadily be worth less and less, so that after ten years or so your capital will hardly buy anything. So when assessing the appreciation of an investment, it is desirable to remember this fact, and avoid crowing with delight because some catalogue value climbs 10 or 20 per cent a year. It has to do this just to keep level with inflation. In any case, the serious investor would do well not to worry too slavishly about the ups and downs of catalogue prices. Like the expert player of the stock market, one ought not to bother too much with how the market reacts, or over-reacts, but should be able to know with fair accuracy how things are going to come out in the long-term.

The harassed catalogue editor tries to write down a fair price for every item anything from three months to a year hence. Some of the biggest catalogue publishers have to do their repricing eight to ten months before the date of publication. They look at past price movements, talk to their sales staff and perhaps to other dealers to discover what is on every 'wants list', look at their own stocks, and use their own judgement of the fashions and the market to predict what will be a valid price when the catalogue is on sale.

Many collectors think that big catalogue publishers buy an item furiously and then, when they have a huge stock, smartly whip up the price. In fact, it is impossible to run a business in this way. I doubt if any single publisher or dealer can really manipulate the market, and the gross across-the-board price movements are based on the inexorable interplay of supply and demand with which no individual or company can greatly interfere (except in the case of strongly demanded rarities, and even then the outcome is doubtful). Admittedly, catalogue prices do influence market prices, but any catalogue that tried to exert a sustained, gross influence on the market would not only fail to do so but would be discredited. If a stamp is repriced in the catalogue (and it can move down, as well as up) this simply reflects the price the item is fetching in the market.

Fig 48 illustrates the way some particular 'blue-chip investments' have moved in relation to the inflationary rise in the cost of living. The inference is that such items are probably a good investment, but in fact the experienced collector can show a much better return than this. Obviously it would be impossible for me now to include a supposed comprehensive list of items the philatelic investor ought to buy, but it is possible to give a great deal of general guidance. The basic, inescapable requirement is the greatest possible knowledge of one's chosen country or class of material. A second need is experience of the market, of sources of supply and, on any particular occasion, of the price at which a particular item or lot would be worth buying. The source of supply may be a giant auction, an opulent dealer's shop, an unknown person who has put an advertisement in a stamp magazine, or a street trader's barrow. I consistently buy from all four kinds of source, and the experienced collector will learn to judge very quickly whether a particular source is going to be good or not.

If you go to a top-flight auction, especially one dealing mainly with your own choice of country or class of material, there will be no shortage of desirable items. All will be fairly and accurately described (although some auctioneers are fairer and more accurate than others), but every intending buyer should inspect the lots in which he is interested most carefully. In general, nobody will get anything knocked down to him at a silly price, although people who bought slightly imperfect valuable items ten or twenty years ago can today make a killing. Most big auctions are battles royal, and almost every desirable lot goes right to the limit of what seems reasonable, and sometimes beyond. Yet it sometimes happens that, if you keep on the alert, you can get a bargain. Sometimes a lot is unaccountably unwanted, and one can get it for well below estimate. Sometimes two dealers will fight like cats for the first of three essentially identical lots, and it will go for a very high figure. You may then fight the loser for the second lot and let him have it for almost as high a price. Then you *may* be able to pick up the third, identical lot for very much less. Sometimes, for no very obvious reason, the first of two identical lots will fetch its full market value and the second will fall to your bid of half as much. Sometimes you can do very well towards the end of a big sale, when most of the fierce dealers have gone and almost everyone else has overspent his budget. Always remember that there is rarely an occasion when you simply *must* buy. Do not be deceived into thinking it is now or never. Always remember the price at which you can sell something, and the undoubted fact that any particular kind of item is bound to turn up again. If the price goes up far beyond the level you have set, wait and bid again another day.

I am thinking solely of investment here. The investor who also collects stamps as a hobby may well wish to buy something that precisely fits his own collection, or fills a long-time awkward gap, but I am discounting such considerations. Indeed, it might just be that the investor could do well buying damaged material! I mentioned earlier how twenty years ago one could buy really very rare and inherently valuable classic stamps cheaply if they were damaged. People who bought such stuff were despised, and not even fit to bid against. As I commented earlier, we now have dealers putting in their advertisements comments about 'quite small tears' and bad thins and creases that are 'not visible from the front'. So one must expect to see even this class of merchandise rising swiftly in market value. Hopefully, perfect items, which I shall continue to insist on, will move ahead even more strongly.

In the case of modern stamps, there are two kinds of investment. One is the stamp that is already standing high in the catalogues. It may be expensive because it is rare, or fashionable, or because it is in some way incorrectly made. Anything with a major missing colour, for example, commands a very high price, as does a modern stamp with gross errors of perforation. But it is not worth deliberately trying to find such scarce items. Invariably you have to buy them through the philatelic trade, and the very first dealer to get hold of them will sell for what he thinks is a fair price. Only time will show if it is. In some cases, the investor who had the money to snap up the whole of a dealer's stock of a really good variety – if the dealer allowed it all to be bought by one person – was on to a very good thing indeed. But it is a risky business. Maybe one quarter-sheet is known to exist, and you are able to buy most of the quarter-sheet for £60 a stamp. How do you know that next week someone will not find a dozen sheets with the same error? After a year has gone by you can begin to get a better picture, but by this time the market price has settled down. Fig 58 shows the curve of realisations (a very good indication of market price) for a modern rarity and demonstrates the sort of appreciation one can expect. I would not think such items were either safe or rewarding to the pure investor, though, as a collector, I find them captivating.

The other good investment among modern stamps is the item that later will become rather scarce. It must be an item that is in the catalogues, so that all future collectors know about it, and ideally it should appear in the printed albums so that it shows as a gap. The investor can exercise his skill in spotting such items while he can pick them up at face. When stamps had watermarks such items were more abundant. For example, consider an investment-minded collector walking into a British post office in the spring of 1961 with a ten-shilling note in his hand. According to tradition, his best bet would have been to buy a ten-shilling stamp. Had he done this he would have invested quite well. Had it been a tiny sub-office, there is just a chance the ten-shilling stamp would have

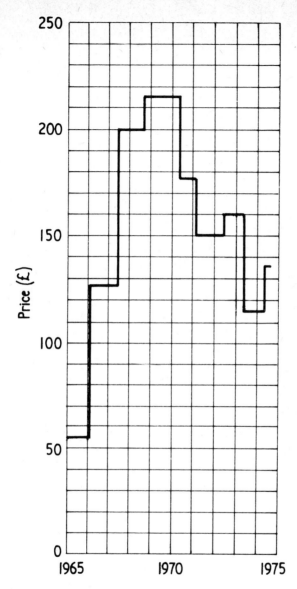

Fig 58   Can one be 'on to a good thing' with a modern rarity? Obviously one can if it is picked up at face value, but a modern rarity purchased philatelically soon after discovery will probably appreciate no more rapidly than most other philatelic material. These curves show typical prices realised by a famous missing colour.

219

been the first De La Rue printing, which he could today sell for well over £10 (I have seen one fetch £20), or twenty times face. More probably it would have been the second DLR print, which would today fetch at least £5. Both these rates of appreciation are higher than those for most high-face stamps; for example, if he had bought a ten-shilling stamp two years later, in 1963, he would do well to get twice face (£1) for it today. But suppose he was thinking about possible future rarities. He could have bought a ten-shilling stamp booklet containing a pane of six 2d stamps with inverted watermark. Today he could sell that pane for anything up to £40, or 800 times face.

Booklets and coil strips are invariably worth buying, and it is a good idea to maintain a large stock of them. After a year or two it is usually pretty clear which ones are going to be really scarce and which have become common. You can then use up the common ones for postage, if you wish, if you doubt their probable rate of appreciation. In general, any catalogued uncommon variety that can be bought at or near to face at the time of issue is bound to be a good investment, and so is any stamp that for any reason has an unusually short active life. For example, on 26 August 1964 the Australian Post Office completed its splendid new set of high-face stamps by issuing a 7s 6d (the first of this face-value in Australia) and a £2. As the date of the changeover to decimal currency had already been fixed as 14 February 1966, less than eighteen months away, these were obviously going to be fairly definite investment items. In the event, even though a million or more collectors must have realised the situation, only 501,165 of the £2 were sold (and most of them were postally used and thrown away) and a mere 303,687 of the 7s 6d. Both are today very good stamps indeed, worth about ten times face in either mint or fine-used condition, which is quite good for an item where probable appreciation was blindingly obvious before it had even been placed on sale.

In general, the suggestion that something will be a certain winner is bound to depress its value and in the long-term may markedly reduce its appreciation. For example, in Britain, Edward VIII was monarch from 20 January to 10 December 1936. With such a short reign it might be thought his stamps would be super investments. In fact, it was so obvious that they would be worth collecting that most Great Britain collectors are ankle-deep in them. There is the occasional rarity, such as the 1d and 1½d values with perforated bottom sheet margins, but Edward VIII is one area most GB collectors have little time for. In the same way, if I wanted to kill an item stone-dead, the surest way to do it would be to broadcast to the world's collectors that it was the best investment in the history of philately. That is why it would be silly to try and produce a list of current or future items that every investor ought to buy.

Before I go on to other forms of investment, there is the obvious fact to be faced that an investor must be able to realise his assets. Obviously the good philatelic investor is likely to wish to keep his material as long as possible, because hopefully it will rise in value rather faster than the cost of living. On the other hand there is no reason why an item which happens to be bought for an abnormally low price should not be sold straight away. The only thing you need when selling valuable stamps is to be an expert. If you are not, then the only thing to do is to put everything into an auction, and rely upon the diligence of the auctioneer in discovering precisely what is being sold. As I have pointed out earlier, one bad stamp will put the auctioneer (or his customers) right off, so that the search for value will become half-hearted and suspicious. It is highly desirable that, before selling, everything in good condition is carefully put into albums and properly written-up, and damaged items taken out. If you are an expert, then you ought to have a very good idea of the market value of what you are selling, and can make a proposition to a dealer. The advantage of selling to a dealer is that he will pay you the whole amount agreed as the price, whereas an auctioneer will keep a percentage of the realised sum as his commission. Different auctions have different scales of charges, and some levy a lot-charge from the vendor while others impose this charge upon the buyer. Again, the taxation systems of some countries include a tax on capital gains or upon the sum realised by a sale of possessions, and this tax may have to be borne by either the vendor or the buyer. One advantage of stamp-collecting is that the large number of separate items in most collections makes it easy to evade such taxes, which generally are payable only on single trans-actions above a stipulated sum. (In the UK value-added tax is payable only on certain stamps or auction lots, which can make things complicated in selling big collections!)

For very many years good philatelic material has been a buoy-ant, firmly appreciating kind of property. There is no obvious reason why it should not continue that way. So most collectors are likely to want to put off selling as long as possible, and many of the finest collections come into the possession of heirs and other ben-eficiaries who may have neither philatelic knowledge nor interest. As outlined in Chapter 8, anyone with a valuable collection *must* make arrangements either to sell it properly or to have it stored safely. All too often I find that a collection has passed into the hands of someone with no idea of its true market value and no idea how it should be looked after. It would serve our clever investor right if, after he was suddenly run over by a bus, someone took his priceless asset to a dealer and emerged five minutes later delight-edly clutching a five-pound note.

Of course, dealers who can pull off deals like this (and most of them are much too honest to do so), can live off stamp-collecting very nicely. But the collector cannot do this. He gets a return on his capital only when he sells. The same holds true for practically every other kind of collecting. On the other hand, he could put his

Fig 59 Generalised curves of the rising cost of living (heavy line) and various kinds of investment. These curves happen to apply to the United Kingdom at this particular period in time, but they are not untypical of many of the devel-oped countries. The ups and downs of the stock market are obvious – and, of course, any one company's shares can fluctuate even more wildly and may, in the case of bankruptcy, suddenly become virtually worthless. The '1936 type-writer' is typical of items which may suddenly come into fashion, and which may later ease to lower values. Good philatelic material has never shown any sign of a general easing in value.

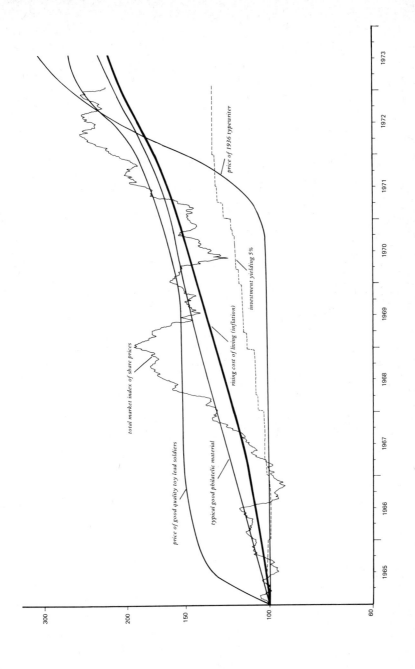

price of good quality toy lead soldiers

total market index of share prices

typical good philatelic material

rising cost of living (inflation)

price of 1936 typewriter

investment yielding 5%

300

200

150

100

60

1965 1966 1967 1968 1969 1970 1971 1972 1973

money into other forms of investment that show recurring dividends. There are gross differences between 'collecting' and 'investing'. Collecting is at least partly a hobby, and the hoped-for capital appreciation is a bonus. Buying and selling prices are variable and indeterminate, and there is no ready yardstick to tell either a buyer or a seller what a proper price might be. On the other hand the prices of bonds, equities and all other forms of investment are clearly stated at all times. There is always a 'perfect' market, and at any moment one can always buy or sell at a precise price known in advance.

It is hard to think of anything that has not been collected by people at some time or other. From the pure investment point of view I have known people make massive profits on soap, ground black pepper (carried in air force kit-bags), and bars of nickel, but these have limited aesthetic appeal. As soon as aesthetic appeal comes into the picture, one is in a more or less fickle market where fashion exerts a powerful and often unpredictable influence. Of course, there are some things that are supposed to have 'intrinsic value', so that, whatever fashion may say, these items never become worthless. Gems and precious metals are obvious examples. A piece of jewellery might be judged not merely unfashionable but downright unpleasant; but if it was made of solid platinum, studded with fine diamonds, it would fetch a high price anywhere. There is absolutely no reason for this idea of intrinsic worth, beyond popular agreement. At present a damaged piece of gold is worth much more than a damaged rare stamp, because no intrinsic worth is attached to early hand-made paper. Gold is one of many substances which does not deteriorate when reasonably handled and which is regarded by most of the world's population as having a particular value. This value is by no means constant. Early in 1973 the price of gold rose from $68 to $90 per fine ounce, a staggering jump. By 1974 it had almost doubled, to $170. It may well fall again, but one can be sure that it will never fall very far. On the other hand few people literally 'collect' gold. There are very restrictive legal sanctions on the hoarding, movement, and selling of gold, and one can get much better results with other commodities.

Probably the nearest hobby to collecting stamps is collecting coins (the science of coins, and of all forms of money or exchange token, is numismatics). Here the object usually has an intrinsic worth, although this is often low. Condition is generally of vital importance, and the market value of seemingly rare and valuable coins is often very disappointing unless they are in very good condition. Although thousands of dealers around the world trade in both stamps and coins, the stamp market is generally much larger, more active and more likely to yield an elusive item in what is considered fine condition. The manufacture of coins is much less suitable for the existence of rarities within a given set of items than is the case with stamps. Numismatics tends to be much more limited and unrewarding than philately. Give a philatelist a hundred seemingly identical old stamps and he will show you that all are quite different, with sharply contrasting values. Give a numismatist a similar quantity of seemingly identical old coins and, usually, he will only be able to comment on their varying condition.

As soon as something of intrinsic worth is fashioned into an artefact, its value may be increased by its fashionability, by the quality of workmanship and, in rare cases, by the reputation of the craftsman. Typical of this class of merchandise is fine Georgian silver. The dictates of fashion do not cause violent fluctuations in such items, because it is safe to predict that silver will always be valuable, and that beautifully worked silver will always command a premium. The finest porcelain and pottery will likewise never be subject to a slump, even though in this case there is no intrinsic value attached to the raw material. Wedgwood has always been collectable in its own right, whatever fashion may say. But other manifestations of similar materials have strong ups and downs. Heavy Victorian ironstone was so out of fashion it was ignored; then a few years ago it went ahead strongly, and today still commands very high prices. Today, Chelsea figures sell for almost exactly as many pounds as in 1960 they sold for pence. Until 1960 the table pottery of the 1920s – for example, items by Clarice Cliffe – was spurned by 'the trade', and could be disposed of only at jumble sales; today, as one might guess, individual items fetch £40 or £50. This is a chancy business. The bright speculator can guess right and make a lot of money, but eventually the item that has no intrinsic value is judged too expensive. Isolated buyers refuse to pay the price asked, and very swiftly indeed the whole class of commodity is judged 'oversold'. The price slumps dramatically because, in falling to seek a level that buyers will pay, the commodity automatically kills its attraction as an investment. When it seems to have touched rock-bottom it might again be worth buying in quantity, because all collectable items of this kind appear to go in cycles of down, up, and down again.

What about antiques? These cover such a multitude of descriptions that the only two rules I can think of are: don't touch anything unless you are an expert; and put the quality of workmanship first. Perhaps one has to have a certain flair to judge what will appreciate most strongly. Today, anything Georgian or Victorian that contains fine craftsmanship is eminently saleable. Even mass-produced toys of the early twentieth century are fetching very high prices. Provided they are in good condition, tinplate clock-work toys or high-quality lead soldiers can be relied upon to fetch at least twenty times the price at which they were originally sold. Everyone knows the worth of lovingly restored vintage cars, and the same goes for steam traction engines, barrel-organs (street organs), slot machines, and lamp-posts. Old lamps, optical instruments, early cameras and typewriters are all obvious items that, if in pristine condition, can be sold for many times their original price. If you were given a set of huge carousel horses from a fairground you might consider them only as fire-wood, but a friend of mine sold such a set within hours at £100 each. The world is littered with erstwhile rubbish which an affluent society is eager to buy at high prices. The days when 'antique' meant fine glass, porcelain, pistols, swords and silver have gone for ever. Even the 'Chippendale' and 'Hepplewhite' chairs seem today to be 10 per cent original and 90 per cent restored by a later hand. Today's big profits in general collecting are made by sharp operators who spot something quite new – I must go and snap up some discarded electronic computers dating from before 1960!

Certain classes of painting, of course, have always been judged of value. With Canaletto and Rembrandt the only place to go is up, and fashion does not enter into it. But with less-exotic paintings that more of us can afford, the situation is hazardous. There is only one of each painting. My friend Dr Edward De Bono has written perceptively of the way people would judge the values of, say, an original classic painting; a copy produced by some modern photographic or printing process; a copy produced by a computer-controlled system that could reproduce the artist's exact brush-strokes, using as nearly as possible the original pigments and canvas; and a copy produced by a skilled human copy-painter. The expert (which means the scientific expert) will always be able to tell which is the original, and this will never be degraded in value no matter how many seemingly identical copies there are. And the reason is simply the vague and inexplicable fact that people are prepared to outbid each other in offering fantastically high prices for the original. Obviously there is an element of pride and self-aggrandisement in possessing such a thing, but one can muse on the possibility of a new generation of society saying 'This original painting is very little different from these computerised copies that retail for £1.99; why should anyone pay more?'

My own view is that the man who pays £535,000 for a single painting is likely to get a greater sum when he sells. Paintings in this class are a recognised form of investment, but it is impossible to say what one's return on capital will be. Far higher appreciation has been shown by material once judged out of favour. Pre-Raphaelite paintings are a classic example of items that suddenly shot upwards in price. Another example is the Victorian animal painting. Ten years ago one could have bought fine horses by Stubbs for £150; today they fetch around £40,000. I doubt if they will suffer a slump.

Traditionally, the finest and safest investment imaginable was land and property. We all know of the tycoons in this market who began twenty-five years ago with a couple of pound notes, but this area is today a good one to stay away from (in most of the 'advanced' nations, at least). Prices are already astronomic, and one has to deal in units of money right outside the reach of any people except millionaires or large institutions. Taxation has destroyed its investment appeal, most countries have introduced legislation limiting the number of properties or tracts of land one person can own, the supply of mortgage money is often crucially limited, and altogether the individual speculator who puts his money into land and property today must be either stupid or else possessed of second sight and able to see a totally changed political scene.

For most people a much more attractive place for their money is a bank or the stock market. A few people still keep money in the form of money, hidden in places like an old tin or mattress, but I suspect inflation has shown most of them the crass error of their ways. If they put it into a bank or a national form of investment, their money will at least earn enough compound interest for its true value to stay roughly constant. Almost everyone today wants 'a hedge against inflation'. This is what the modern interest in investment and in collecting is all about, and it justifies this chapter. Property, the traditional hedge, is now difficult or impossible. Unfortunately, the stock market is also highly variable, and confidence in it as a sound investment has rarely been so low.

When you buy a company's stock you receive a share certificate which states that you own a certain percentage of that company. Unlike stamps, the 'condition' of the certificate is immaterial; you need not insure or take care of it. One's investment is conceptual, and on a particular day is worth a particular amount. One buys the stake in the company partly on the strength of the company's management, products and marketing, and current trading figures; but a far more important factor is the trading position of the company in the future. Sometimes an improvement seems obvious; for example, proposed legislation regarding pollution would appear certain to benefit a company specialising in effluent control. More often the improvement seems likely to come about through complex factors. Indeed, many investors buy on 'hunches'. There are two basic ways in which one can measure the performance of a company. One is the obvious factor of 'yield'; if a company's stock returns a divided of 9p per share and the price of a share is 100p, then the yield is 9 per cent. The other measure is the 'price/earnings ratio' or P/E; this is the price of a share on a particular day (usually today) divided by the money which that share would have earned over the previous year. If the share is currently priced at 150p and the earnings over the previous year were 10p, then the P/E is 15; if people believe the earnings over the following year will rise to 15p per share then they predict a P/E of 10. People buy stock either because they are 'high fliers' with soaring P/E, and thus fast capital growth, or because the yield is high and thus returns a good income. Usually it is a bit of both.

Value of stock can fall as well as rise. In the UK, a man who invested in equities in February 1968 would have found just five years later that he had an average capital gain of 215/135, or 59 per cent, which is ahead of the rising cost of living (but I am not allowing for capital-gains tax payable upon sale). If he had delayed for a year, his result over four years would have been 215/190, worse than the progress of inflation. If he had bought average stock in February 1969 and sold it in June 1970, his result would have been 145/190, or a thumping loss. So correct timing is as vital as correct judgement. Today economics, the price of money, and government regulatory actions, are wholly international. The problems are very large indeed, and the ambition of almost every intelligent citizen throughout the developed countries to buy a hedge against inflation is thwarted by poor market performance, by taxation, by restrictive legislation, and by the investor's basic lack of knowledge. Often the savings of a lifetime are just put into a bank, where they appreciate at about the same rate as inflation, or they are used to buy a unit trust which, as it is based on the performance of a large group of equities chosen by experts for security and either P/E or yield, ought to do distinctly better than just keep pace with inflation – but nothing like so well as the stock bought by the experts who really know the market.

Of course, there are also the pure gamblers. People who play the stock market may often appear to be gambling; but many of them are operating on the basis of knowledge, which is a totally different thing. If you wish to back horses or a football team you may again be able to use judgement and experience, but in this case the scales are unbalanced by the fact that the losers must pay all the winners as well as all the large overheads and profits to run the system. The same goes for true games of chance, where judgement is probably not applicable. It is a far cry from the roulette table to the stamp auction room, because in the latter one's performance depends almost wholly upon judgement. If you have neither knowledge nor judgement you will do at least as well at the roulette table. I prefer to bet on certainties.

One can become an expert on particular classes of valuable stamps in a matter of a few years – say, about as long as it takes to become an expert on particular classes of equities – but one can give a passable imitation of being an expert in a few weeks. Suppose you pick a single stamp, the Great Britain 1841 2d. In a matter of minutes one could learn most of the salient facts about this stamp. Within a day one could learn most of the ways in which a particular copy might be worth far more than the average value. With familiarity gained over a few days one could learn to judge condition swiftly, to notice all the pros and cons accurately, and to put a mental price on any particular copy. This is a good stamp when in fine condition, and a collection soon begins to mount up to a value that would interest most investors. It has its parallels in early France, Germany, USA, and most other 'good' countries.

Stamps of this kind are extremely interesting investments, because not only do they appreciate very firmly in value, but they are available in quantities large enough for the investor to find copies that can put him 'ahead of the game'. All he has to do is understand what rarities exist and then not fail to notice them as they come along. If he buys them at the price for the rarity he is still on the appreciation curve; if he buys them at the regular price he is way ahead of it. The fact that the stamp has no intrinsic value is immaterial. If somebody set out with the deliberate intent of discouraging stamp-collecting, and tried to prove that these small pieces of paper were 'oversold', he would have a very difficult task. For a century they have been of increasing interest to collectors. The number of collectors around the world has never ceased to grow. The prices realised by good stamps have never ceased to rise. Today we face a world in which wealthy people of every creed and colour are wondering how they can best invest to beat inflation, and many of them also feel there may be better things to do with their spare time than playing cards or watching television.

I play cards, at times, and also watch television. The turner in the machine shop who makes up a four for a card game in his lunch-hour can hardly be expected to turn away from his mates and start examining a choice auction lot under the light of his lathe, even if he does carefully wash his hands first. But, if he did, he would no longer be judged wholly eccentric or childish. The chaps around him would be interested to know what he was doing, what sort of return on investment he expected to get, and why he preferred philately to other ways of spending money. Practically everyone today is interested in money, and an increasing proportion of the world's population is interested in philately. Buying and storing postage stamps can be one of the finest forms of investment, quite apart from bringing immense pleasure. All you need is to know exactly what you are doing.

Glossary of Terms

accumulation   Any large collection of stamps arranged with insufficient care to merit the title of a collection.

adhesive   (1) The gum used to affix a stamp. (2) Any postage stamp originally issued with adhesive on the reverse (especially used to denote stamps stuck on a cover bearing other postal markings such as handstamps).

advertisement pane   A pane from a booklet in which one or more of the stamp-sized areas bears an advertisement or slogan.

aerogramme   Printed and gummed writing-sheet designed to be folded and sealed to form a lightweight air-mail letter. Usually made of thin paper and printed with the appropriate postal duty.

albino   Literally, white or without colour; a stamp or overprint in which absence of ink has resulted in a colourless impression.

alphabet   A particular distinctive set of letters used to print a stamp or overprint and which helps a philatelist identify the item precisely.

aniline   Oily liquid, originally distilled from coal-tar, used as the basis of certain dyes; in particular a bright-red ink, manufactured partly from aniline, which immediately penetrates between the fibres of uncoated paper.

APO   Army Post Office.

approvals   Stamps or other philatelic items sent on approval by a dealer to a customer who can study them at leisure whilst knowing the price asked.

backstamp   Handstamp impressed on the reverse of a postal item giving date received at a transit office or at the office of destination.

bilingual   Stamp printed in two languages.

bilingual pair   Se-tenant stamps each printed in a different language.

BIOT   British Indian Ocean Territories.

bisect   Half a stamp postally used for half its original value and tied to cover across the cut edge.

block   Any se-tenant group of stamps extending over more than one row and more than one column; ideally, a perfect rectangle, of any size.

blued   Stamp printed on paper showing irregular, usually faint, blue colour, often imparted deliberately.

BNA   British North America (Canada, Newfoundland, Nova Scotia etc).

bogus   Fraudulent stamp either of a non-existent issue or a non-existent country.

booklet   (1) Small, convenient book containing panes (pages) of mint stamps (and often slogans or advertisements). (2) Booklet issued by an exchange club in which a member mounts material for disposal (more properly called a 'club booklet').

booklet pane Complete pane (page) of stamps (plus slogan or advertisement labels, if any) from a booklet, preferably with selvedge.

boxed Postal marking, or printed marking in margin of stamp sheet, surrounded by rectangular lined 'box' frame.

burelage Pattern of fine wavy lines, often fugitive, printed on face or reverse of some stamps.

BWI British West Indies.

C (1) Chalky paper. (2) Common (in scale of rarity).

CA Crown Agents.

cachet Special handstamp, manuscript note, adhesive label or printed design borne by a postal item and confirming unusually interesting usage; eg a first flight on a particular route.

cancel, cancellation Any indelible design printed or written by hand or machine across an adhesive to render it invalid for further postal use.

cat Abbreviation for catalogue value (unless there is no possibility of doubt, the publisher should be named).

CC, cc Abbreviations for Crown Colony or colour changes (ie a second issue of stamps printed in different colours from the first).

cds Circular date stamp, the preferred type of cancellation for most modern stamps.

centred to . . . In a perfectly perforated sheet, each stamp has the same size of margin on each side; in describing a valuable stamp it is desirable to comment on the centring by stating the stamp is 'perfectly centred' or 'centred to bottom', 'centred to top-right' etc. 'Centred to bottom' means the top margin is larger than the bottom one. The term is not applicable to imperf stamps.

chalky Describes stamps printed on heavily coated paper (see Chapter 4).

charity stamp (1) A stamp, not intended for postage, issued in support of a charity. (2) A postage stamp bearing a surcharge which, usually after deductions for overheads, is donated by the postal authority to a charity featured in the design of the stamp.

coated Any paper bearing a coating, chalky or otherwise.

coil Stamps issued in the form of a long strip, one stamp wide, in the form of a tight roll issued either from a machine or by a hand dispenser. Stamps can be arranged in a coil side by side or one above the other.

coil leader Piece of paper in the form of a long tag at the delivery end of a coil; usually printed with the number, denomination and coil price, and sometimes with a date or checker's number.

colour trial Stamp printed singly or in multiple in a particular shade of ink to judge aesthetic appearance, prior to final decision on the issued colour.

column A vertical row of stamps in a sheet.

combination Cover bearing: (1) Stamps of different denominations, not se-tenant. (2) Stamps issued by different postal authorities.

comb perf Sheet or individual stamp perforated by a comb machine, each beat of which perforates three sides of one column or row of stamps (one of the three sides completing the perforating of the preceding column or row). Distinguished by perfect registry of the holes at every stamp corner.

control Letters and/or figures printed in a stamp-sheet margin to indicate time of accounting (eg a particular period of six months) or other manufacturing data.

cover Envelope minus the letter it contained when postally used.

cto Cancelled to order, a stamp bearing a cancel (invariably a neat *cds*), but never postally used. Provided as a service by some postal administrations.

cylinder   The cylinder used to print photogravure stamps. In many cases the cylinder is numbered and is large enough to print two PO sheets of stamps simultaneously. One of the sheets is often called the 'dot sheet' and the other the 'no dot sheet'; thus, the ninth cylinder made for a particular issue would print sheets bearing the numbers 9 and 9., the latter being read as 'nine dot'.

cylinder block   Block of stamps (usually six) from that part of the sheet where the cylinder number(s) can be seen in the margin.

cylinder number   The number(s) printed in the margin of a stamp sheet by each cylinder used to print the sheet; thus, a nine-colour stamp will have nine cylinder numbers, each in the colour of one of the chosen inks, with an additional number for any cylinder used to print phosphor tagging.

datestamp   Any postal marking impressed by a hand or machine stamp containing a date; sometimes used to mean a cds.

demonetised   No longer legal tender; in particular, a stamp bearing a duty in an obsolete system of currency, or of an issue stated by the postal authority to be no longer valid for postage.

des   Abbreviation for 'designed by'.

die proof   Single, very carefully impressed proof of a new die, invariably in black ink on smooth white card or fine-calendered or coated paper. When dry, inspected in great detail to check that the die is perfect.

dot, no dot   See *cylinder*.

doubly printed   Stamp or part of sheet bearing more than one clear impression of the printed design, invariably both on the same side of the sheet and both in the same sense (ie not an *offset*).

dry print   Stamp image or overprint grossly deficient in ink, but not albino (which is devoid of any ink).

due   Adhesive label to record postage due on delivery because of insufficient prepayment.

duplex Hand obliterator comprising a cds, intended to be impressed on the cover, and a second portion intended to cancel the stamp.

duty plate Portion of a stamp design containing the postal duty (face value) when printed separately from the frame, head, or key plate; in particular, the plate used to impress the duty (see *value tablet*).

end delivery Coil in which stamps are arranged one-above-the-other and dispensed by a machine.

eng Abbreviation for 'engraved'.

entire A complete postal item, especially a cover complete with the letter and any adhesives.

essay Hand-drawn or printed design for a proposed postage stamp.

est Abbreviation for 'estimated price' which an auctioneer thinks would be a fair price for a particular lot.

exchange club Stamp-collecting club whose members circulate material (usually individually priced in booklets), generally by post, but which does not normally arrange meetings of members.

extension perf hole Pattern of perforation in which each horizontal (rarely, each vertical) row of perforations is extended by one hole into either or both margins.

face Face value, the price at which a stamp was first sold; in the case of charity or surcharged stamps, the total amount payable.

facsimile Printed copy of a (usually rare) stamp, with no intent to deceive.

fake Stamp or other postal item fraudulently altered to appear to be a different item of greater value.

fdc First-day cover, an entire bearing one or more adhesives and postally used on the day of issue of those adhesives.

237

file crease Cover or other postal item that has obviously been kept folded over a long period.

fine Philatelically sound and desirable; in particular, an adhesive in undamaged condition (if postally used, with a clear, light cancellation).

first-day cover See *fdc*.

flaw Visible change in the printed design of a stamp due to damage to the printing surface of the plate or cylinder; 'constant flaws' are seen, either unchanged or very slowly progressing, over a very large number of stamps printed by the same impression.

forgery Stamp fraudulently manufactured with intent to deceive.

FPO Field Post Office, a post office for military forces on active service.

frame Printed border of a stamp.

franking (1) Loosely, any postal obliteration. (2) Hand or machine impression on a postal item in lieu of adhesives to denote prepayment (thus, 'a franking machine' as a term for a postal meter). (3) Postal markings to indicate that the item is to be carried free of charge.

fresh Postal item, especially an adhesive, in fine original colour.

front The front of a cover, cut from the remainder but bearing any adhesives, cancellations and the address.

fu Abbreviation 'fine used'.

fugitive Ink that runs when moistened by water.

gauge Number of perforation holes in a length of 20mm (in the case of most definitives, the number of teeth counted across from left to right).

granite Paper containing countless very short hairs (fibres) of colour(s) contrasting with the main mat of the paper.

graphite   Adhesive bearing one or two vertical lines of black electrically conductive graphite on the back, under the gum.

gravure   Photogravure (see Chapter 4).

grill   Adhesive bearing fine pattern of criss-cross embossing to break up the paper structure and prevent erasure of a cancellation.

guide dot/line   Dot or line appearing on a stamp as a result of failure to erase punched or inscribed marks on the plate intended to guide the platemaker in entering the stamp impressions. Usually such marks are close to the frame of the stamp.

gum   General term for the adhesive substance brushed or printed on the back of most stamps and activated by moistening with water or saliva. See *gum arabic, pva.*

gum arabic   Widely used adhesive applied as a glossy coating that is transparent when pure, but yellowish when less highly refined; obtained from the acacia tree and often called gum acacia.

gum crease   A crease ironed out of the paper of an unused stamp but clearly visible in the gum; in some cases the crease is actually caused by warping and subsequent cracking of the gum.

gutter   The unprinted strips between rows and columns on a sheet of stamps; in a correctly perforated sheet of most modern stamps the perforations run along the centres of the gutters.

hair line   Any very fine line in a printed stamp design, either a printed (coloured) line on unprinted paper, or an unprinted (white) line on the printed design; in particular, unprinted diagonal lines across the corners of certain British typographed stamps of 1862–4.

handstamp   (1) Any device for printing that is held in the hand and struck first on an ink pad and then on paper. (2) To print with such a device. (3) The impression thus printed. Handstamps may be used to cancel adhesives or postal stationery, but many serve to give information.

head plate   In a stamp printed by two or more impressions, usually in contrasting colours, the portion of the design containing the central portion (which in early stamps generally contained a portrait).

heavy cancel   Obliteration which, either by its design or overinking spoils the appearance of the stamp by covering most of its surface.

hinged   An unused stamp to which a hinge (stamp mount) has been affixed is described as 'lightly hinged' or 'heavily hinged', depending upon the degree of gum disturbance.

imp   Abbreviation for imperforate (imperf is more common).

imperforate   Never perforated; early stamp sheets were issued in imperf condition, but with modern issues an imperf copy is usually a prized rarity.

impression   (1) The image of a stamp transferred by pressure to a duplicate die or transfer roller. (2) The similar image transferred by pressure to the surface of the plate. (3) The printed image impressed on to the paper.

imprimatur   In philately, usually a stamp cut from one of the first sheets to be printed of a new design or new plate, often on ungummed paper and usually imperf; frequently the issued stamps were perforated and of a different shade of ink.

imprint   The name of the printer printed on the margin of a stamp sheet or on any other printing job; thus, an imprint block is a marginal block of four, six or more stamps including the imprint.

intaglio   Line-engraved or recess printing.

inv   Abbreviation for inverted (usually referring to the watermark).

item   General term for any philatelic object such as a stamp, cover, booklet, die proof or even a postally used piece of wrapping paper.

jubilee line   Marginal rule.

key plate   A basic design of stamp issued by a colonial power or other central postal authority within which are spaces for the insertion of different names of territories and different postal duties. Many different issues might all use an identical key plate which would normally include the frame and the main design.

kiloware   Unsorted modern material, typically stamps off paper or on piece, sold in kilogramme bags at a flat rate.

label   (1) Original term for a postage stamp. (2) Proper term for dues (which are, strictly, not stamps). (3) Stamp-sized area of a booklet pane either left blank or printed with a slogan or advertisement. (4) Any small adhesive, other than a valid postage stamp, affixed to a postal item. (5) Bogus stamp of non-existent issue.

laid paper   Paper watermarked with close parallel lines, with other lines, much wider spaced, crossing at right angles.

to lift   To unstick an adhesive from a cover or any other substrate.

line engraved   Stamp printed by a plate produced by impressions from an engraved die, the recesses in the plate accommodating the ink; also called intaglio or recess printing.

line perf   Abbreviated description for a stamp or sheet perforated in straight lines, all the horizontal (or vertical) lines being done first and then all the crossing lines. The two sets of perforations need not register at the corners of the stamps.

litho   Short for lithography, in which the inked image is determined by the ability of a flat (or gently curved) surface to repel ink in some places (where it is wet) and hold it in others (where it is greasy). See *offset*.

M, m   Mint.

make-up   The contents of a booklet, usually in total number of stamps of each denomination.

241

Maltese cross   More properly called a croix paté, the form of the obliterator used to cancel British adhesives in 1840–4, also later used as a watermark.

margin   The unprinted area around the edge of a stamp or stamp sheet; in the case of an imperf stamp the width, number and regularity of the margins strongly affects the value, the ideal being a wide, even margin along each side.

marginal rule   Printed line, usually about 0.1in (2.5mm) wide, surrounding the stamp impressions on a sheet. Usually there is one line for each ink used to print the stamps, and the rule is often broken at the gutters. It is impressed by a raised edge around the printing plate which reduces or eliminates the shock that would otherwise be felt as the inking roller struck the first row of stamp images on the plate.

maximum card   Envelope or postcard bearing a printed, usually illustrated, feature linked with the subject of commemorative stamps with which it is postally used (not necessarily on day of issue).

mc   Abbreviation for Maltese cross.

miniature sheet   Small sheet bearing in the centre a small number (typically one or four) of a feature or charity stamp, often with imprint and other details in the wide margins; perf or imperf.

mint   Exactly as issued by the Post Office or other original source.

mixture   Assorted stamps from many countries in a loose condition.

mount   Any device for attaching a stamp or other item to an album page or other substrate; the commonest mount is the hinge.

m/s   Abbreviation for manuscript, ie written by hand.

multiple   Three or more unseparated stamps, mint or used, on cover or off, in any arrangement.

N Abbreviation for normal (price); thus, a sideways watermark may be priced 8N and a block of four may cost 15N.

n/h Abbreviation, 'never hinged'; the inference is that the item has full original gum, and to some degree n/h is a North American way of saying 'mint'.

O Abbreviation for ordinary (as distinct from chalky paper, or some other distinctive printing).

obliterator Hand or machine stamp used to cancel an adhesive, especially a device other than a cds.

obsolete No longer on sale by the Post Office.

official Stamp specially printed, or overprinted, for use solely by a designated 'official' department.

offset Partial or complete impression of a stamp printed in error in the wrong place, eg on the gummed side of another stamp or on top of an existing stamp, as a result of the impression being transferred to an intermediate surface such as part of the printing press. Usually an offset impression is a mirror image (reversed left to right). Thus, offset litho, a printing method in which the stamp impressions are printed on an offset cylinder which in turn prints the paper.

og Abbreviation for 'original gum', ie bearing most of its original gum in undisturbed condition (but hinged at least once).

omnibus issue A set of stamps featuring a particular topic issued simultaneously by a number of countries, usually with most of the issues sharing a common design (note: Christmas is not an omnibus issue; each administration chooses its own design and release date).

on, off paper On paper means a piece has been torn from a postal item containing one or more adhesives (but not necessarily including any complete postmarks); off paper means a stamp has been lifted.

overprint (abb ovpt) Inscription added to all stamps in a sheet, either at or after the original time of printing, to: (1) Turn a definitive into a commemorative. (2) Turn a definitive into an official. (3) Render a stamp exclusive to a particular organisation (in Britain today overprints are legal only for fiscal use) so that it cannot be used by anyone else. (4) Change the issuing authority (eg British stamps were formerly overprinted for use by administrations throughout the Middle East and North Africa).

P Abbreviation for 'proof'; ie the item is a die proof, or an impression taken to prove the accuracy of the impression.

packet (1) Early term for a fast mailboat operating, as far as wind and weather allowed, to a stated schedule between stated ports. (2) Small envelope, with transparent front, filled with dealer's common stamps (either a mixture, or one-country or selected sets); thus 'packet-maker' for a dealer who buys kiloware or other large assortments and makes it up into packets of off-paper stamps sold as a packet for a stated price. (3) The box of exchange-club booklets circulated between members.

packet letter Early letter conveyed by packet, usually for an additional fee. See *ship letter*.

pair Two se-tenant stamps, taken to be se-tenant horizontally unless described as 'vertical pair'.

pane (1) Page of stamps (and labels, if any) from stamp booklet. (2) Portion of a sheet of stamps forming a simple fraction of the whole ($\frac{1}{2}$, $\frac{1}{4}$ etc), especially in the case of a sheet printed in the form of a number of panes separated by very wide gutter margins.

paper fault Clearly visible irregularity in paper introduced at the time of manufacture of the paper (or, at least, prior to stamp printing or other use of the paper).

paquebot French term internationally used to cancel stamps on mail posted on board merchant ships.

p/c Usual abbreviation for postcard.

pelure Type of paper calendered under extreme pressure and thus very thin and often brittle.

pen-cancelled Adhesive used postally and cancelled by hand-writing across it (not to be confused with similar stamp used on a receipt).

percé en arc Rouletted by lines of small curved arcs.

percé en scie Rouletted by lines of zigzag cuts (literally, 'saw teeth').

perf Perforated.

perfin A stamp perforated across the centre with the initials of a company or other organisation.

phos Phosphor.

phosphor Any substance emitting visible light when stimulated by visible or invisible electromagnetic radiation. Modern stamps may be printed with colourless inks containing a phosphor, either in the form of bands (visible when viewed at an acute angle) or as 'all-over phosphor', or the phosphor may be coated on the paper before stamp printing begins. The word should not be confused with phosphorus, a chemical element which has no connection whatever with phosphors.

photo Abbreviation for a stamp printed by photogravure.

piece Portion of a cover front or other postal item containing not only the adhesive(s) but also the complete cancellation.

pinhole Any small hole in a stamp other than perforation applied officially, and thus construed as damage.

pin-perf Pin rouletting.

Pl, pl Abbreviation for plate (thus, 'printed by Pl 6').

plain Stamp issued without phosphor tagging (to distinguish it from otherwise identical phosphor issue).

245

plate block   Block of four, six or other number of stamps complete with portion of sheet margin containing the printed number of the plate used; this is the recess-print counterpart of the cylinder block of gravure printing.

pmk   Abbreviation for postmark.

poached egg   Popular term for many kinds of testing label bearing a design resembling such an object.

positional piece   Portion of a sheet of stamps, usually containing a variety, extending to the corner of the sheet or other part of the margin containing marks sufficient to identify the exact location of the variety, and thus confirming that the variety is genuine.

postmark   Any mark deliberately impressed on a postal item, and especially one impressed at the time of posting (to serve as an obliterator or otherwise).

pp/c   Abbreviation for picture postcard.

precancel   Adhesive postage stamp issued to a customer using a large number of stamps, already printed with cancellation (usually the name of the place of despatch between parallel bars).

printed on gum   Printed in error on the reverse side of the sheet (note: if such a stamp becomes wet the printed design will be detached).

proof   Piece of fine card or other high-quality substrate on which an impression has been carefully taken from a new die or other printing hardware to check that the design is correct in all respects.

provisional   Temporary issue of stamps used in the absence of an awaited specially designed issue (provisionals may be crude local productions, overprinted issues from another country, or an issue overprinted by a successful revolutionary administration).

pva   Abbreviation for polyvinyl alcohol, the preferred gum of many modern postal administrations (the correct abbreviation is

PVA1, but this is hardly ever used in philatelic literature even though the common abbreviation could be confused with another adhesive, polyvinyl acetate, PVAc).

quartz lamp   One of several kinds of electric lamp giving radiation mainly in the ultra-violet part of the spectrum.

R   Abbreviation for a reprint.

R, RR, RRR   Degrees of rarity in ascending order.

recess printing   Line engraved or intaglio.

reconstruction   In the case of stamps whose individual position in the sheet is known (eg from corner letters) or can be deduced (eg from flaws or other characteristics), a complete sheet assembled from used copies (very rarely, from unused). The reconstruction may be wholly made up of singles, or it may include strips or blocks.

re-entry   Characteristic doubling or thinning of portions of the design of a line-engraved stamp caused by the impression having been entered more than once on the plate (see Chapter 4 and Chapter 5 for discussion of re-entries, fresh entries, and the adjectives coincident and non-coincident).

regional   A stamp issued for use in only part of the territory under the authority of a postal administration (eg Scotland, in the case of the UK).

remainder   (1) Stamp-collection mounted in album(s) from which the best or otherwise most desirable items have been removed. (2) Stock still unsold by the Post Office when an issue is withdrawn from sale.

repair   A corrected flaw in typographed or line-engraved printing.

repp   Heavy, usually soft paper characterised by fine parallel lines impressed in its surface.

reprint Stamp officially reprinted by a postal administration to a design similar, or identical, to a classic early issue (but on more modern paper and often in a different colour).

retouch A corrected flaw in photogravure printing, usually still visible as an irregularity in the design.

reversed A left/right mirror image (usually refers to the watermark).

roll A coil of stamps.

rouletted Perforated by pinholes, short cuts, or other method in such a way that no paper is removed (unlike perforating by the normal modern method, which removes small discs of paper). The term has also been used for imperf stamps cut completely away from the sheet by using a circular cutter, like a pastry cutter, with straight, wavy, or scalloped edge.

row One row of stamps running horizontally across the sheet. See *column*.

rub Surface damage due to abrasion, erasure of a cancel, or other unwanted mark.

run Faded colour due to fugitive ink becoming damp.

S Abbreviation for specimen. (In some reference books it means 'scarce'.)

s/b Abbreviation for stock-book.

selvedge The gummed, stitched, or stapled margin of a booklet pane usually left in the discarded booklet after the pane has been used.

service cover Postal item sent on active service, bearing relevant postmarks, and often carried free of charge.

service overprint Stamp overprinted (with the word 'service' or the initials of a military force) for exclusive use by military personnel, often outside the country of issue.

set A number of stamps of different design or denomination issued together or over a fairly short period to serve as a related group; the term is loose in application and could refer to a set of feature stamps of similar design issued on the same day, or to a group of feature stamps of totally unrelated design issued on the same day, or to a major definitive issue placed on sale at intervals of a year or more. Philatelically the main consideration is that the stamps should be catalogued and sold as a self-contained group.

se-tenant Two or more stamps that have never been separated (the term is particularly applied to stamps of different denominations or designs issued in a single sheet, booklet pane, or coil).

setting The exact geometrical arrangement of the type used for an overprint (thus, a single sheet may contain two or more different settings which an expert can at once distinguish).

SG Abbreviation for Stanley Gibbons (thus, a stamp may have a catalogue number SG145). Many other catalogue publishers are likewise abbreviated.

shade A precise colour of ink used to print a stamp, or part of its design. Several stamps, ostensibly printed in one colour, are catalogued in as many as eighteen shades.

shift A stamp printed in more than one colour in which one colour is noticeably off register (thus, a '4mm shift', a displacement of about 0.17in).

ship letter Early letter carried by private ship (not a packet) in the charge of the captain, and franked as a ship letter when handed over to the post office at the destination port.

short perf Stamp in which one of the teeth around its edge has been shortened or torn off, either in separating it from its neighbour or subsequently.

short set A set of stamps in which the top value is missing (or in which the most 'difficult' value is missing).

short stamp   Stamp in which the top and bottom edges are closer together than usual, as a result of the method of operation of the perforating machine. In nearly all early British perforated stamps the A (top) row is one hole shorter than the remainder.

side   Abbreviation for sideways watermark.

side-delivery   Coil machine dispensing a roll of side-by-side stamps.

single   Individual stamp (thus, a cover may bear 'a pr and two singles').

souvenir sheet   Miniature sheet issued in connection with an exhibition or other (usually philatelic) function, containing stamps which may or may not be valid for postage.

space-filler   Damaged, heavily cancelled or otherwise poor copy of a difficult stamp that fills a gap until a better one comes along.

specimen   (1) A single (usually fine) copy of a postage stamp or other philatelic item. (2) More properly, a stamp thus overprinted and issued by the postal authority as an example of a new issue.

stc   Abbreviation for 'stated to catalogue'; if an auctioneer has a lot consisting of a large number of stamps, he may take the vendor's word for the catalogue value without checking it and will insert, for example, 'stc £145'.

strike   The quality of the impression of a handstamp or cancel is described as 'a fine strike' or 'blurred strike', or whatever adjective may apply.

strip   Three or more unsevered stamps, from the same row (unless described as a 'vertical strip', from the same column, which is considerably rarer).

substitute cliché   A single cliché (line block, to print a single stamp) inserted into a printing plate in place of one irreparably damaged. Can be identified only if it fails to line up exactly with those around it.

surcharge Postal duty overprinted on an existing stamp either to alter or to confirm the amount payable.

tablet Usually rectangular extra piece attached to each stamp in a sheet (sometimes only to marginal copies) bearing an inscription or other design, and which can be removed without postally invalidating the stamp. In modern stamps often called a tab.

tagging Addition of some material to a postage stamp or postal item (postcard or cover) to trigger a sensing device in an automatic letter-facing machine. By far the most common tagging is an ink containing a phosphor or a phosphor contained in or on the paper.

telegraph cancel Cancellation, usually a small cds, showing that the stamp was used on a telegraph despatch form.

testing label Stamp identical in most respects with current postage stamps, but either bearing no printed design or one grossly changed to render it invalid for postal use, issued as a coil to test stamp-dispensing machines. See *poached egg*.

tête-bêche Head to tail, two se-tenant stamps upside-down in relation to one another; tête-bêche pairs can be side by side or one above the other, and may exist by accident or design.

thin A thin is an area in which part of the back of a stamp has been torn away by clumsy removal from a cover or album page.

tied An adhesive is tied to cover by a cancellation clearly extending across both the stamp and the cover, thus assuring that the stamp is still on the cover for which it paid postage.

tinted Paper deliberately dyed a chosen colour throughout its depth.

toned Paper not tinted yet clearly not white; usually a pale shade of cream or brown.

TPO Abbreviation for Travelling Post Office, usually on a mail train, in which the post is sorted and cancelled with TPO marks.

training stamp   Stamp identical in most respects with current postage stamps but grossly altered to render it invalid for postage (eg by crude black overprinted bars) and used to train new counter clerks.

transit marks   Handstamps and other postmarks applied to a postal item between the offices of posting and destination (eg cds from transit offices, notices of redirection, or reasons for non-delivery).

typo   Abbreviation for typographed, or surface printed.

U, u   Abbreviations for 'used'.

u/m   Abbreviation for 'unmounted mint'.

un   Abbreviation for 'unused'.

uncat   Uncatalogued; this usually means it is known to exist, and is listed in the catalogue but unpriced.

underprint   Inscription printed on the back of a stamp, usually under the gum and in the same ink as used to print the front. Some underprints are 'protective'; they state the name or initials of the organisation which bought the stamp and which alone may use it. Other underprints are advertisements, or fine geometric patterns serving a protective function.

unsorted   When applied to an accumulation or loose mixture (eg kiloware) it means that nobody has inspected the stamps to see if anything of value is present; thus the mass may contain a rarity.

used   Strictly, a stamp that has served a complete postal function. This excludes a cto stamp, yet this may be impossible to distinguish from a properly used stamp on a first-day cover.

used abroad   Stamp posted and cancelled at an office set up by a postal administration in a foreign country (especially true of British stamps between 1857–85).

UV, uv   Abbreviation for ultra-violet, invisible radiation which is of very great assistance in the examination of philatelic items of all kinds, and which is also the radiation used to excite most kinds of phosphor tagging.

uw   Abbreviation for unwatermarked.

V, VV, VVV   Symbols sometimes used to indicate 'valuable' to 'extremely valuable'.

value tablet   In many stamps the separate portion of the design in which appears the denomination (often printed in a contrasting colour and sometimes appearing in multiple).

variety   A stamp from a particular position in a sheet characterised by a visible flaw, or a multicoloured stamp in which one colour is missing or badly shifted, or a stamp in any other way incorrectly or abnormally manufactured.

vignette   Small picture occupying an otherwise blank area in the stamp design.

watermark   Characteristic pattern impressed into the paper at the time of its manufacture as a guard against forgery. Today few stamps are watermarked, but many early stamps either bear one complete watermark on each stamp or were printed on paper watermarked with an all-over pattern.

weak   Portion of a stamp that, though imperfect, is not bad enough to be described as damaged; particularly applied to corners, which may be slightly thinned or shortened.

wing margin   Stamps from sheets divided by wide gutters into panes may have a wing margin along one side, there being a wide imperforate margin between the printed design and the perforation.

wmk   Abbreviation for watermark.

wove paper   General term for a range of papers produced by settling fibres on fine wire mesh which imprints a watermark giving a woven appearance.

Index